andrea and trevor

DOW'S

TECHNICAL EXERCISES FOR NOTE READING SUCCESS

BOOK 1: 226 PRIMER PIANO EXERCISES IN MIDDLE C POSITION AND C POSITION

PIANO STUDENT
WORKBOOKS

Andrea And Trevor Dow's Technical Exercises For Note Reading Success, Book 1

www.teachpianotoday.com and www.wunderkeys.com

EXERCISE #1

With 226 technical exercises, this may be the BIGGEST book to ever rest on your piano! To begin, place this book on a table. Turn to pages 20 and 21. Slide your hand firmly down the center so that the book will lie flat. Next, turn to pages 60 and 61. Slide your hand firmly down the center. Finally, turn to pages 80 and 81. Slide your hand firmly down the center. **Now, let's get started!**

andrea and trevor

DOW'S

PIANO STUDENT WORKBOOKS

CONTENTS

4	B | Middle C | Middle C | D
16	A | B | Middle C | Middle C | D | E
28	A | B | Middle C | Middle C | D | E | F | G
44	F | G | A | B | Middle C | Middle C | D | E | F | G
62	Bass C | D | E | F | G | Middle C | D | E | F | G
82	Hands Together

UNIT 1

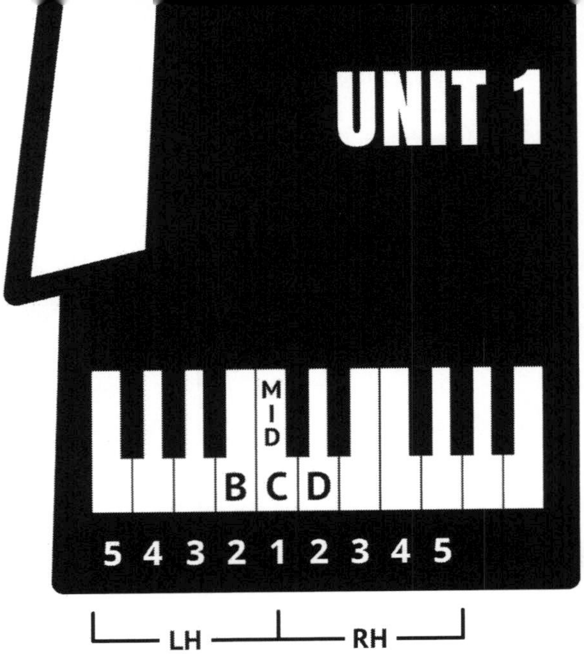

AN INTRO

Let's get started! In each box,
draw a note that matches the first note.

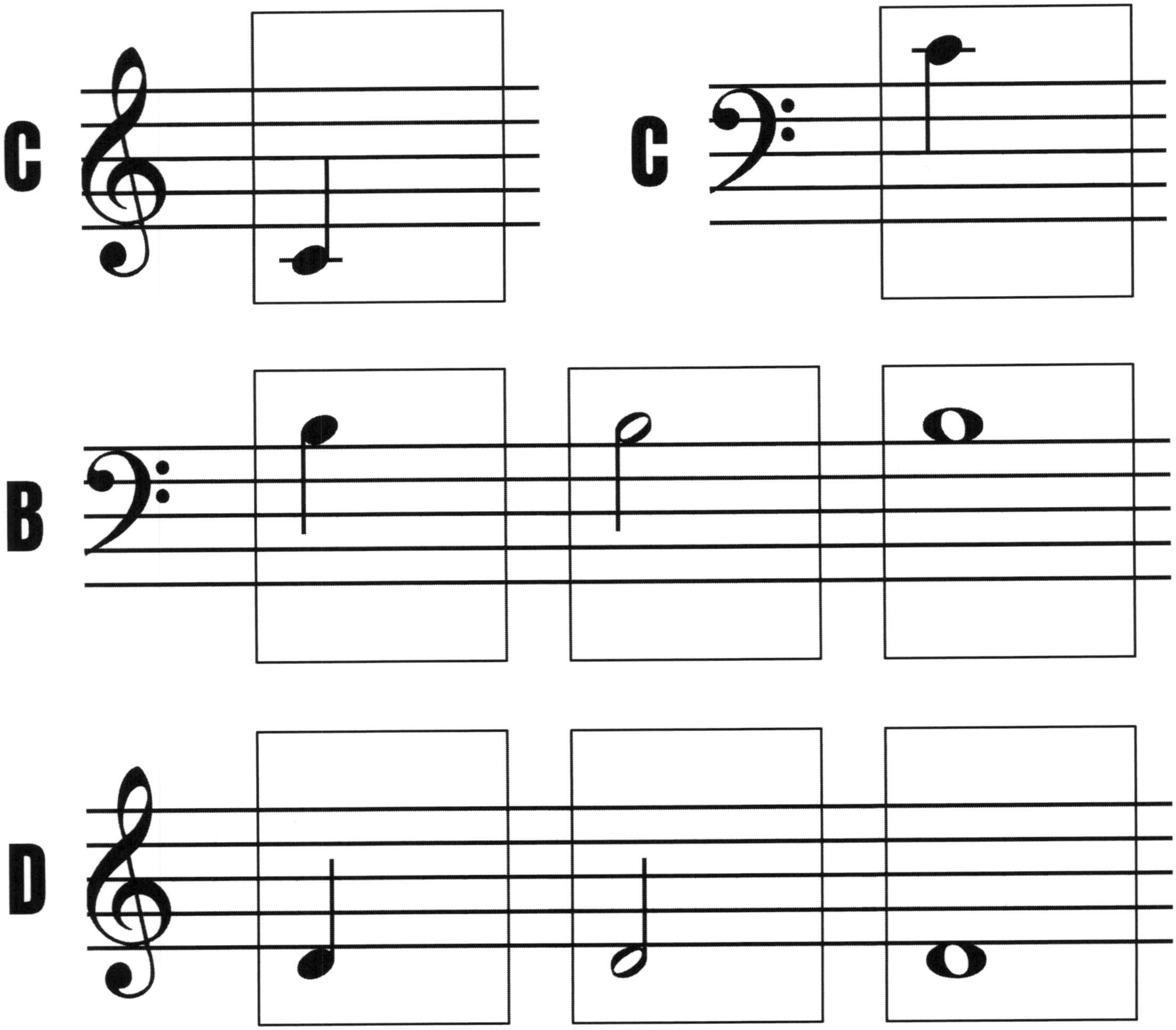

Color in one lettered box each time you practice a line of music.
After all of the boxes are colored, you will be one AWESOME piano player.

PRESS PLAY

A	W	E	S	O	M	E

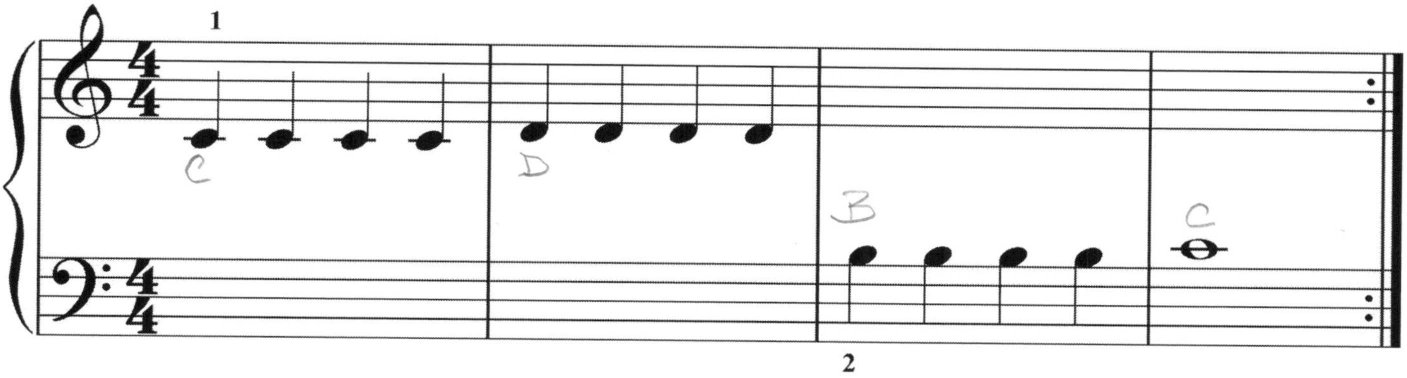

SIDE TO SIDE

P	E	R	F	E	C	T

REVERSE FLY

A	M	A	Z	I	N	G

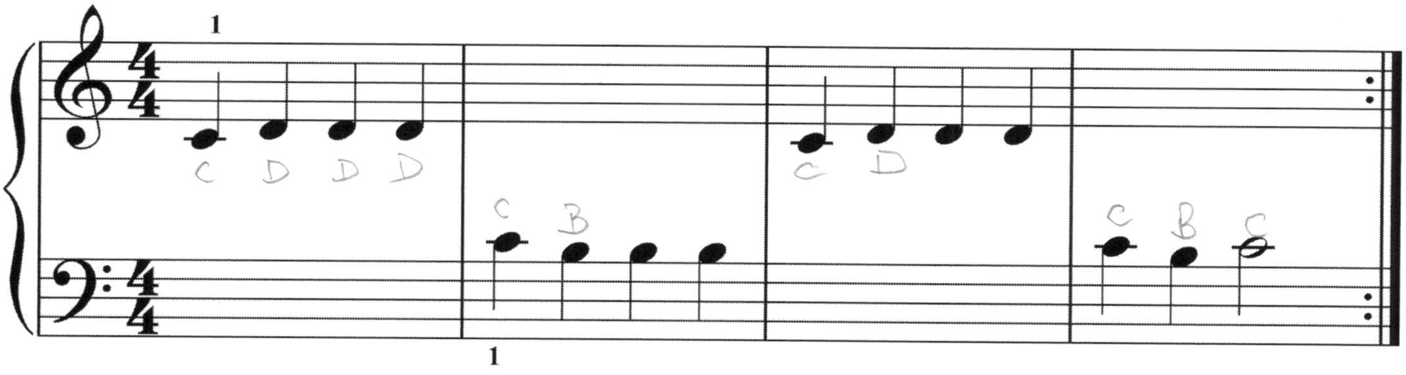

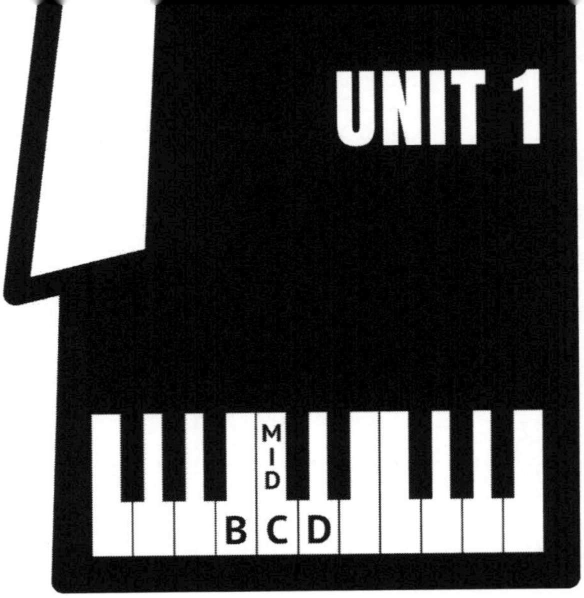

SET 01

Color in one lettered box each time you practice a line of music.
After all of the boxes are colored, you will be one AMAZING piano player.

BENCH PRESS

A	M	A	Z	I	N	G

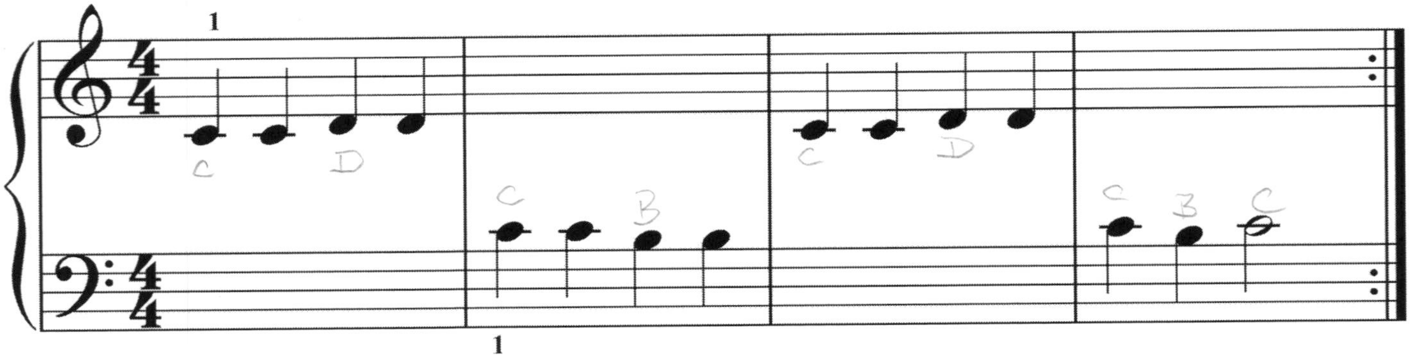

POWER PLAY

S	T	E	L	L	A	R

WOODCHOP

W I N N I N G

CLIMB TIME

P E R F E C T

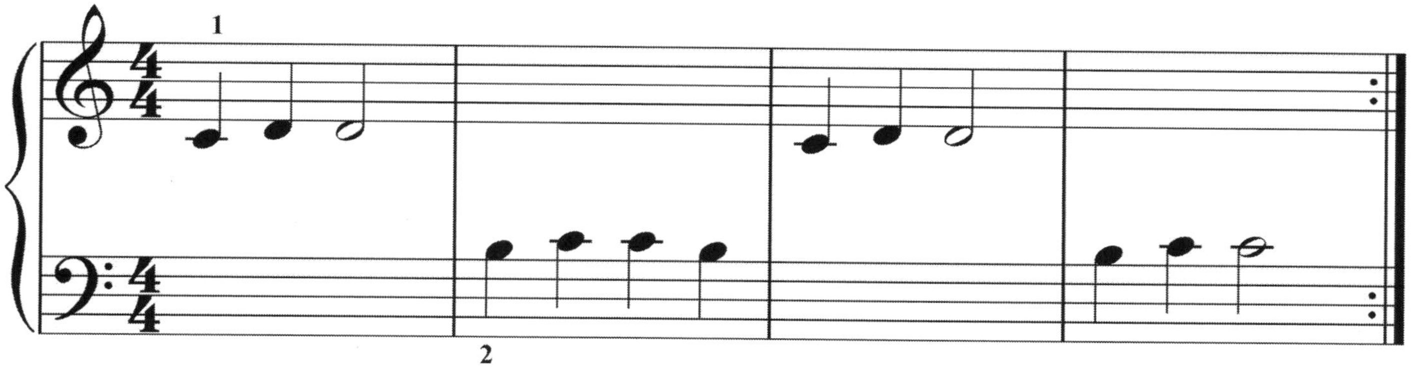

THUMB SWITCH

A W E S O M E

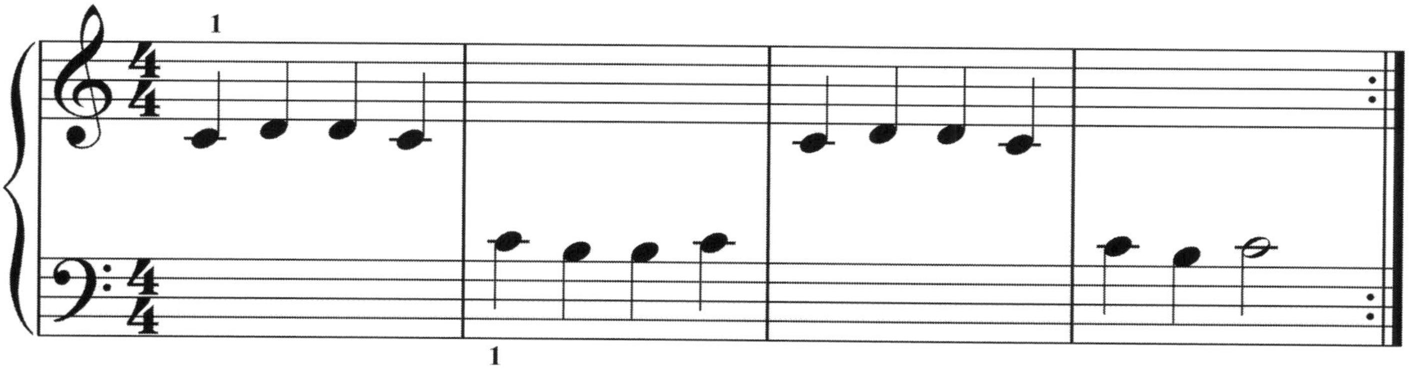

SIGHT READING ONE

SET 2 | PART 1

Look at Sight Reading One. Beginning at the START and ending at the FINISH, play the four measures that rest on the path. Use a colored crayon to draw a new four-measure path. Play again.

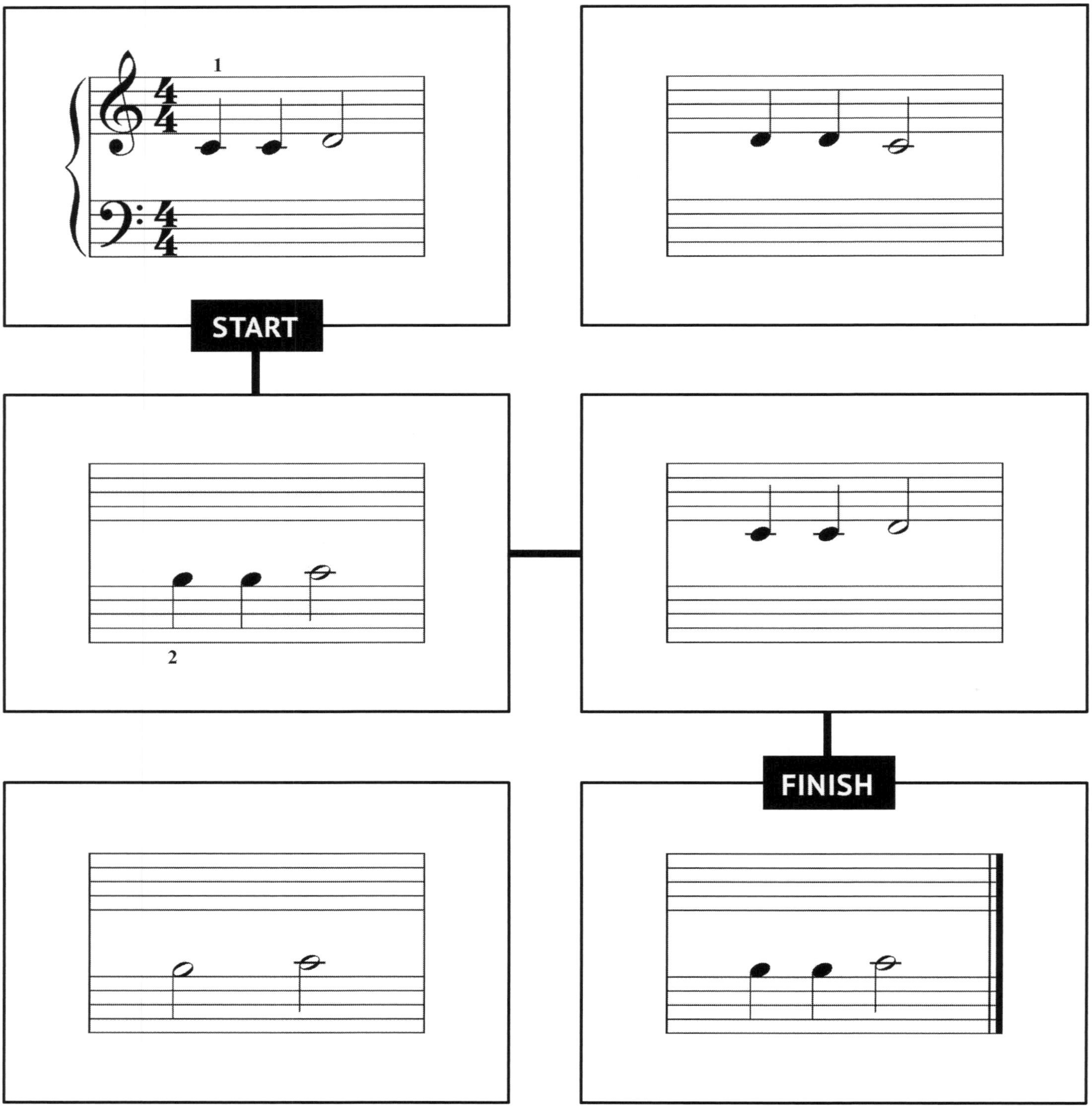

SET 2 | PART 2

Look at Sight Reading Two. Beginning at the START and ending at the FINISH, play the four measures that rest on the path. Use a colored crayon to draw a new four-measure path. Play again.

SIGHT READING TWO

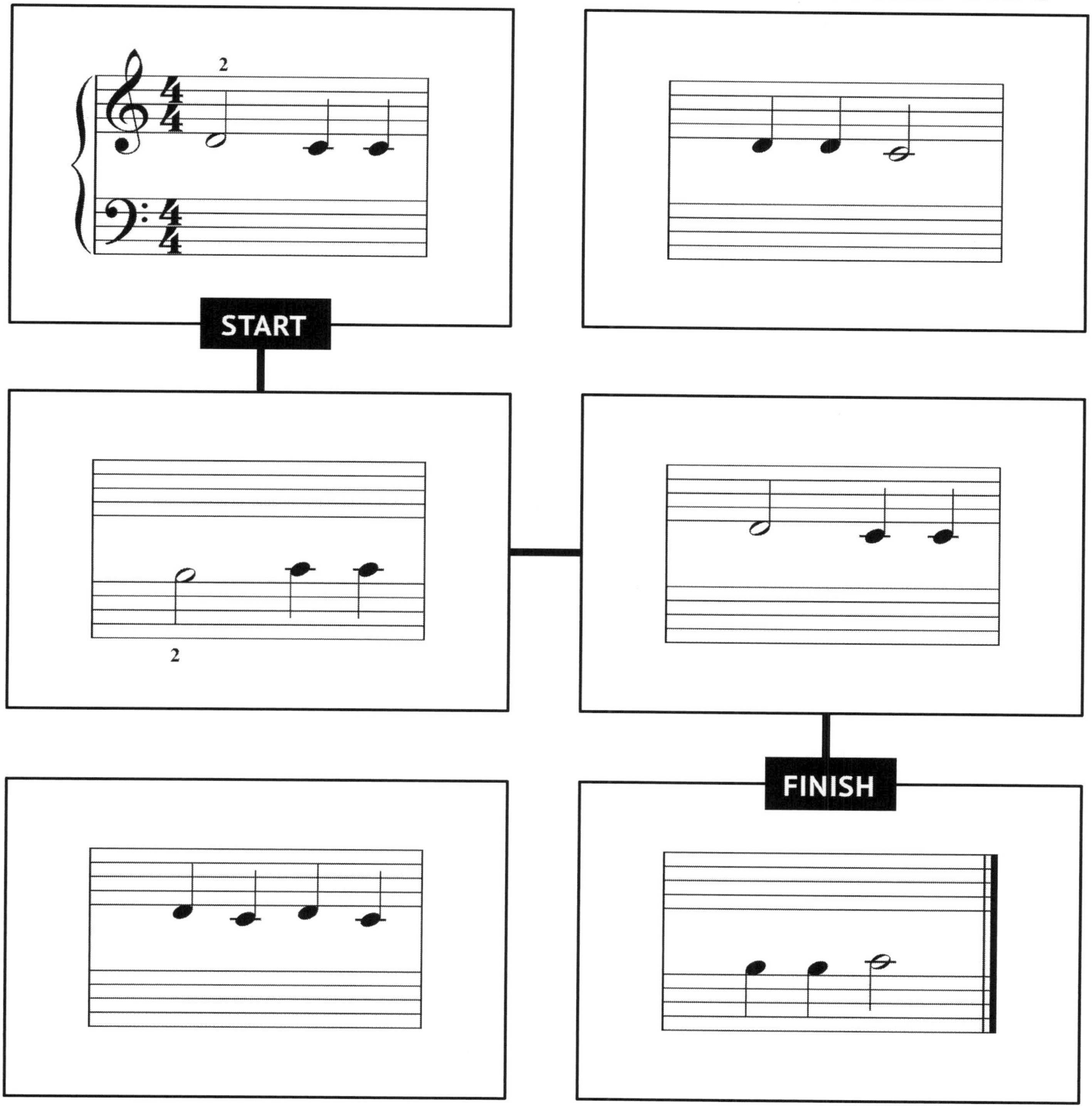

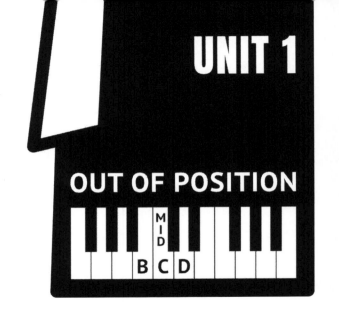

UNIT 1

OUT OF POSITION

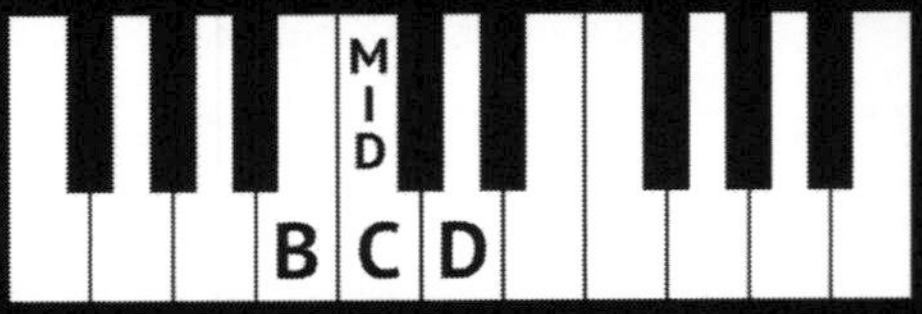

SET 03

In the box above Exercise 1, write the name of the first note. Next, use the finger number to find your starting position. Repeat with Exercises 2 and 3.

MOVE AND GROOVE ☐

S T E L L A R

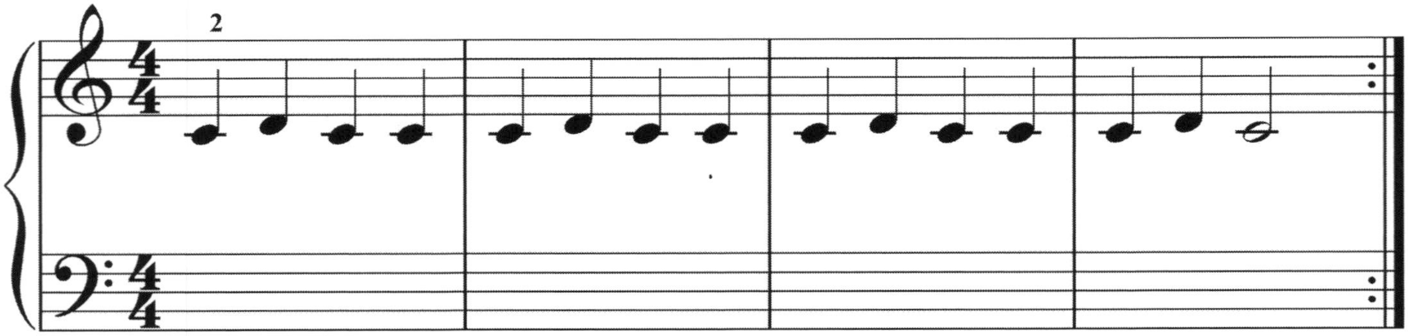

SPACE TRAVEL ☐

A M A Z I N G

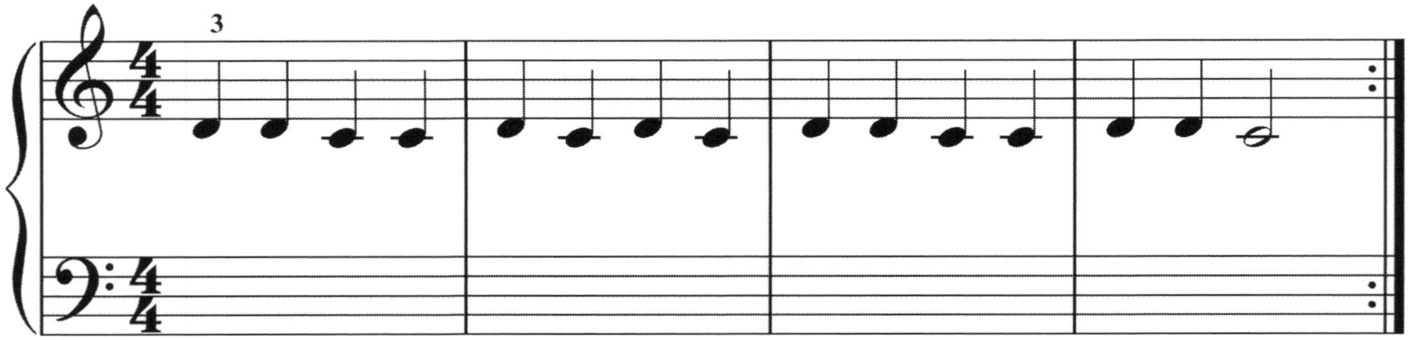

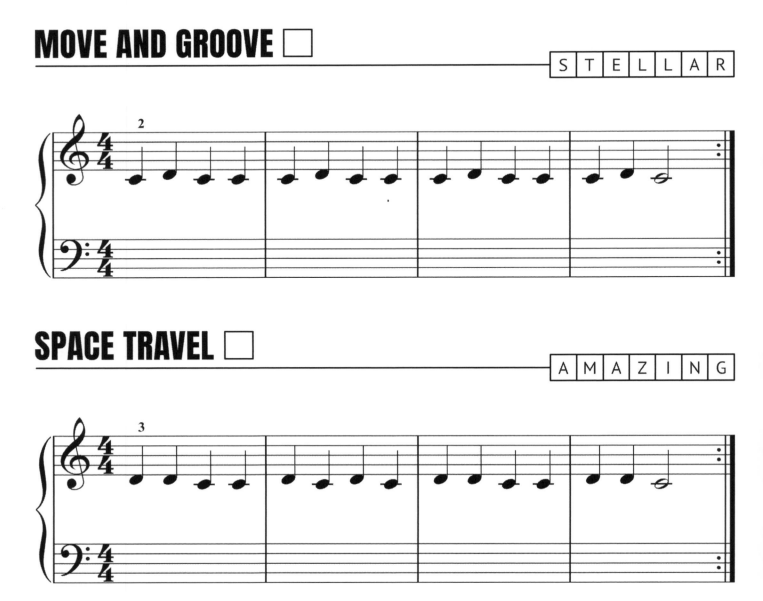

SHIFT WORK ☐

W I N N I N G

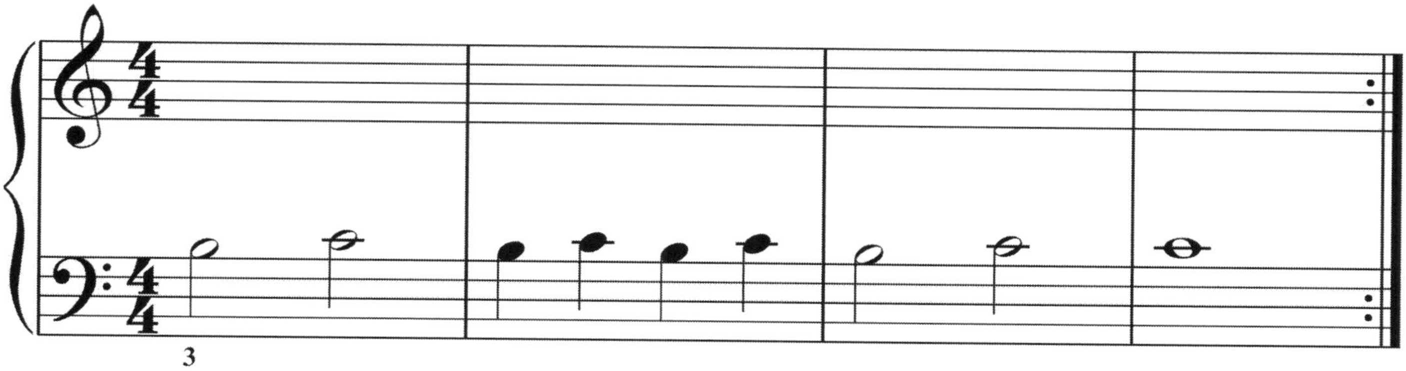

CHALLENGE PIECE 1

P E R F E C T

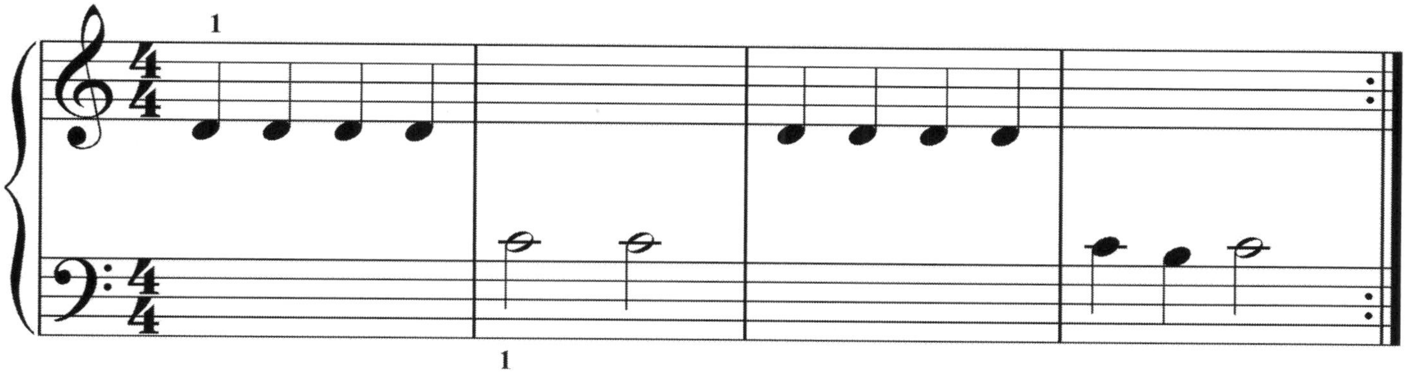

CHALLENGE PIECE 2

A W E S O M E

SET 04

UNIT 1
RHYTHM

Look at the first line of rhythm below. Stem-down notes are performed by tapping both hands on your lap. Stem-up notes are performed by clapping your hands together. After performing the first rhythm, complete the remaining exercises.

RHYTHM CHALLENGE 1

A	W	E	S	O	M	E

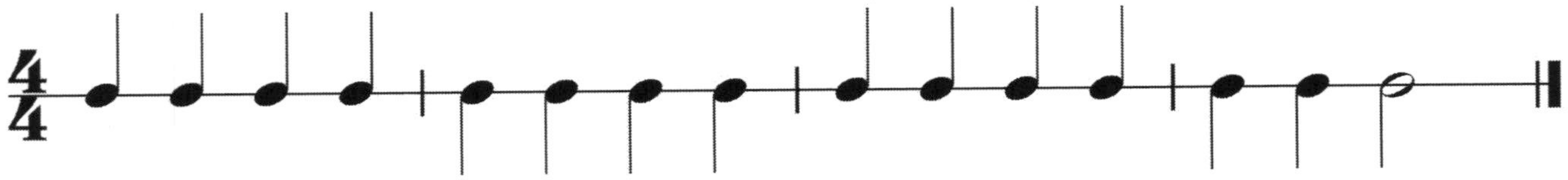

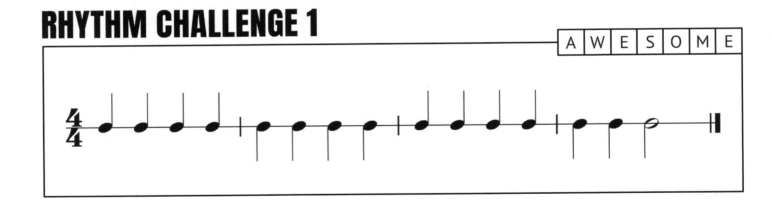

RHYTHM CHALLENGE 2

S	T	E	L	L	A	R

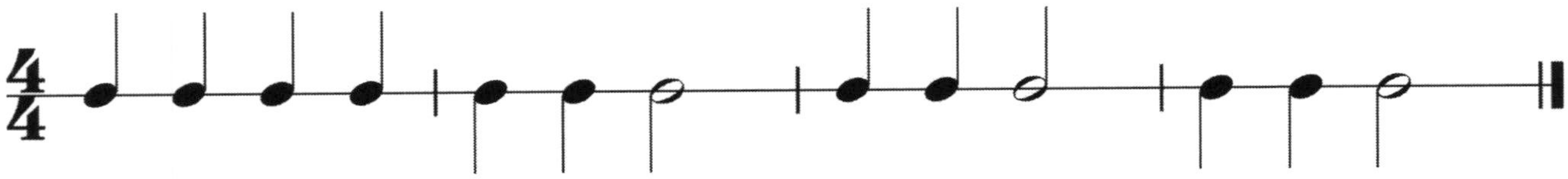

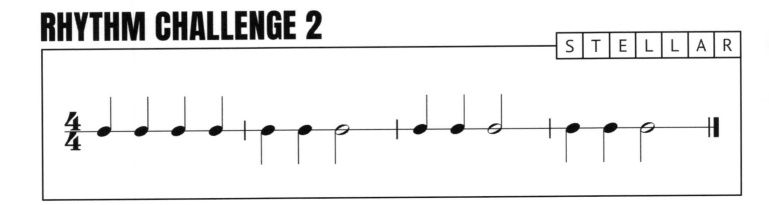

RHYTHM CHALLENGE 3

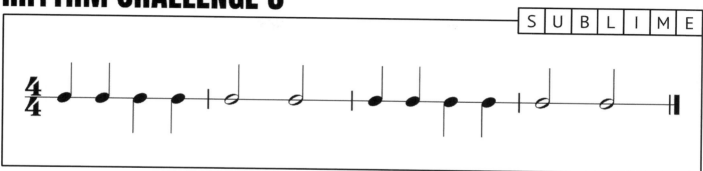

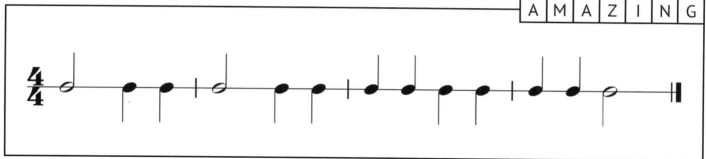

S	U	B	L	I	M	E

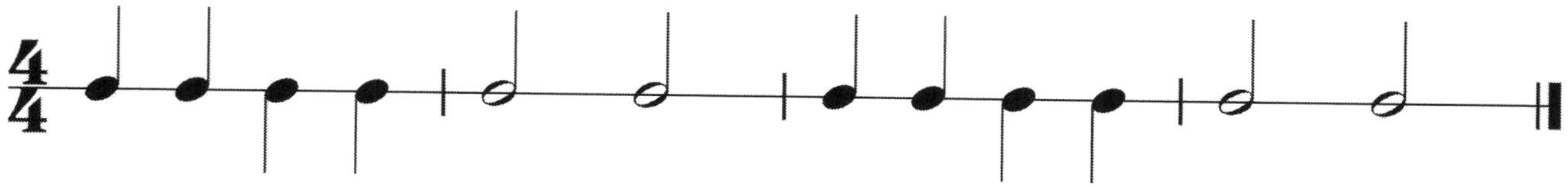

RHYTHM CHALLENGE 4

P	E	R	F	E	C	T

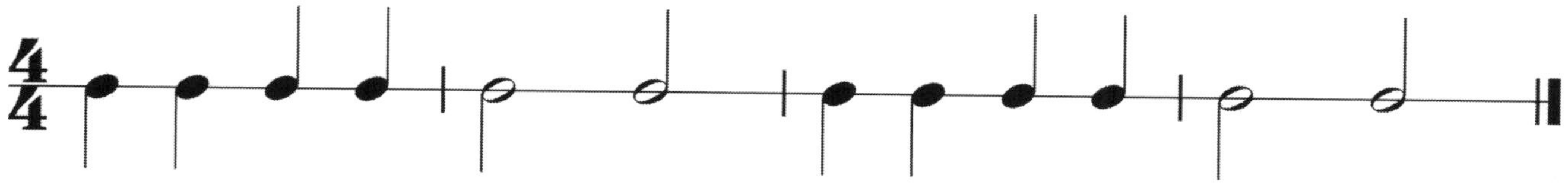

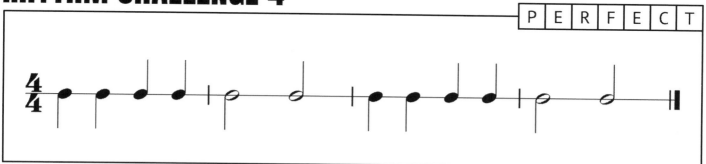

RHYTHM CHALLENGE 5

W	I	N	N	I	N	G

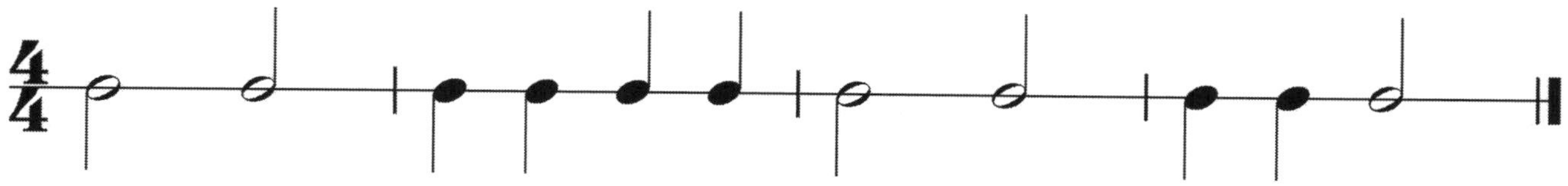

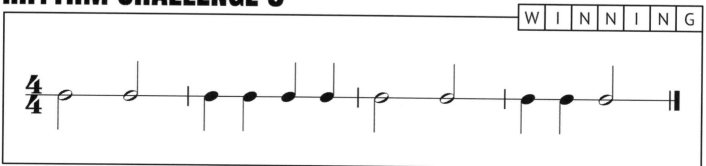

RHYTHM CHALLENGE 6

A	M	A	Z	I	N	G

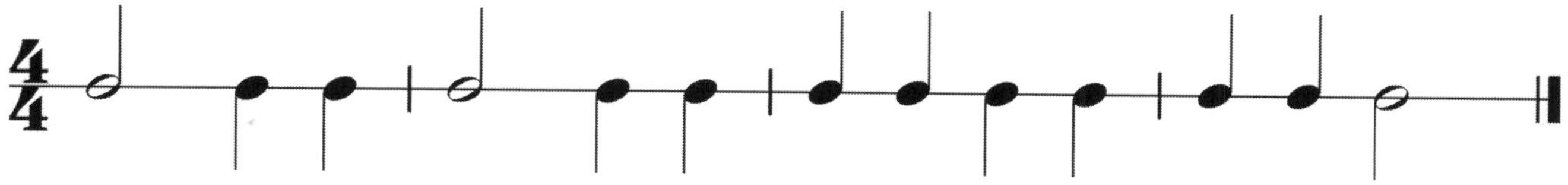

SET 05

UNIT 1

CHALLENGE SET

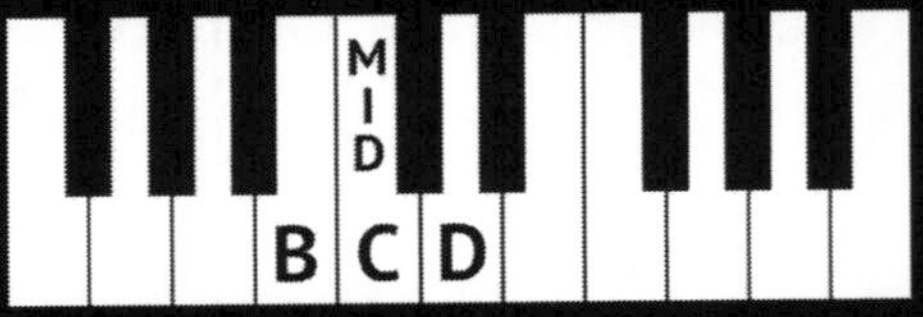

The following cross-staff exercises are intended for
older beginners and students who want to test their skills.

BOUNCE BACK

A W E S O M E

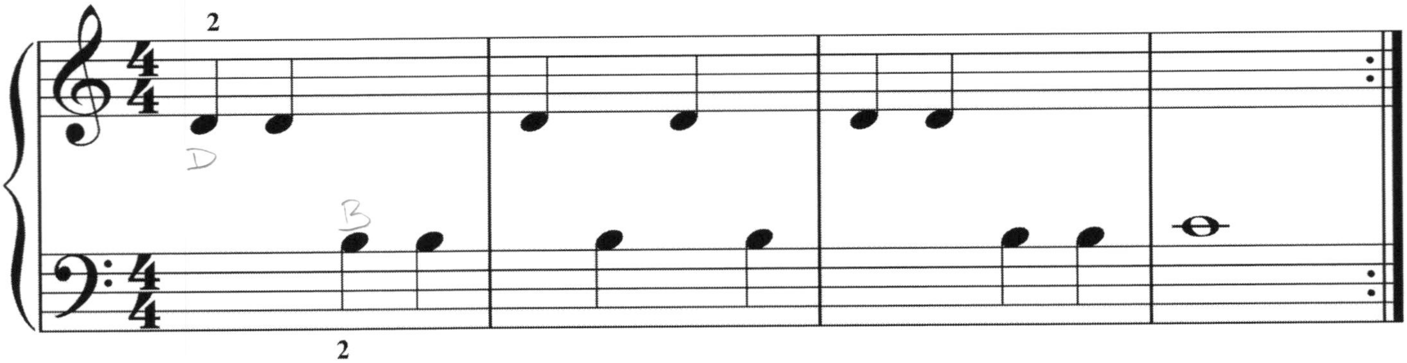

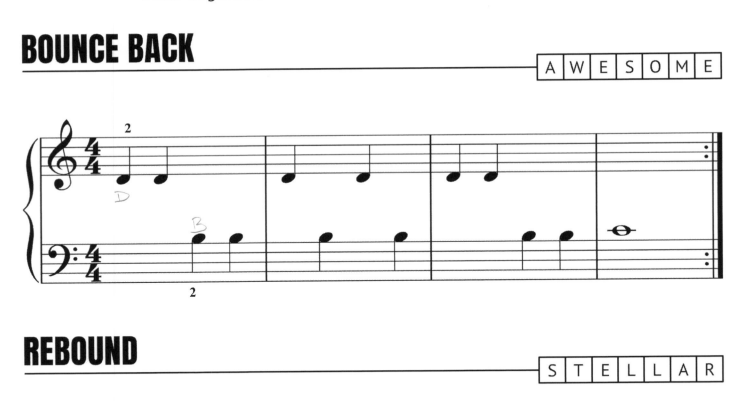

REBOUND

S T E L L A R

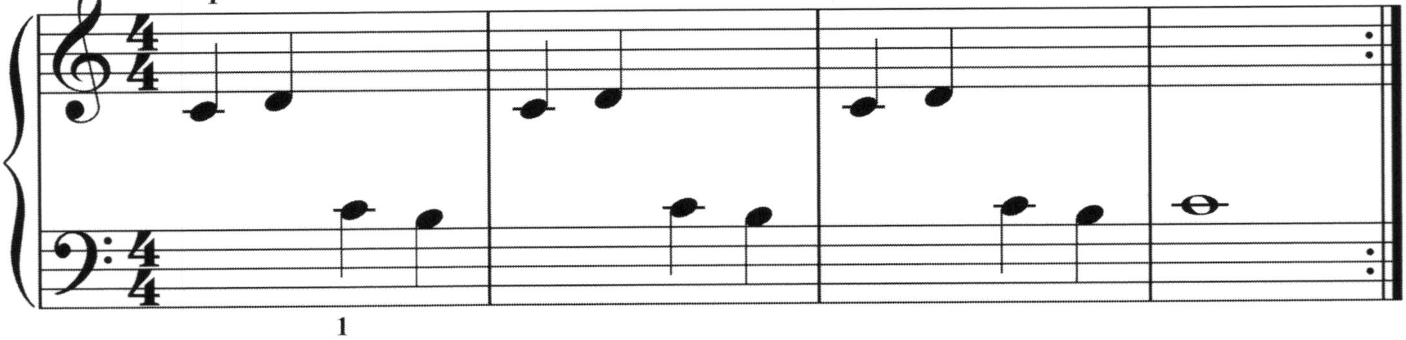

HOMEWARD BOUNCE

W I N N I N G

BOUND TOWN

P E R F E C T

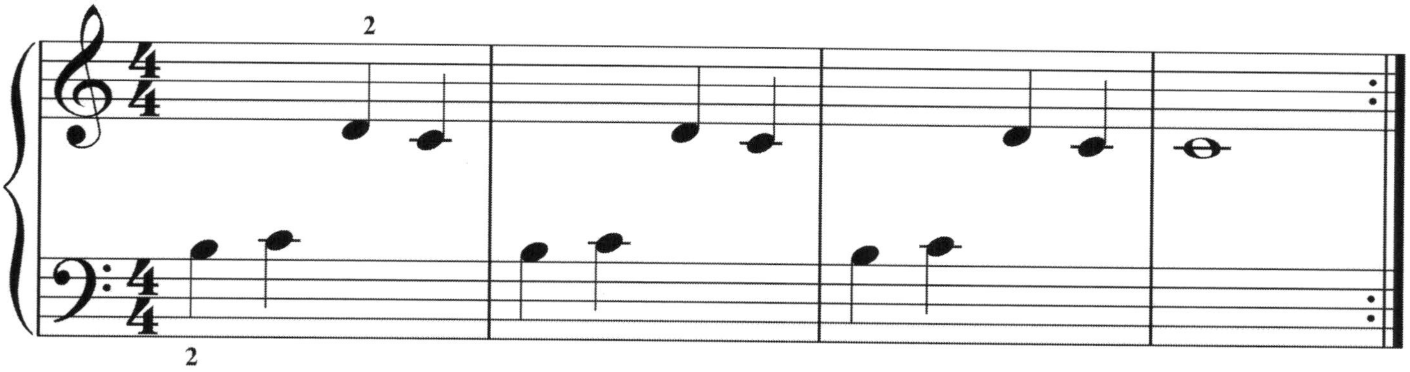

BOUNCE PASS

A M A Z I N G

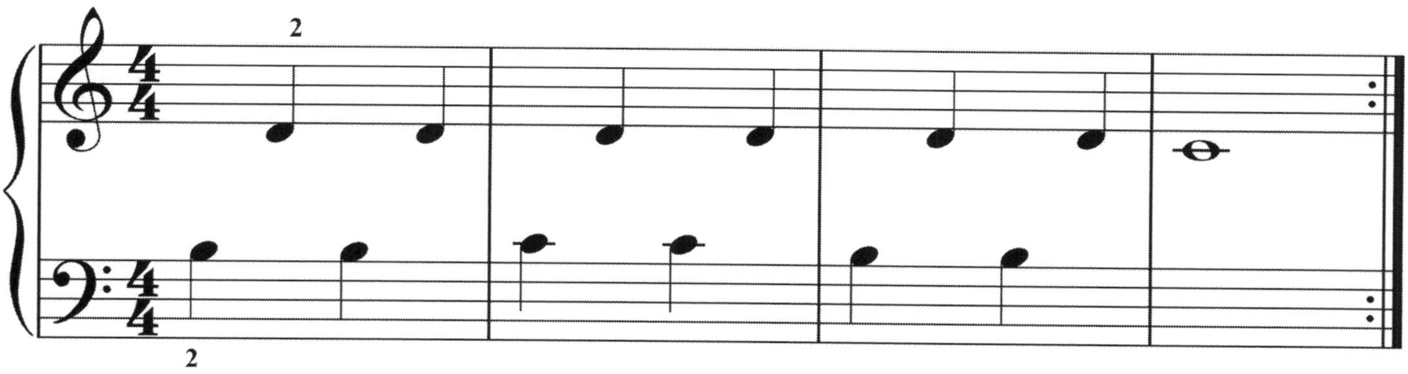

UNIT 2

AN INTRO

Let's get started! In each box,
draw a note that matches the first note.

B

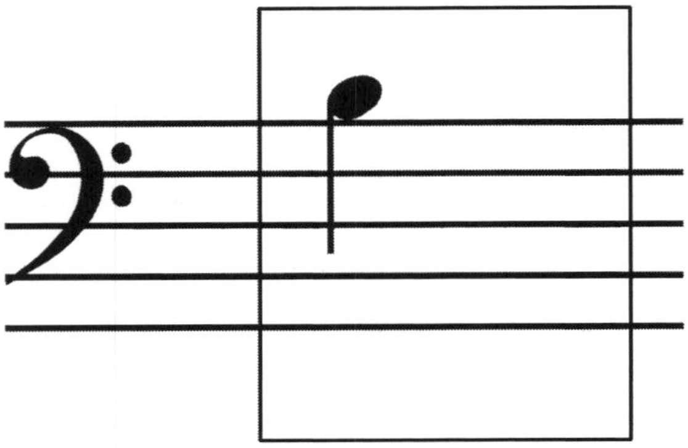

D

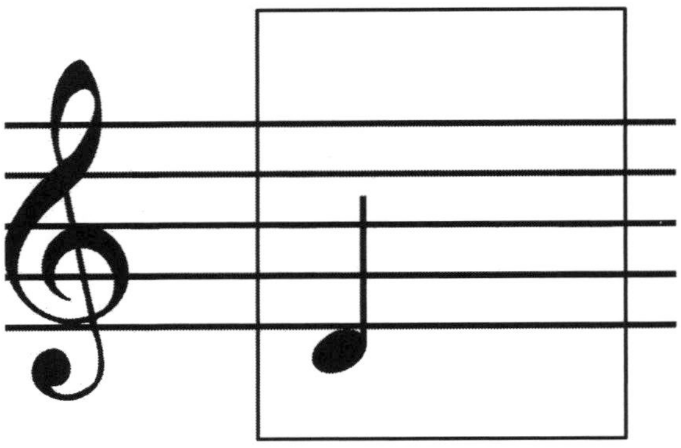

A

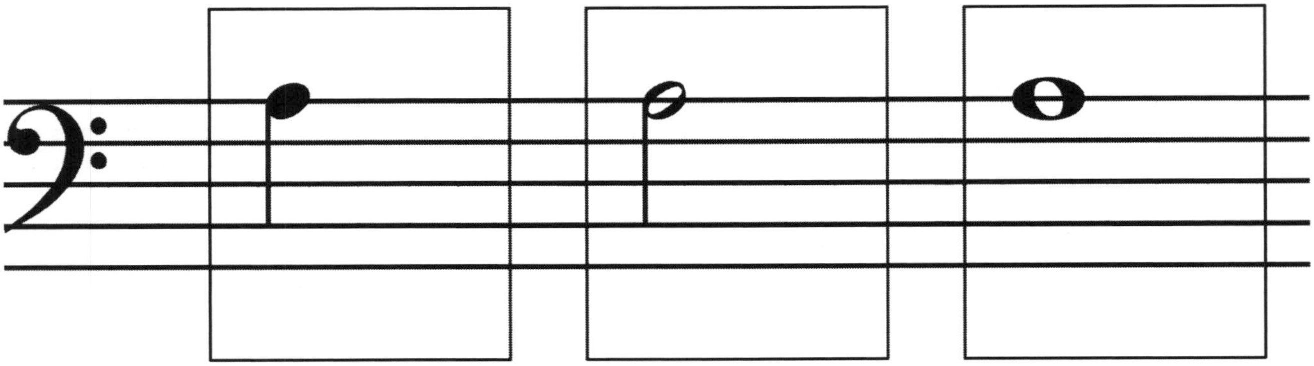

E

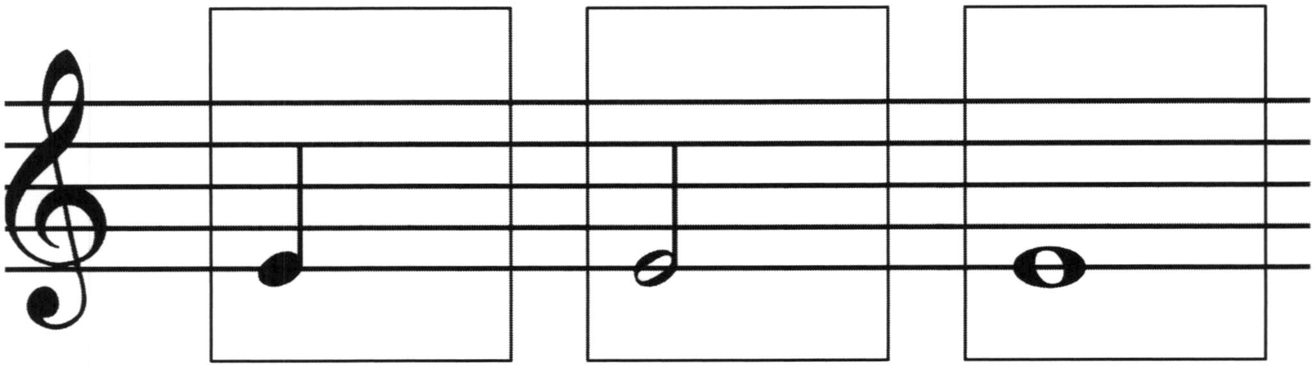

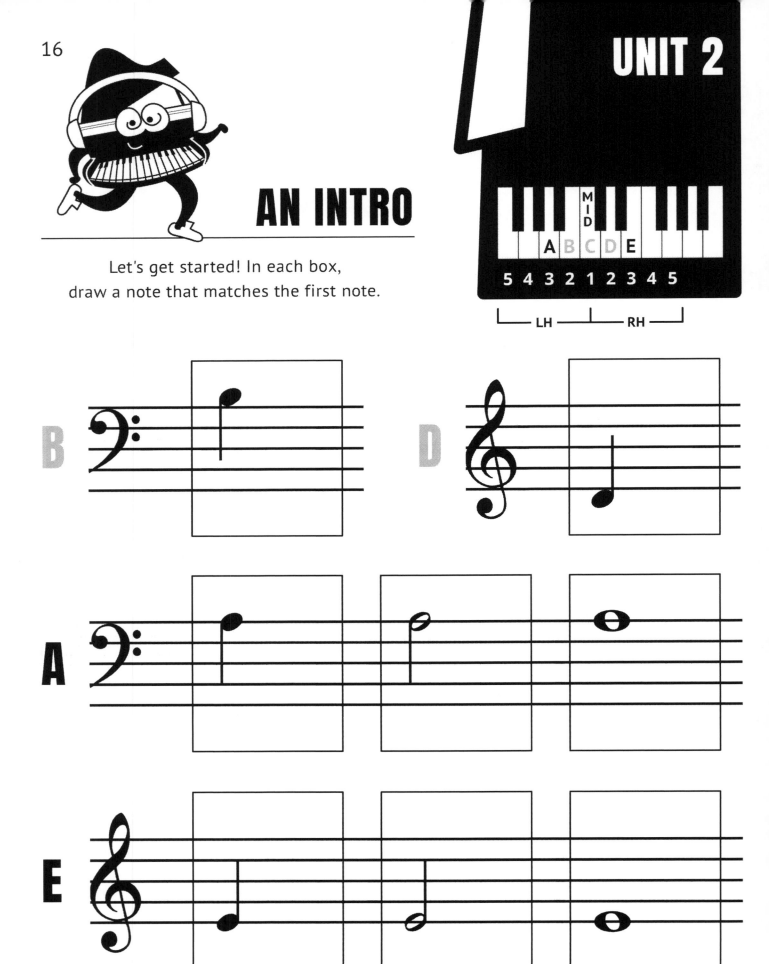

Color in one lettered box each time you practice a line of music.
After all of the boxes are colored, you will be one AWESOME piano player.

PRESS PLAY

A	W	E	S	O	M	E

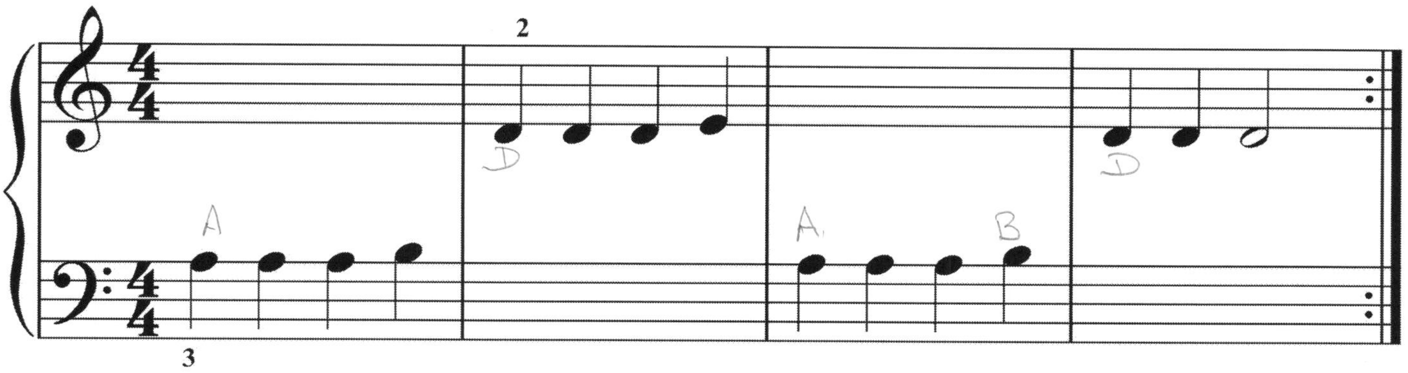

SIDE TO SIDE

P	E	R	F	E	C	T

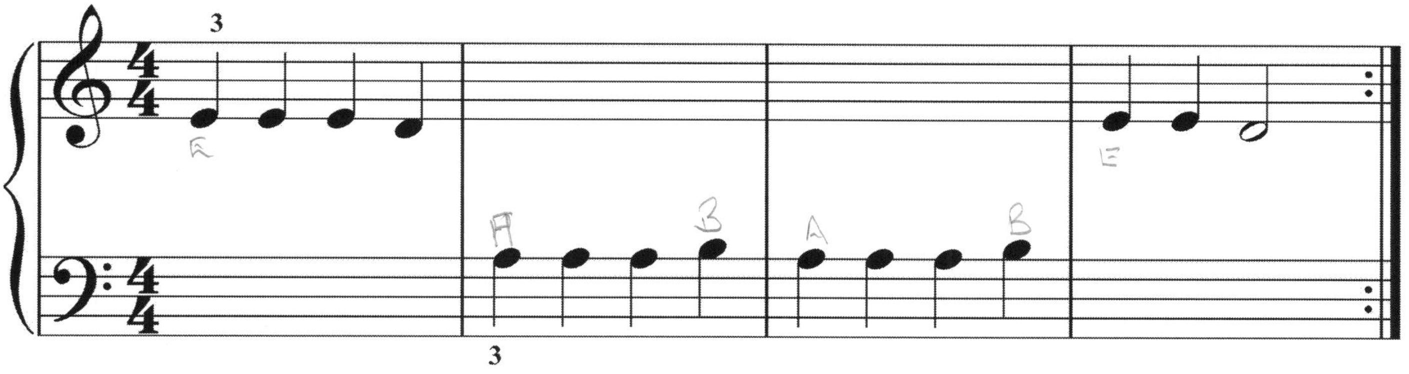

REVERSE FLY

A	M	A	Z	I	N	G

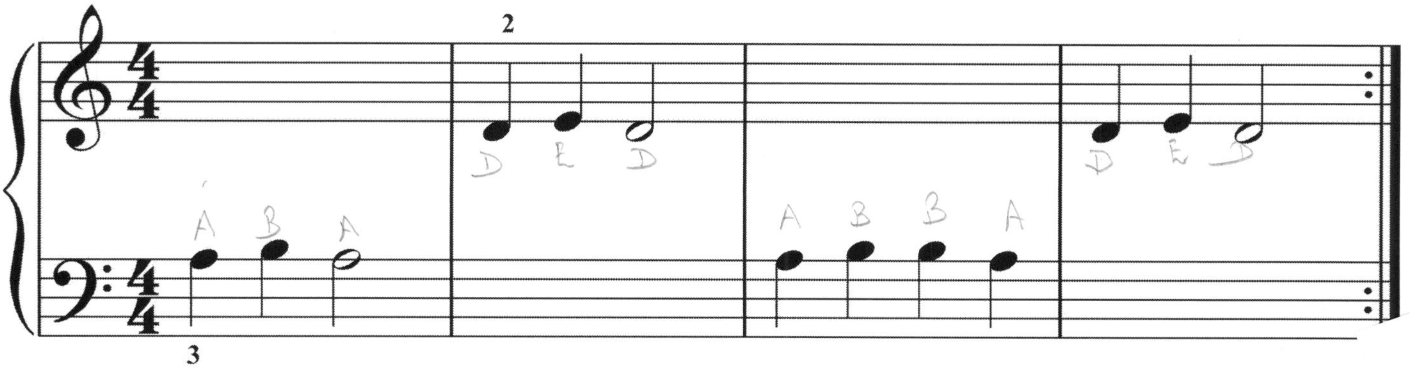

SET 01

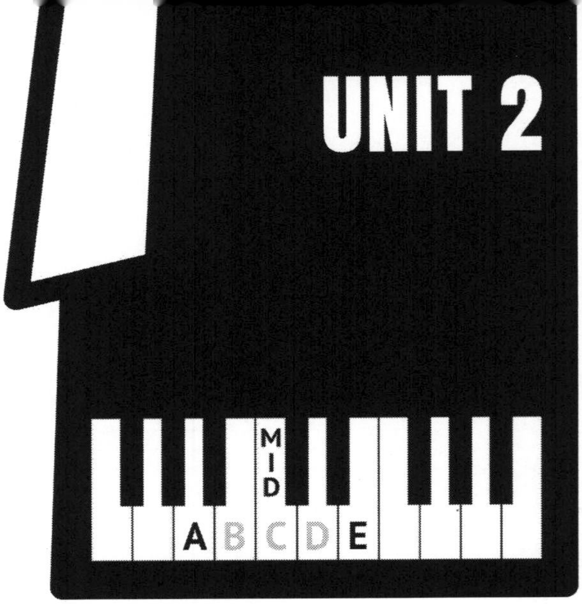

Color in one lettered box each time you practice a line of music.
After all of the boxes are colored, you will be one AMAZING piano player.

BENCH PRESS

A	M	A	Z	I	N	G

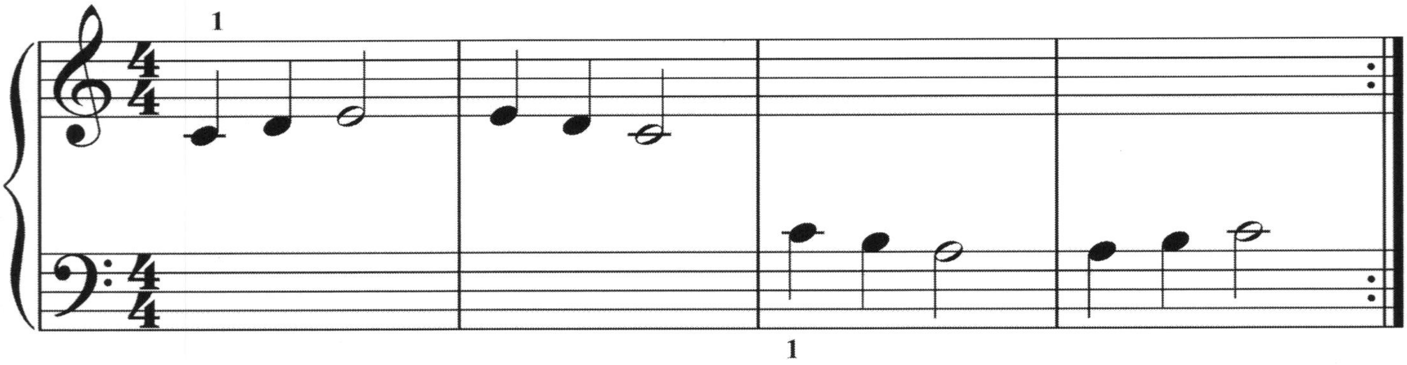

CLIMB TIME

S	T	E	L	L	A	R

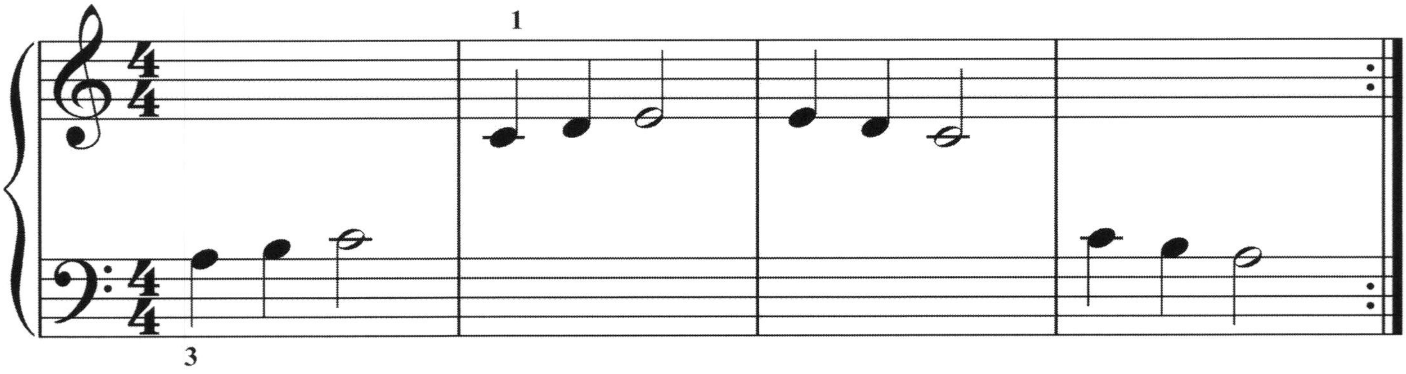

STEP-UPS

W I N N I N G

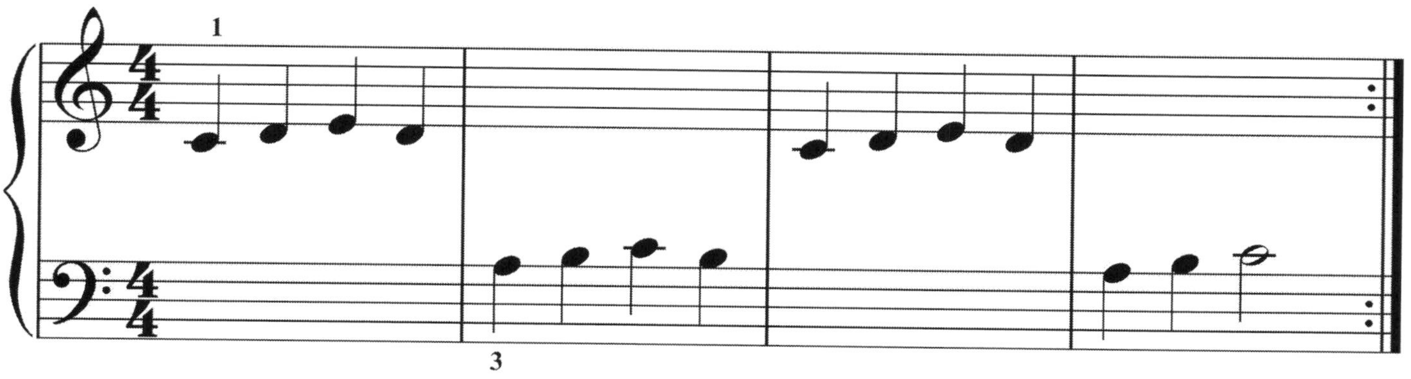

WOODCHOP

P E R F E C T

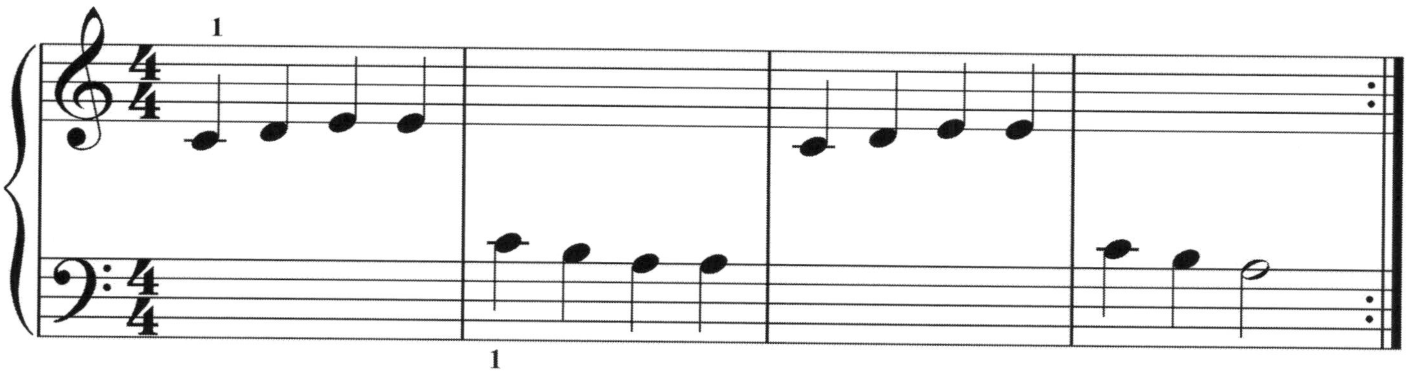

POWER PLAY

A W E S O M E

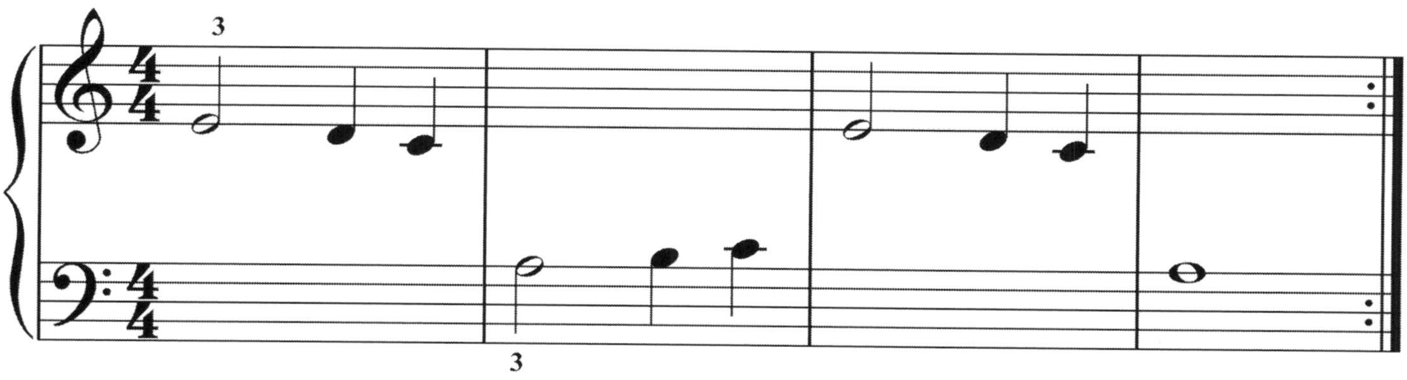

SIGHT READING ONE

SET 2 | PART 1

Look at Sight Reading One. Beginning at the START and ending at the FINISH, play the four measures that rest on the path. Use a colored crayon to draw a new four-measure path. Play again.

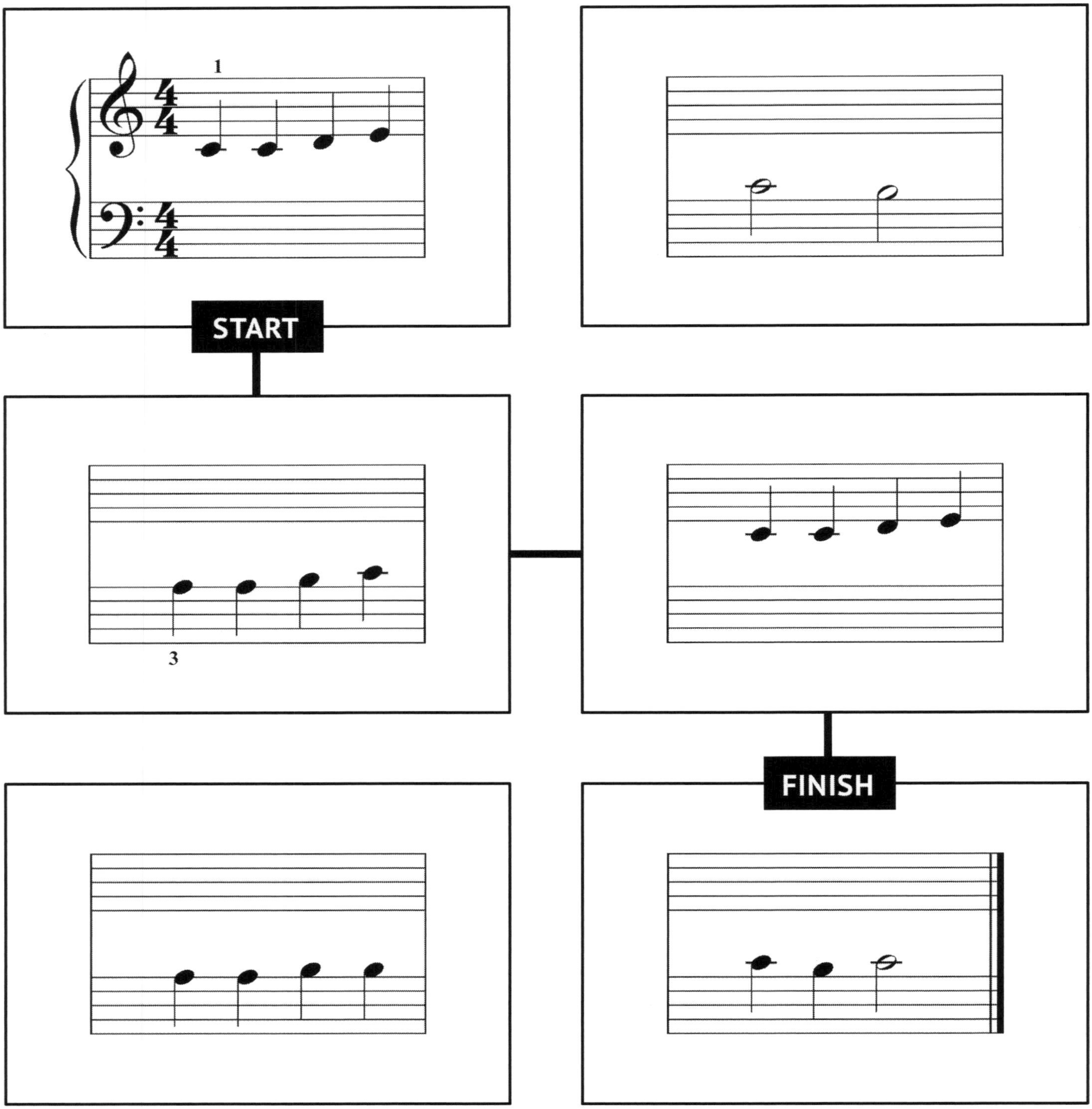

SET 2 | PART 2

Look at Sight Reading Two. Beginning at the START and ending at the FINISH, play the four measures that rest on the path. Use a colored crayon to draw a new four-measure path. Play again.

SIGHT READING TWO

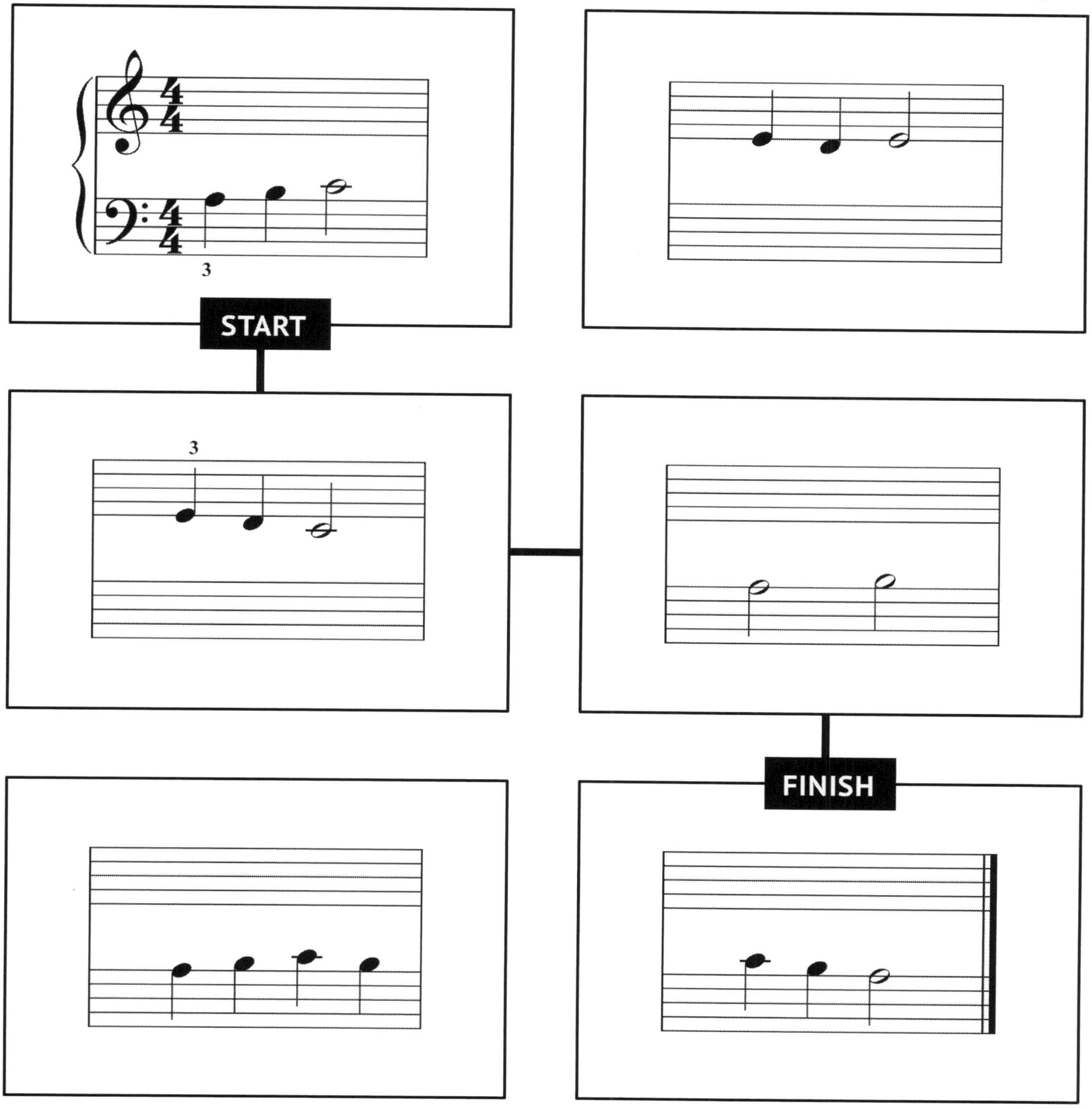

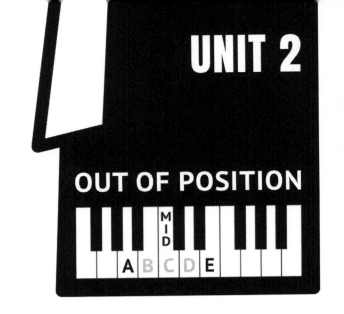

SET 03

UNIT 2

OUT OF POSITION

In the box above Exercise 1, write the name of the first note. Next, use the finger number to find your starting position. Repeat with Exercises 2 and 3.

MOVE AND GROOVE ☐

S T E L L A R

SPACE TRAVEL ☐

A M A Z I N G

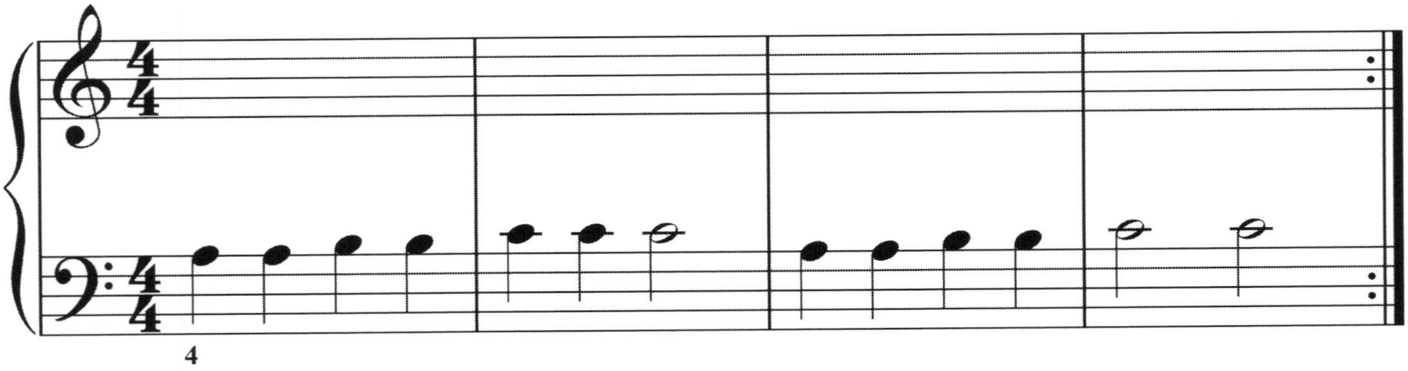

SHIFT WORK ☐

W I N N I N G

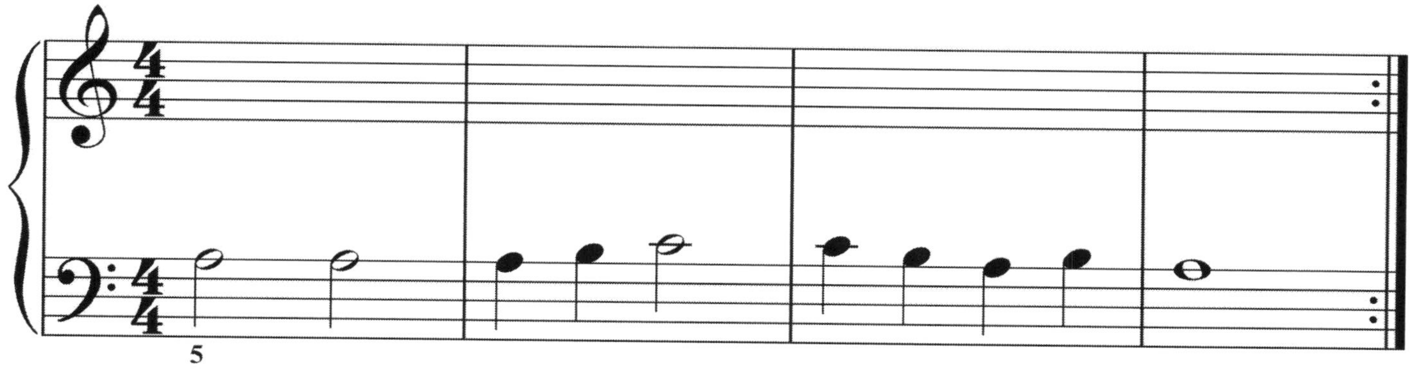

CHALLENGE PIECE 1

P E R F E C T

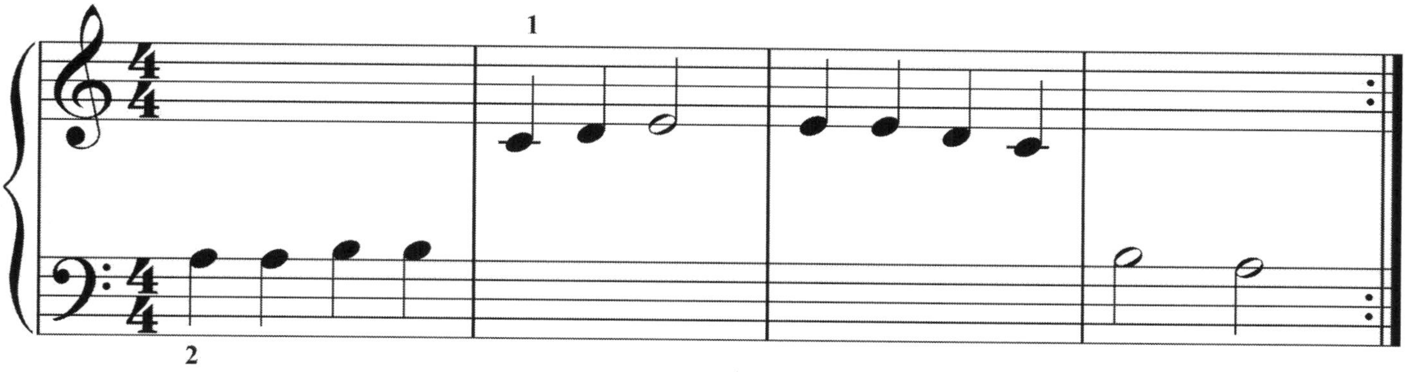

CHALLENGE PIECE 2

A W E S O M E

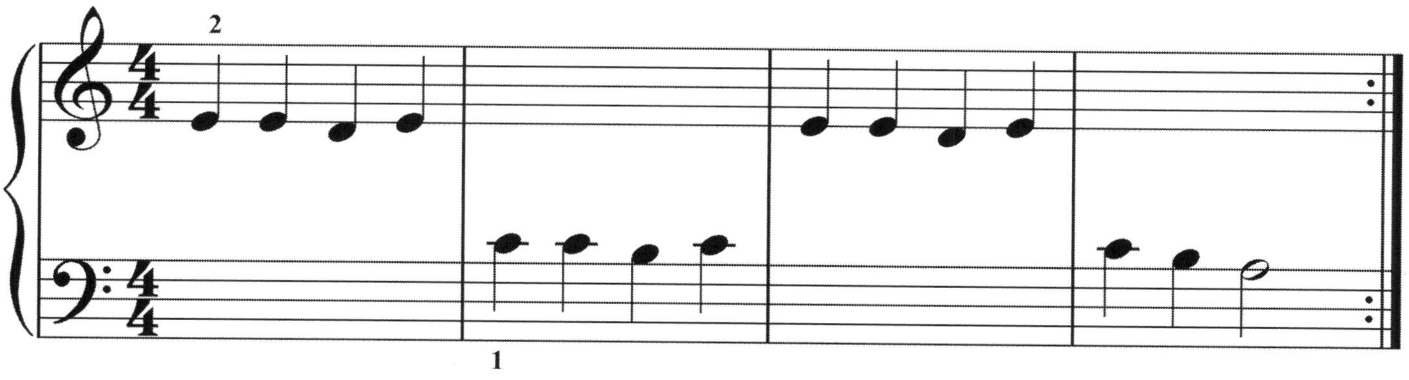

SET 04

UNIT 2
RHYTHM

Look at the first line of rhythm below. Stem-down notes are performed by tapping both hands on your lap. Stem-up notes are performed by clapping your hands together. After performing the first rhythm, complete the remaining exercises.

RHYTHM CHALLENGE 1

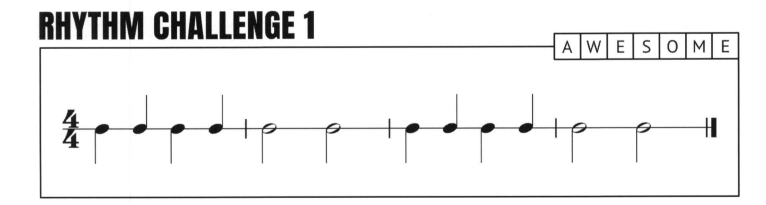

A	W	E	S	O	M	E

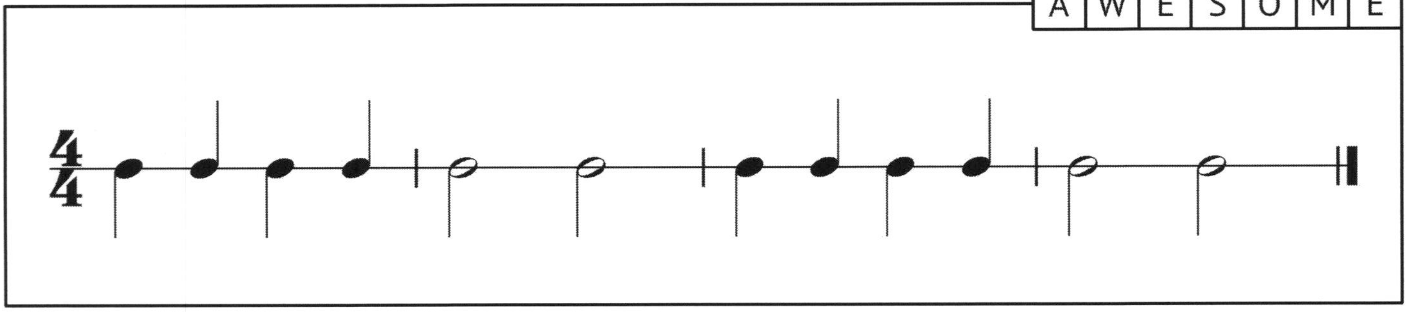

RHYTHM CHALLENGE 2

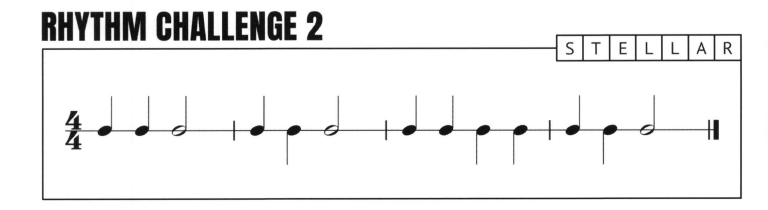

S	T	E	L	L	A	R

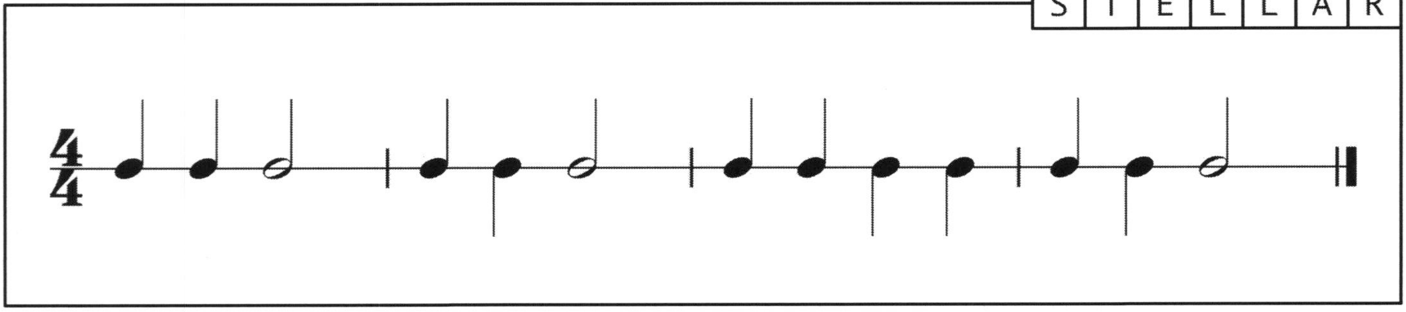

RHYTHM CHALLENGE 3

S U B L I M E

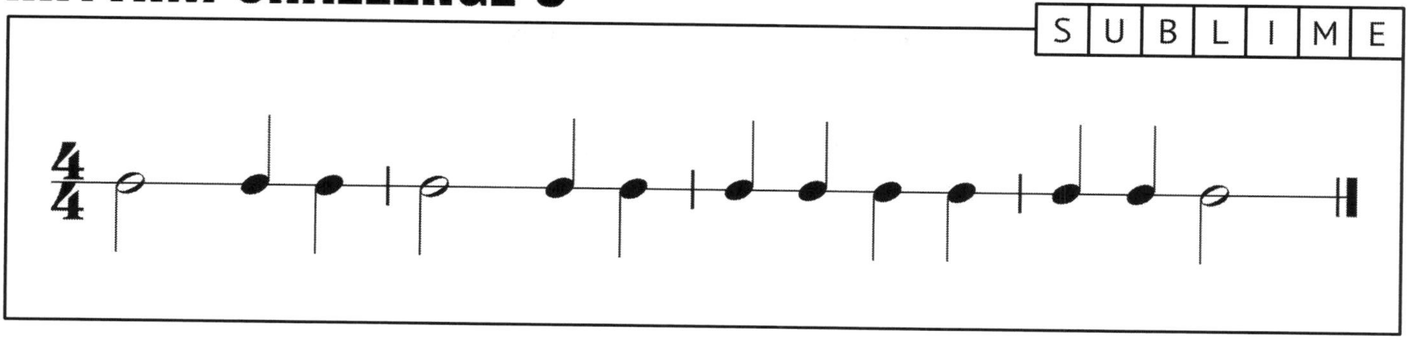

RHYTHM CHALLENGE 4

P E R F E C T

RHYTHM CHALLENGE 5

W I N N I N G

RHYTHM CHALLENGE 6

A M A Z I N G

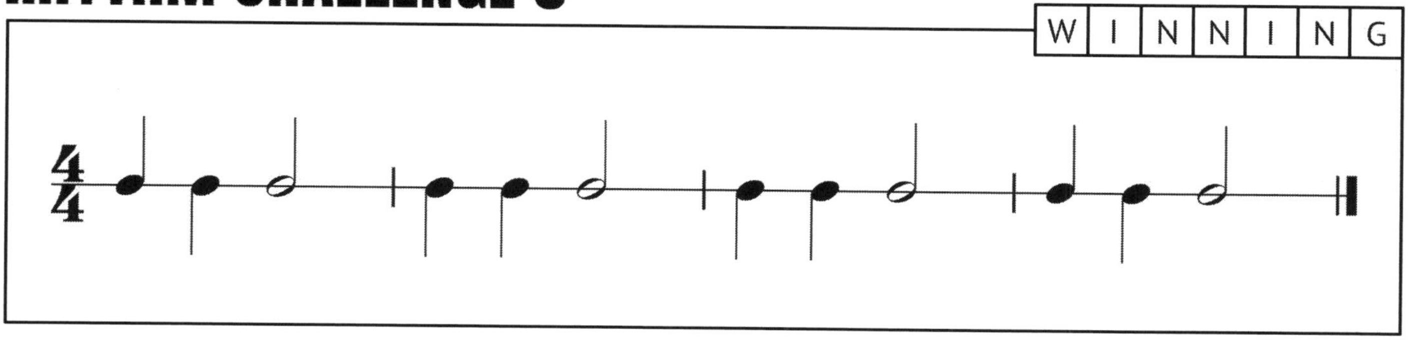

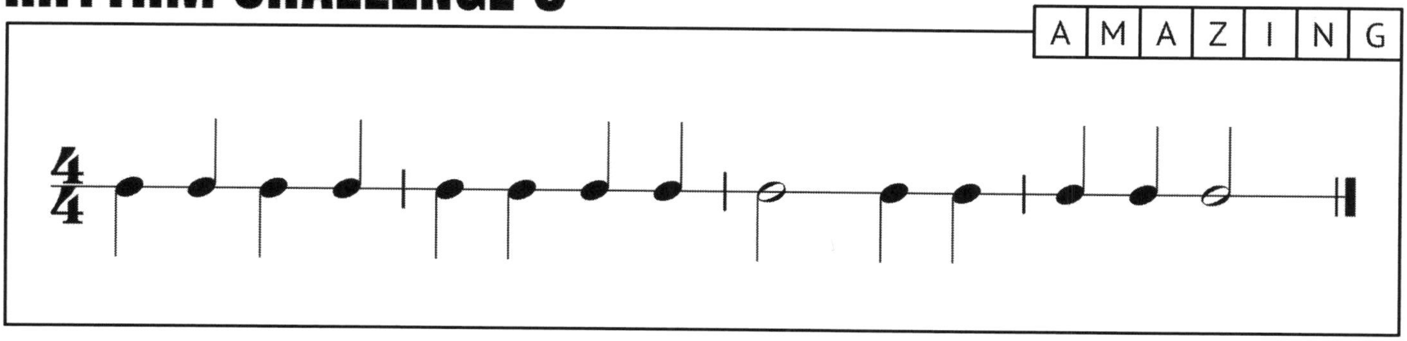

SET 05

The following cross-staff exercises are intended for older beginners and students who want to test their skills.

BOUNCE BACK

A W E S O M E

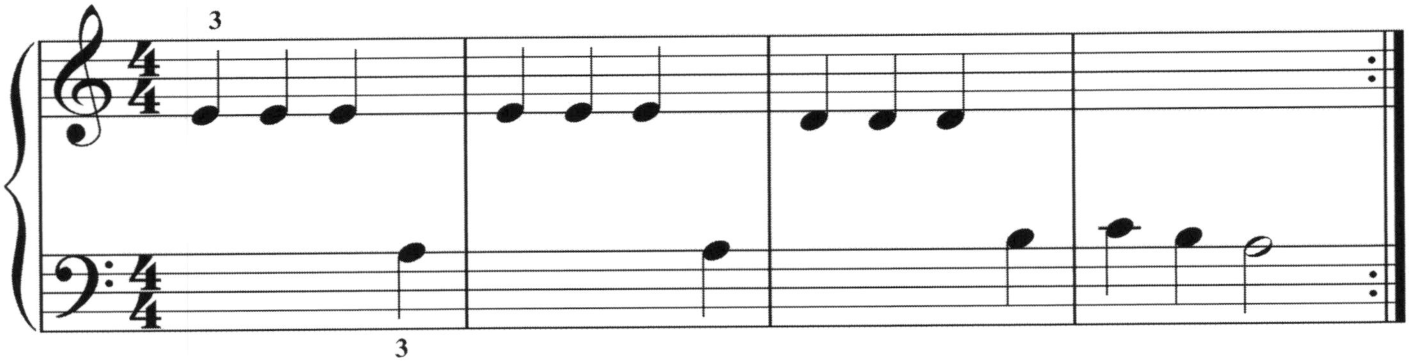

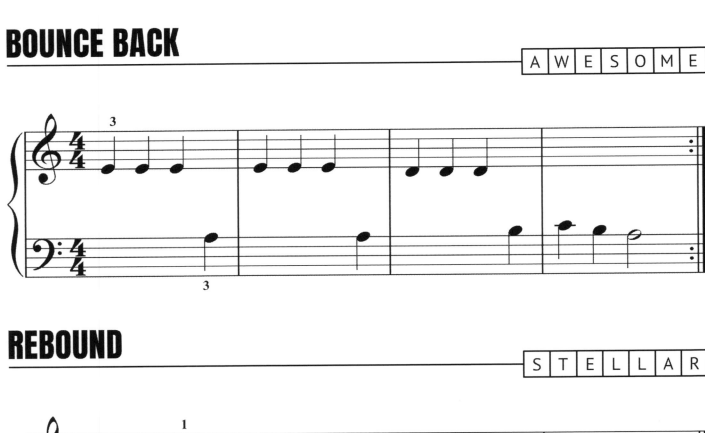

REBOUND

S T E L L A R

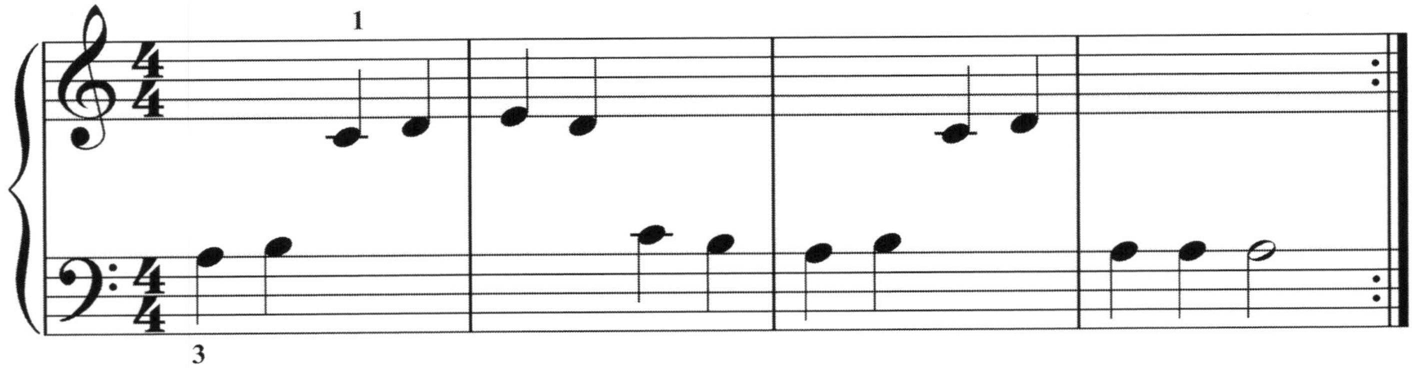

HOMEWARD BOUNCE

W I N N I N G

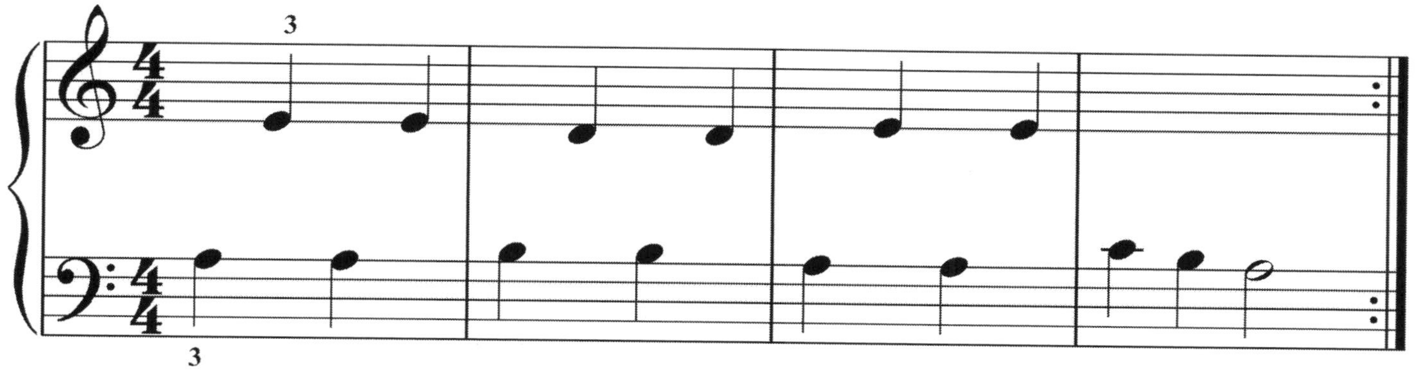

BOUND TOWN

P E R F E C T

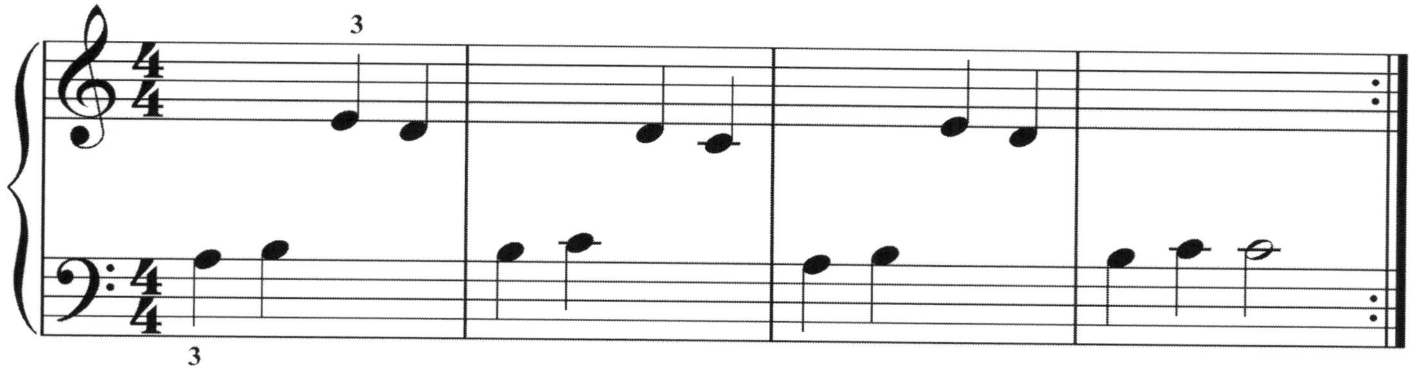

BOUNCE PASS

A M A Z I N G

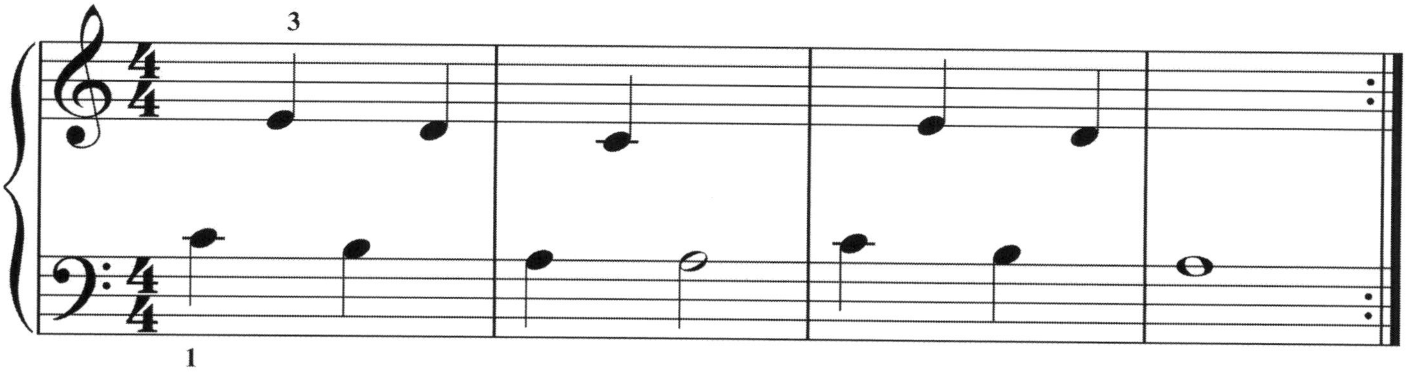

UNIT 3

AN INTRO

Let's get started! In each box,
draw a note that matches the first note.

A
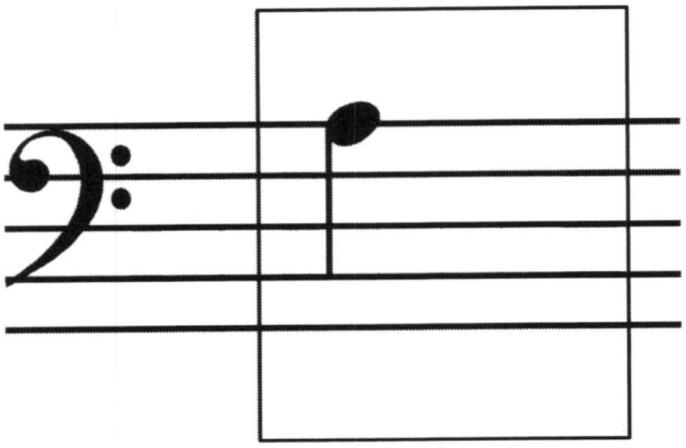

E
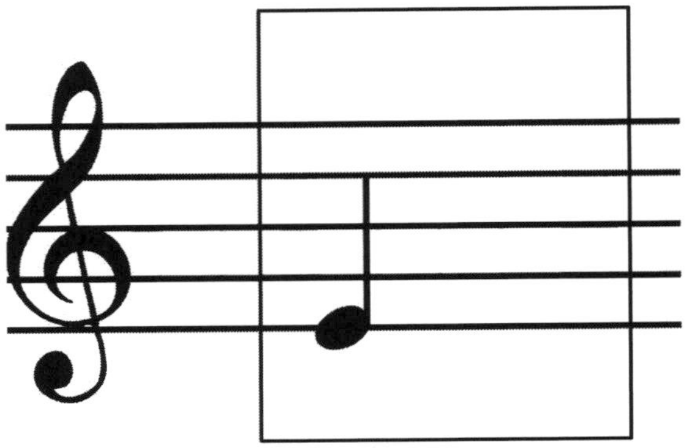

F
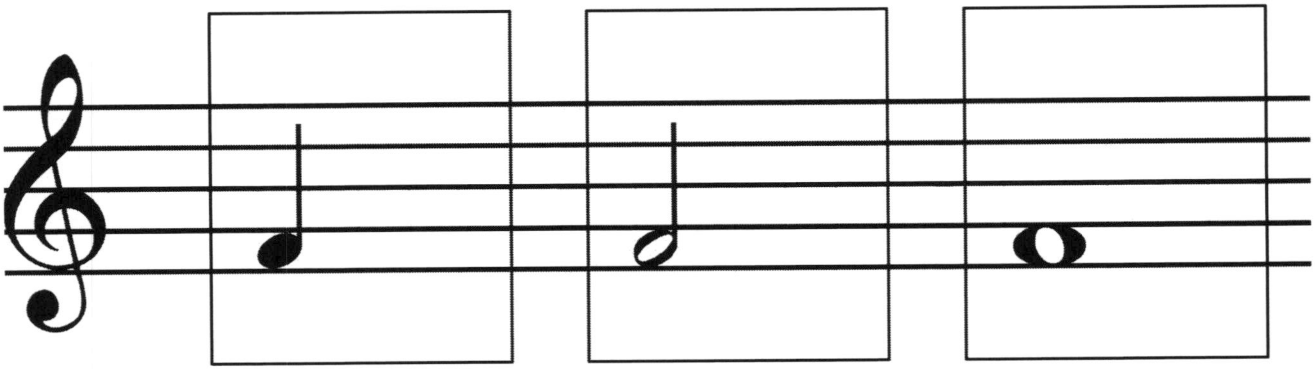

G
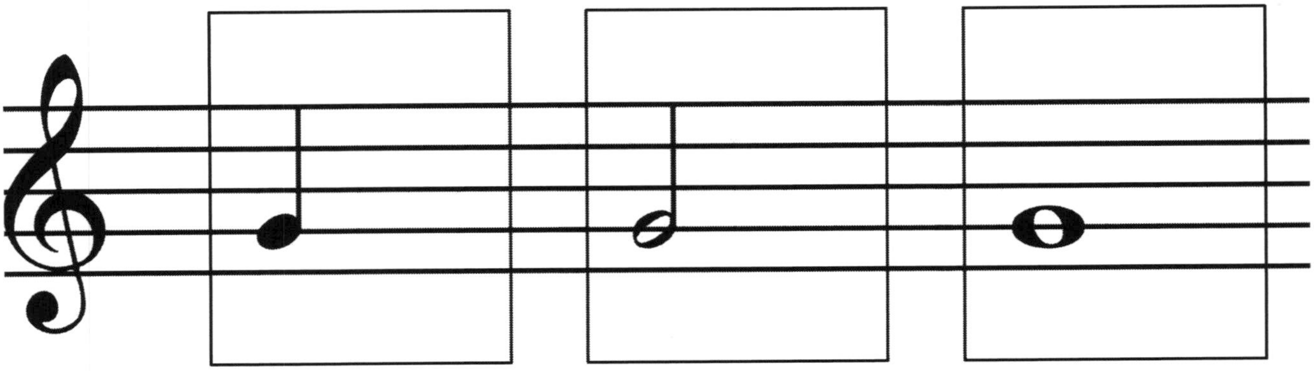

Color in one lettered box each time you practice a line of music.
After all of the boxes are colored, you will be one AWESOME piano player.

PRESS PLAY

A	W	E	S	O	M	E

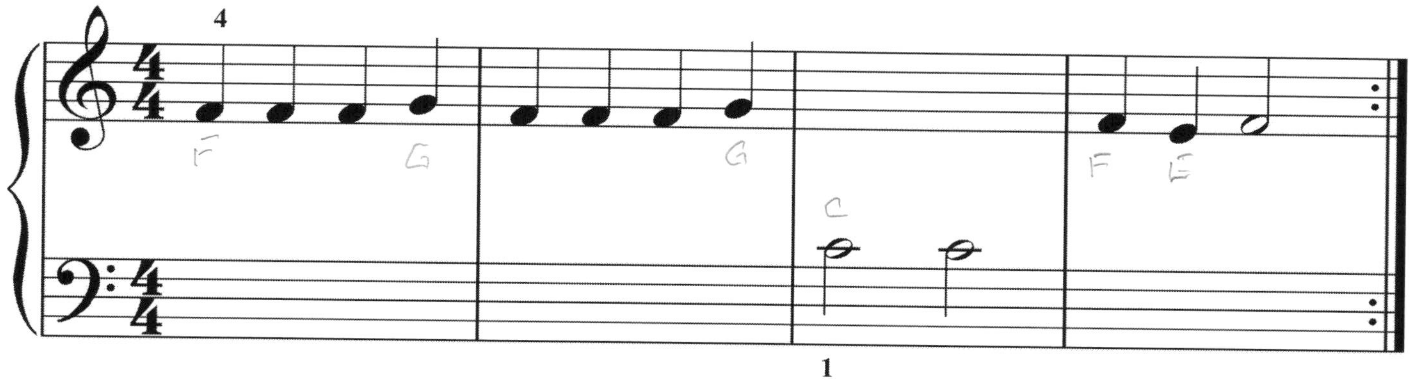

SIDE TO SIDE

P	E	R	F	E	C	T

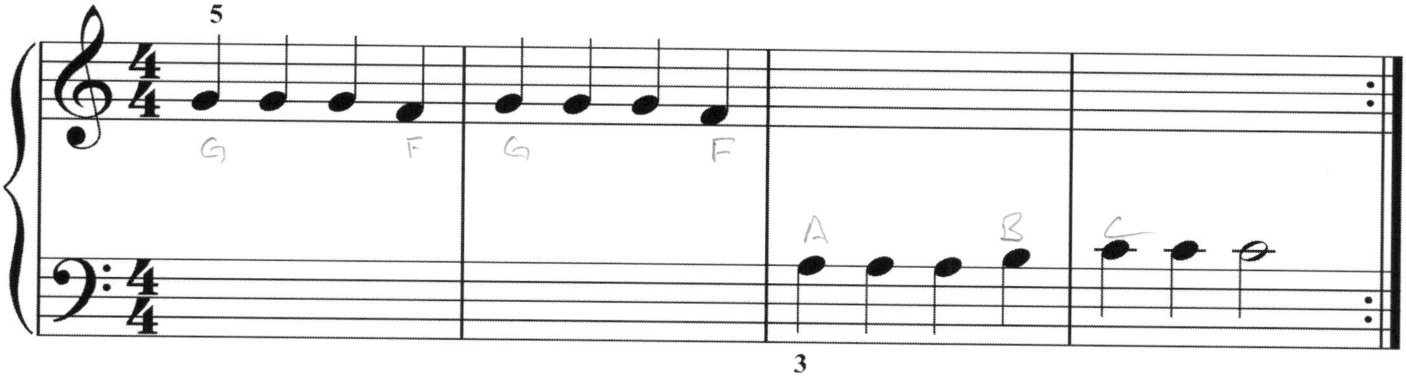

STEP-DOWNS

A	M	A	Z	I	N	G

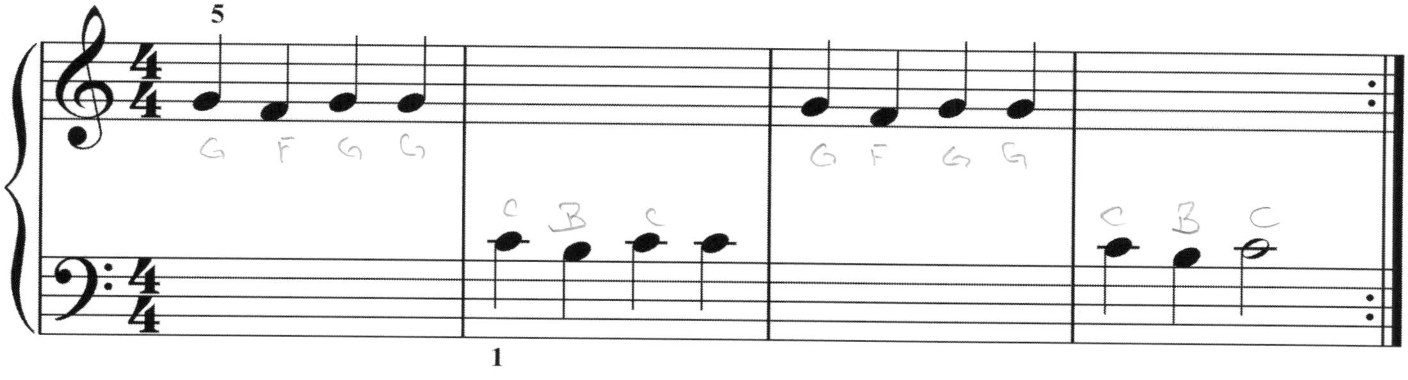

SET 01

Color in one lettered box each time you practice a line of music.
After all of the boxes are colored, you will be one AMAZING piano player.

CURL WHIRL

A	M	A	Z	I	N	G

BENCH PRESS

S	T	E	L	L	A	R

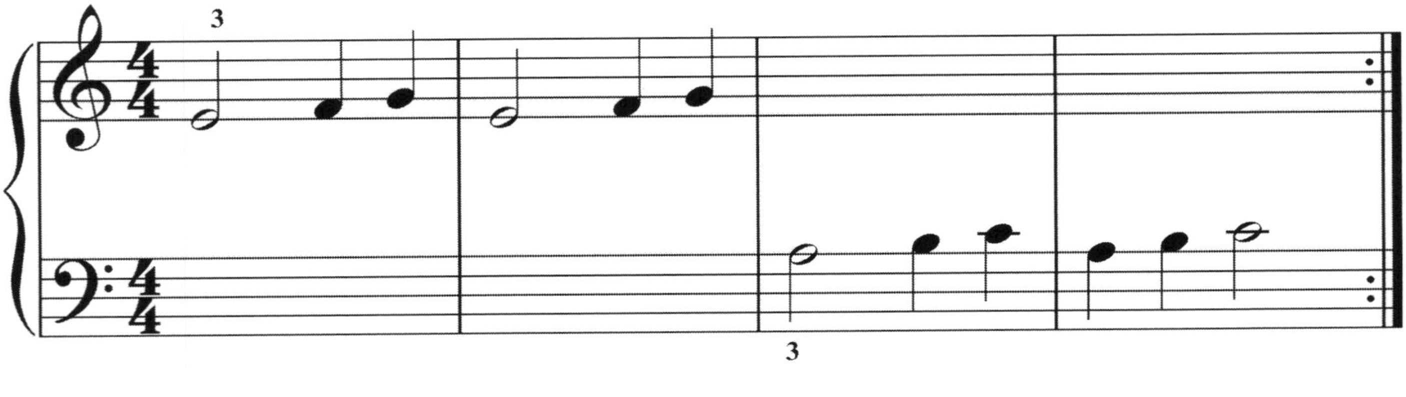

PUMP UP

W I N N I N G

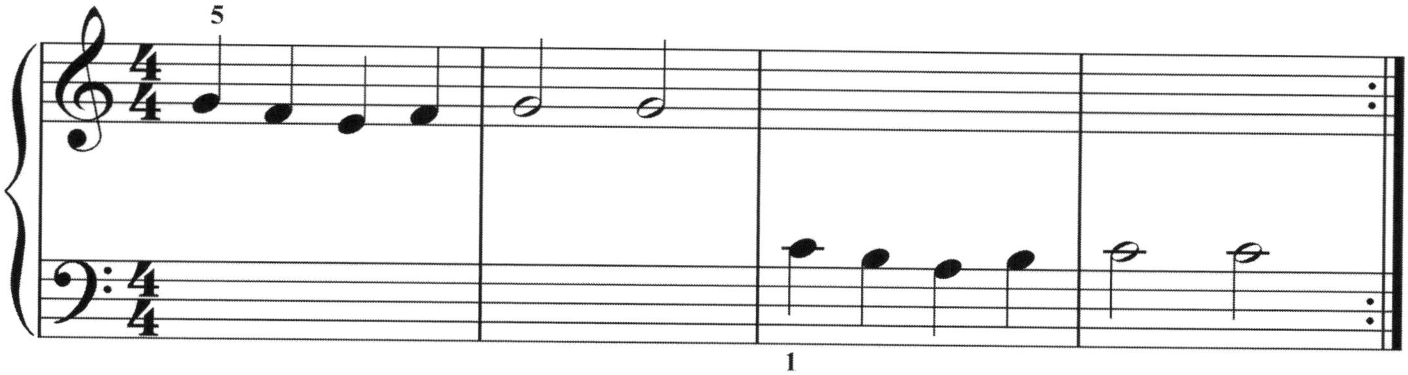

KICKBACK TRACK

P E R F E C T

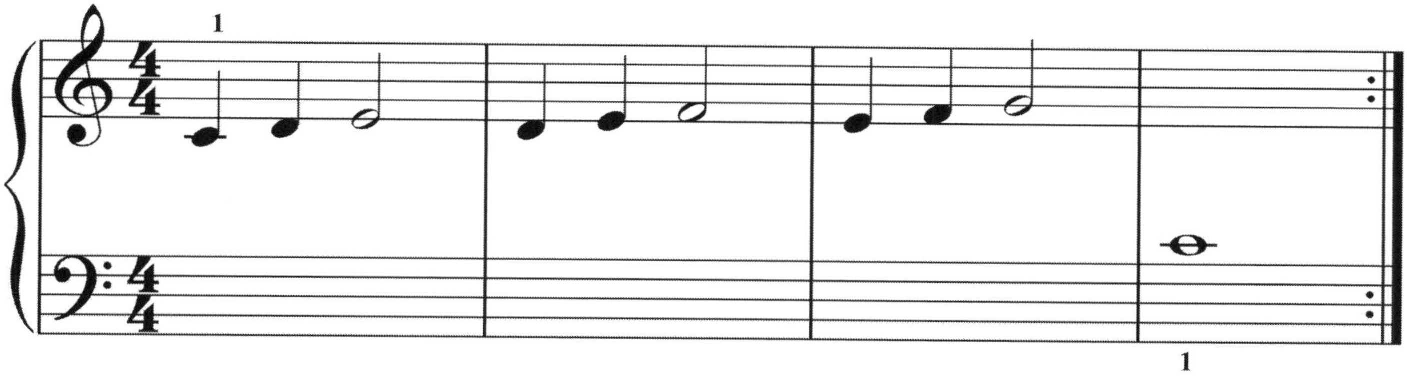

POWER PLAY

A W E S O M E

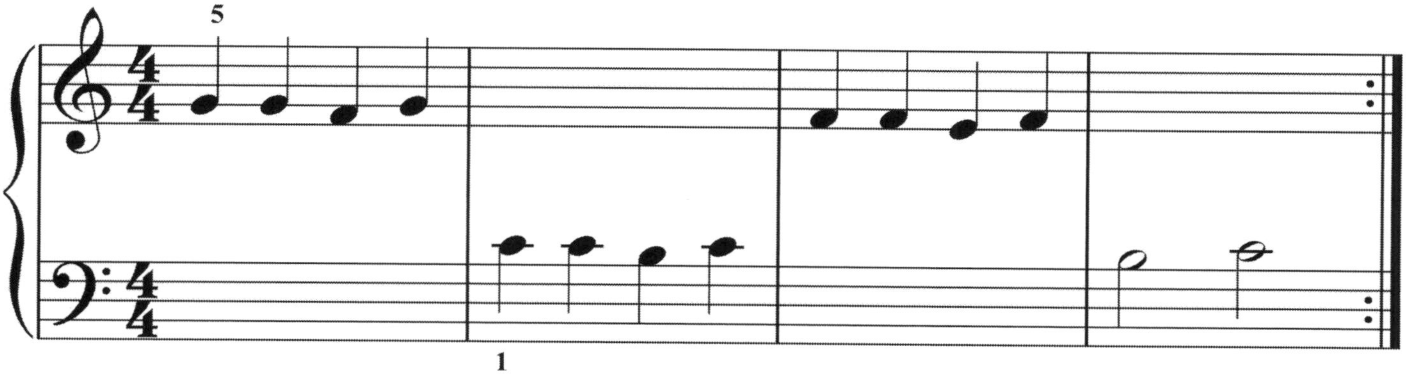

SET 02

Color in one lettered box each time you practice a line of music.
After all of the boxes are colored, you will be one STELLAR piano player.

CLIMB TIME

S T E L L A R

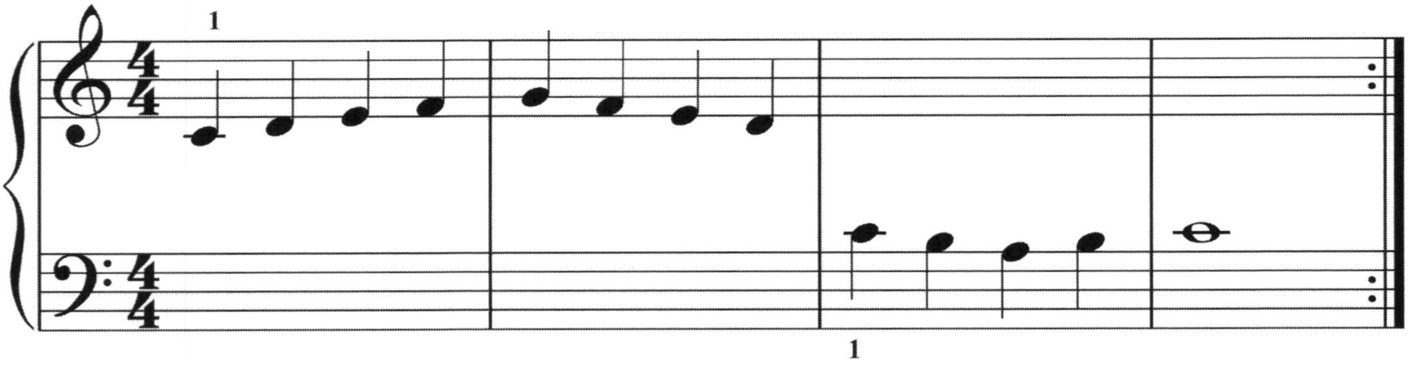

OUT AND BACK

A M A Z I N G

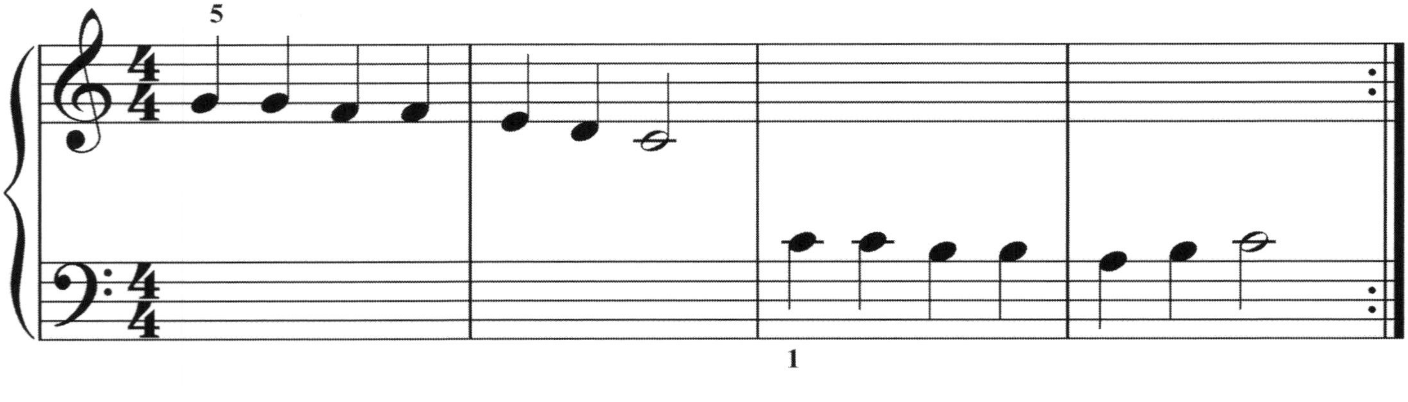

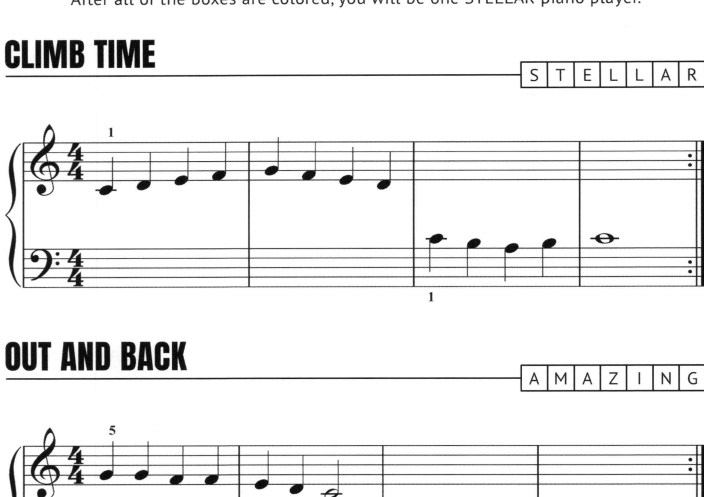

ROLLOUT

W I N N I N G

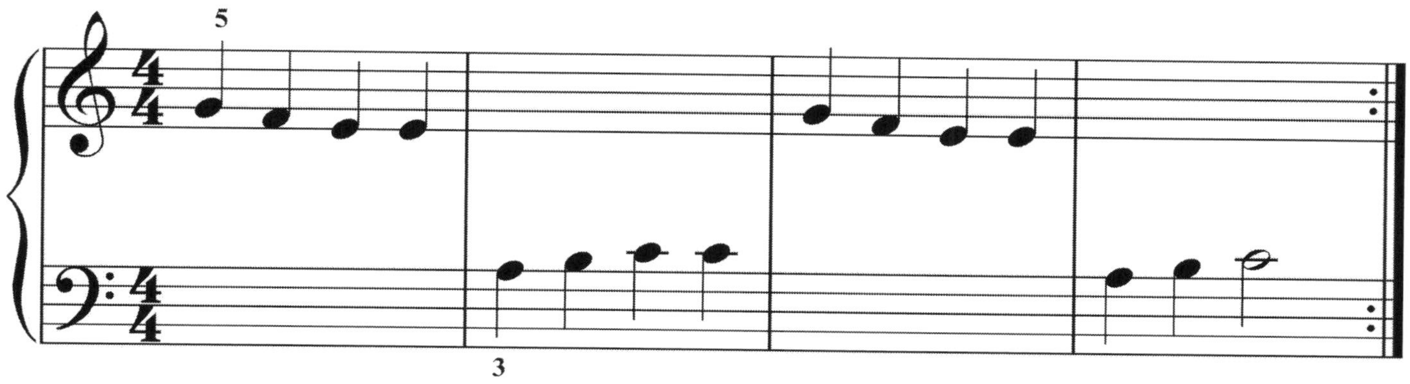

PUSHDOWNS

P E R F E C T

CRUNCH BUNCH

A W E S O M E

SIGHT READING ONE

SET 3 | PART 1

Look at Sight Reading One. Beginning at the START and ending at the FINISH, play the four measures that rest on the path. Use a colored crayon to draw a new four-measure path. Play again.

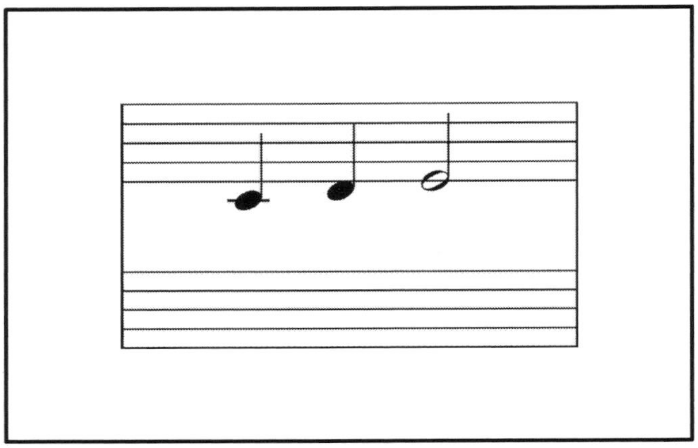

START

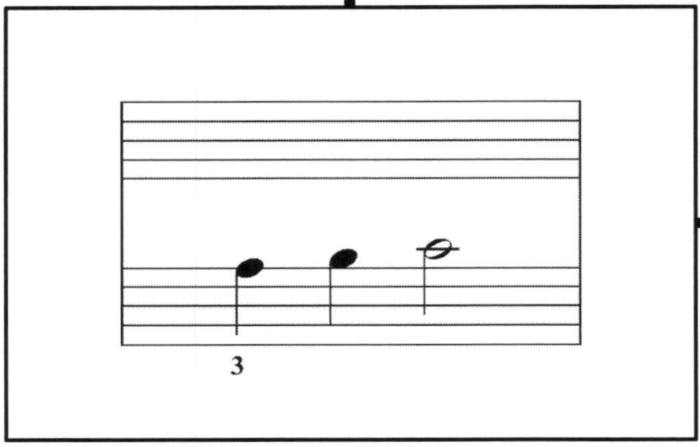

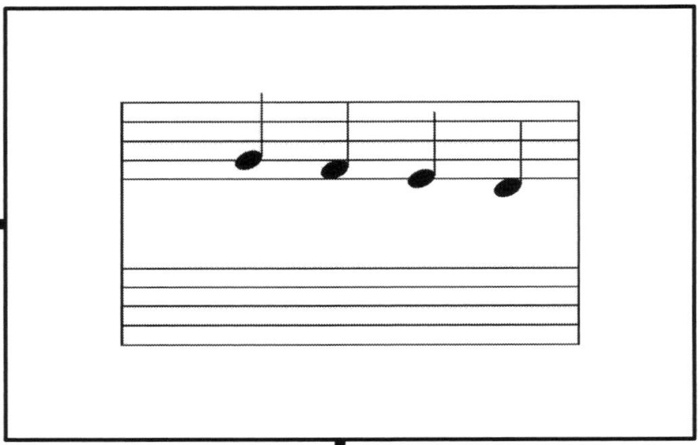

FINISH

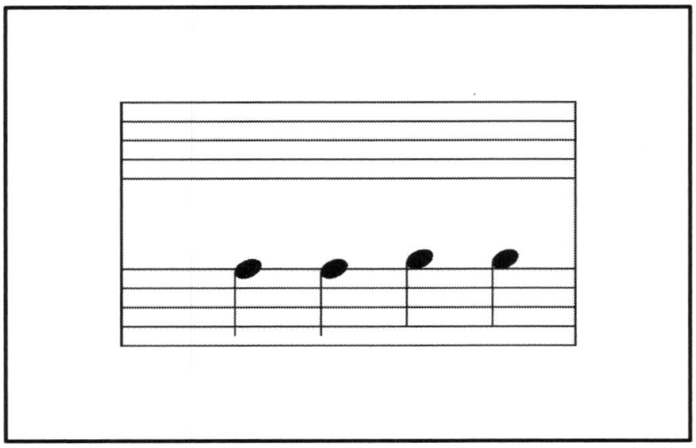

SET 3 | PART 2

Look at Sight Reading Two. Beginning at the START and ending at the FINISH, play the four measures that rest on the path. Use a colored crayon to draw a new four-measure path. Play again.

SIGHT READING TWO

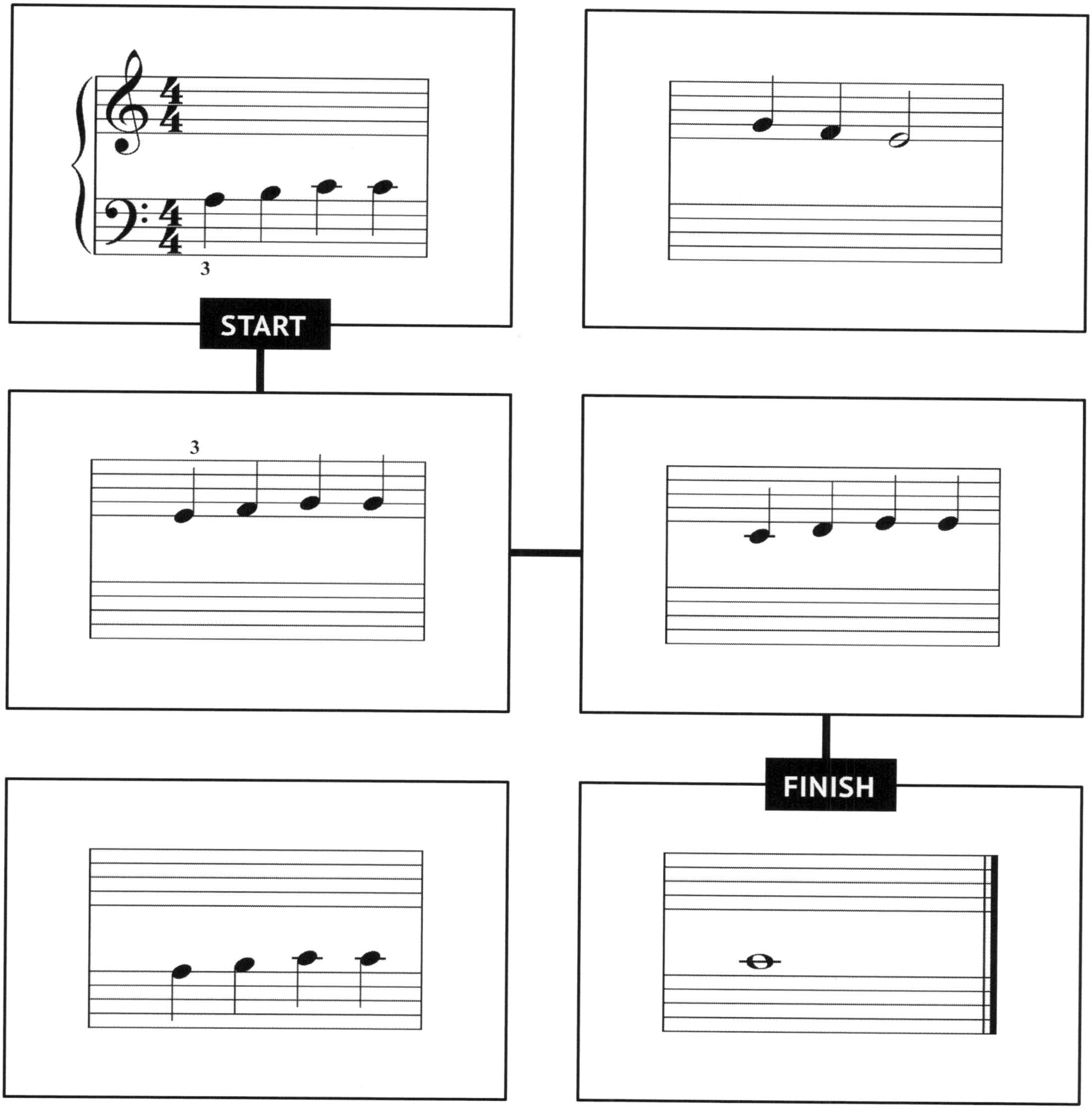

SET 04

UNIT 3

NEW!

TIME SIGNATURE

Color in one lettered box each time you practice a line of music.
After all of the boxes are colored, you will be one AWESOME piano player.

SPROCKET ROCKET

A	W	E	S	O	M	E

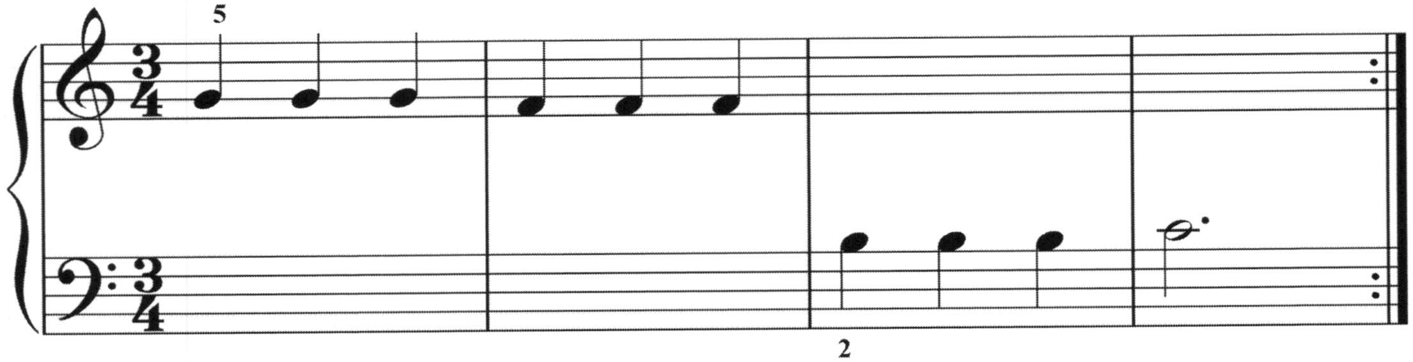

SADDLE UP

A	M	A	Z	I	N	G

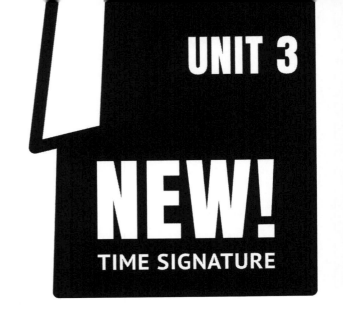

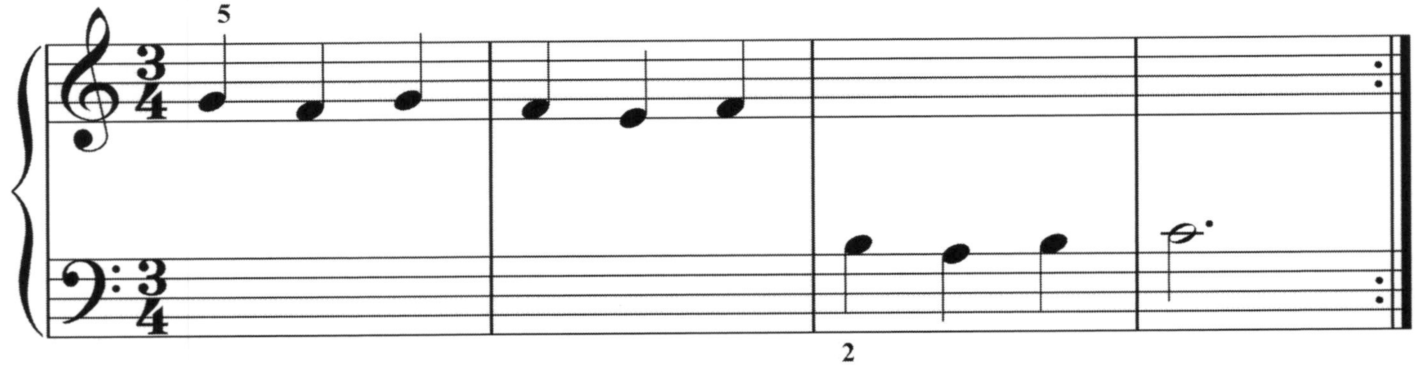

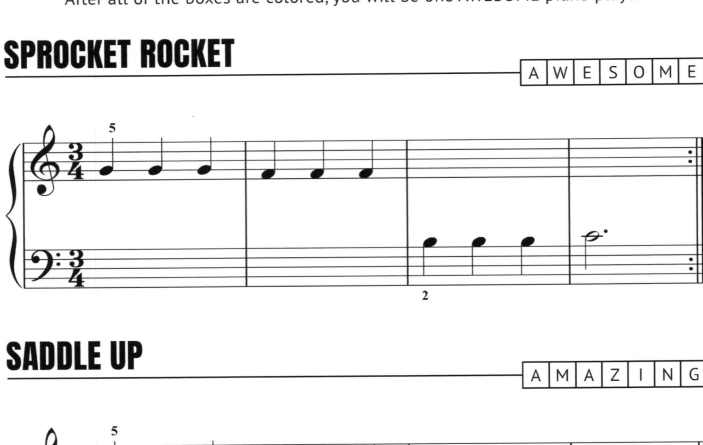

HIGH GEAR

WINNING

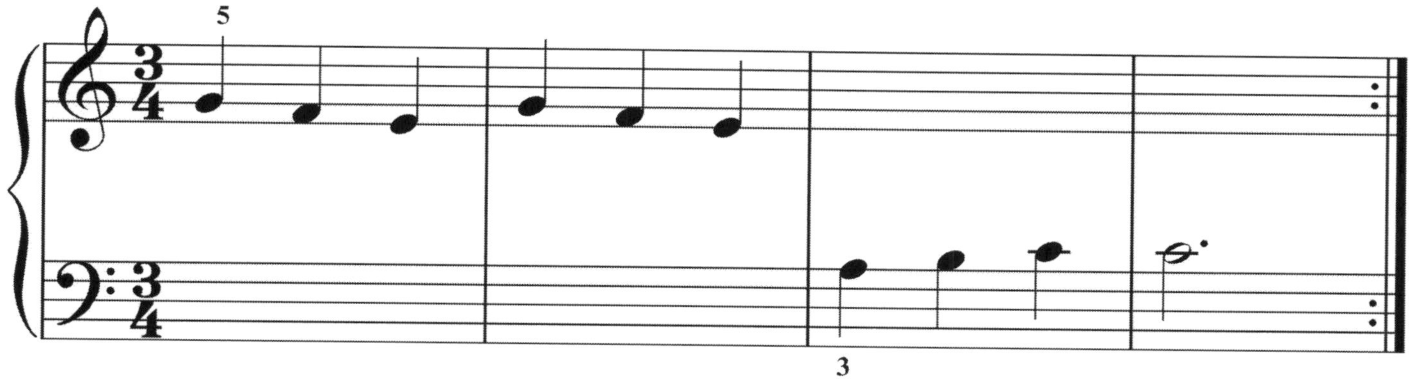

HOP AND HOVER

PERFECT

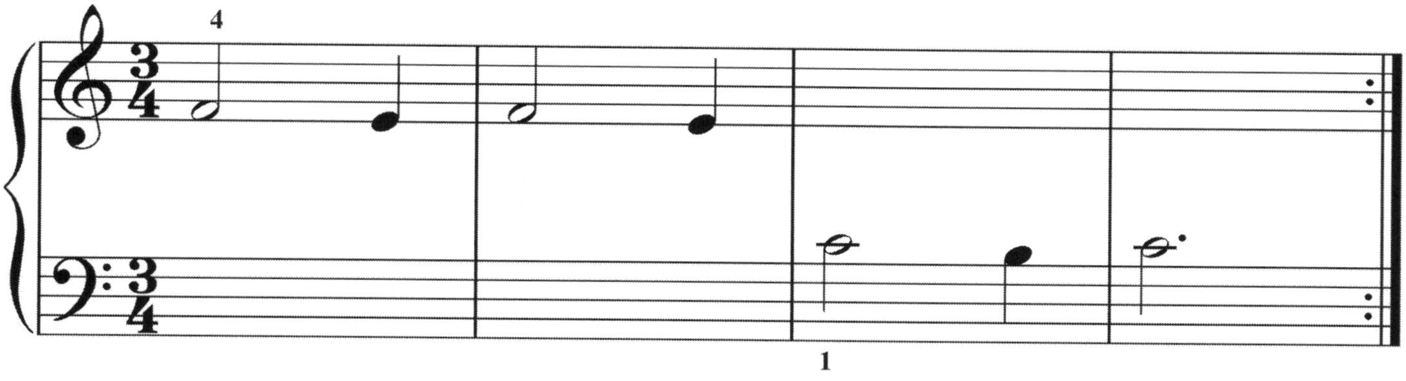

PEDAL POWER

STELLAR

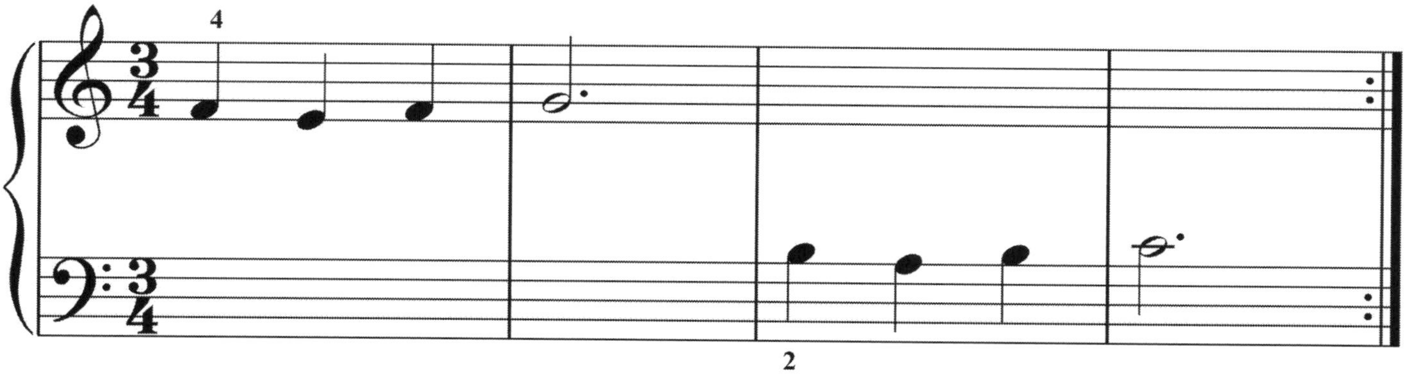

SET 05

In the box above Exercise 1, write the name of the first note. Next, use the finger number to find your starting position. Repeat with Exercises 2 and 3.

MOVE AND GROOVE ☐

S T E L L A R

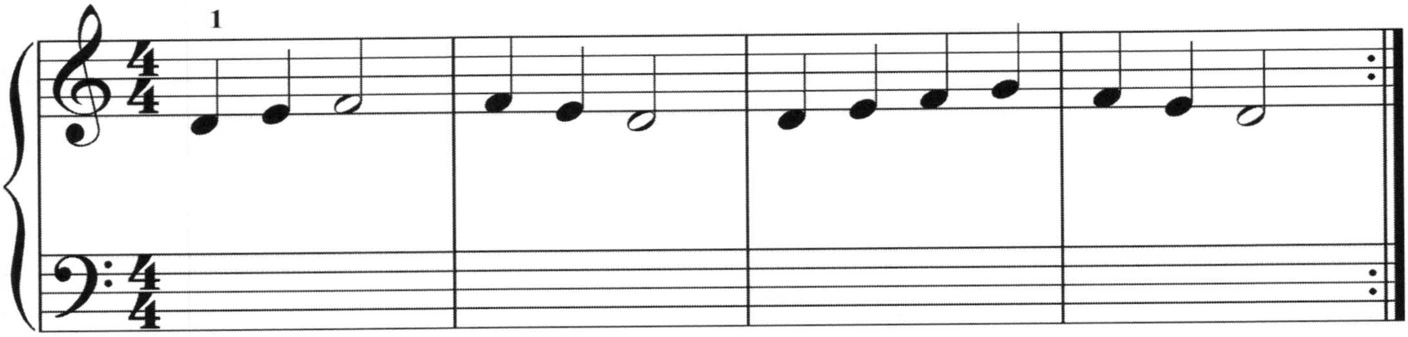

SPACE TRAVEL ☐

A M A Z I N G

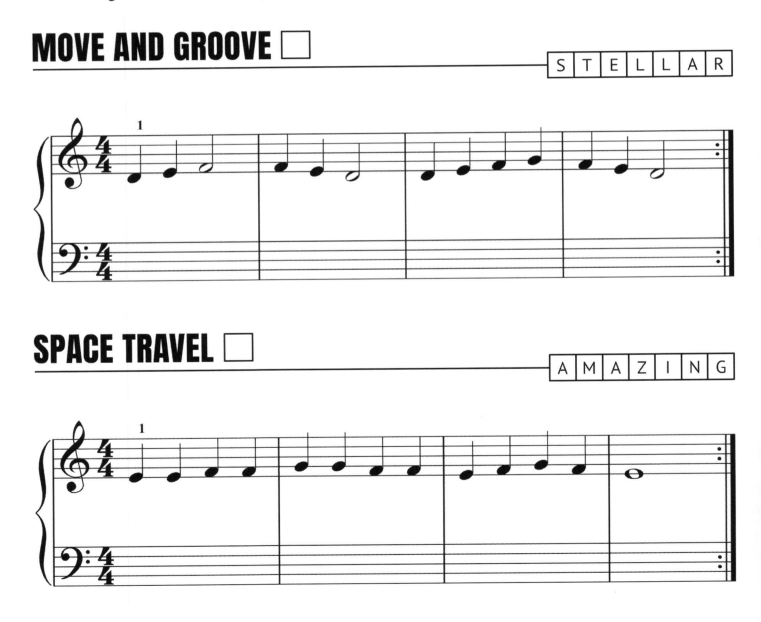

SHIFT WORK ☐

W I N N I N G

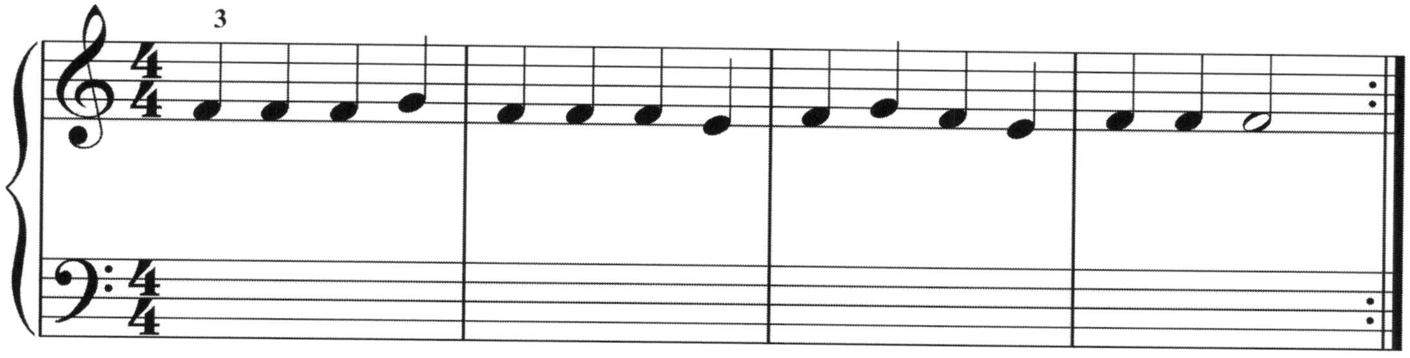

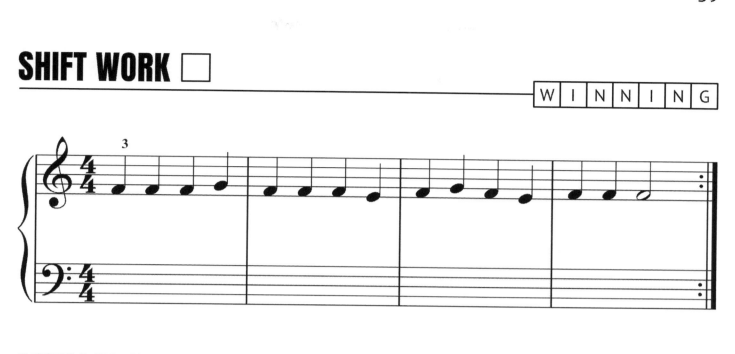

CHALLENGE PIECE 1

P E R F E C T

CHALLENGE PIECE 2

A W E S O M E

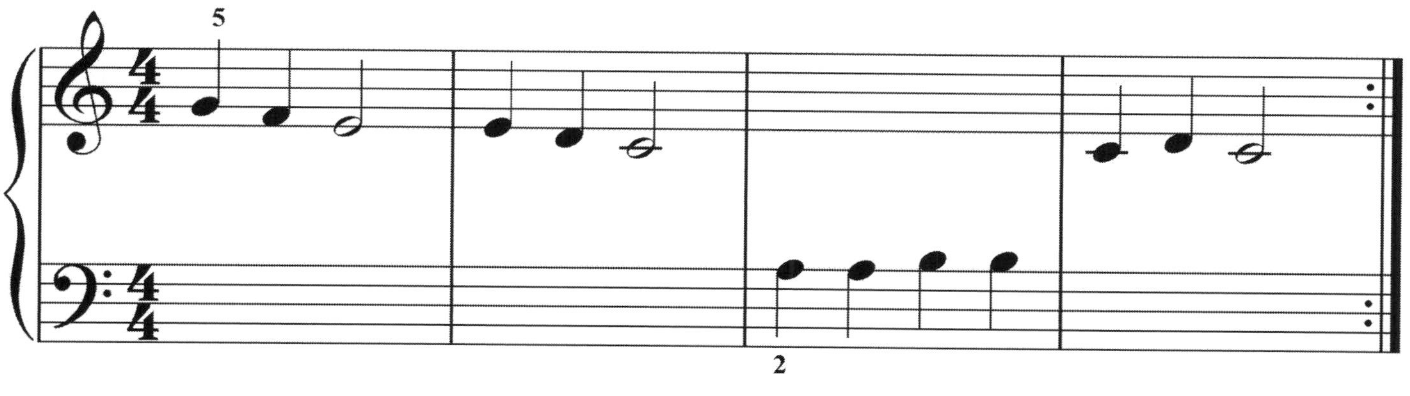

SET 06

UNIT 3

RHYTHM

Look at the first line of rhythm below. Stem-down notes are performed by tapping both hands on your lap. Stem-up notes are performed by clapping your hands together. After performing the first rhythm, complete the remaining exercises.

RHYTHM CHALLENGE 1

A	W	E	S	O	M	E

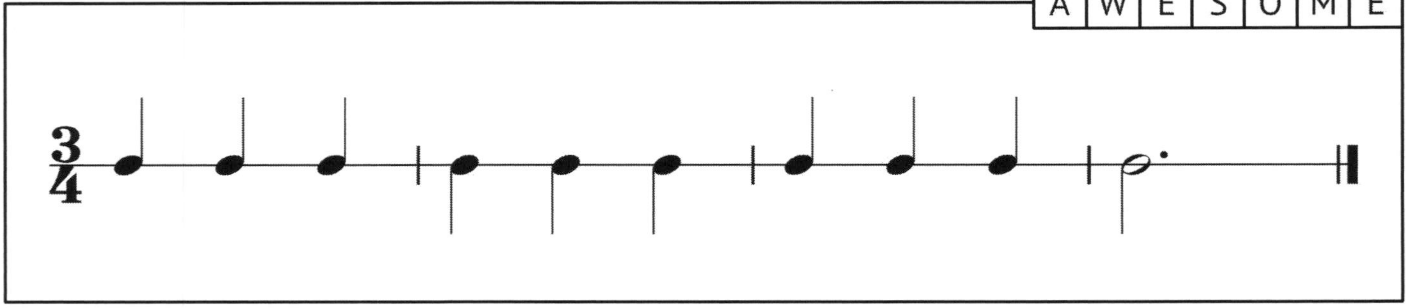

RHYTHM CHALLENGE 2

S	T	E	L	L	A	R

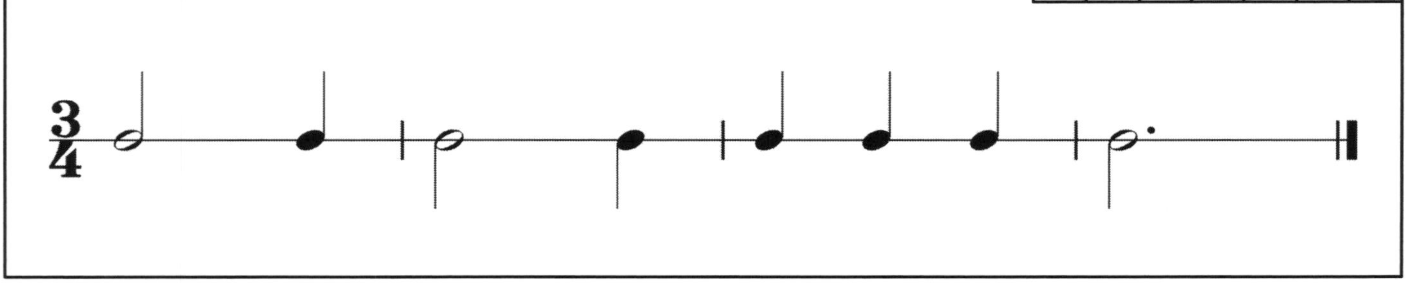

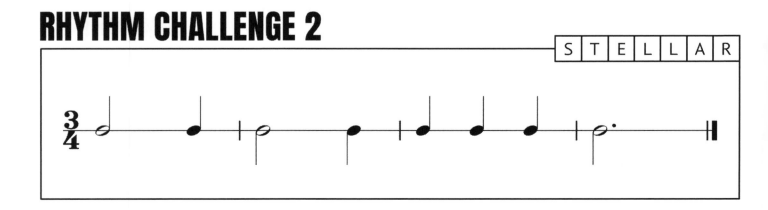

RHYTHM CHALLENGE 3

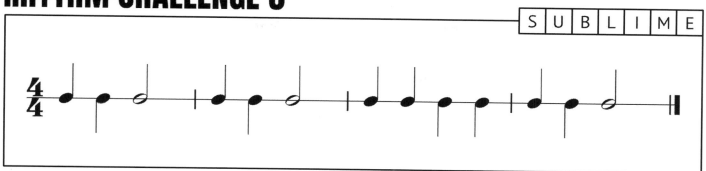

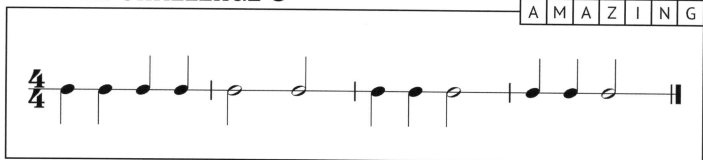

S	U	B	L	I	M	E

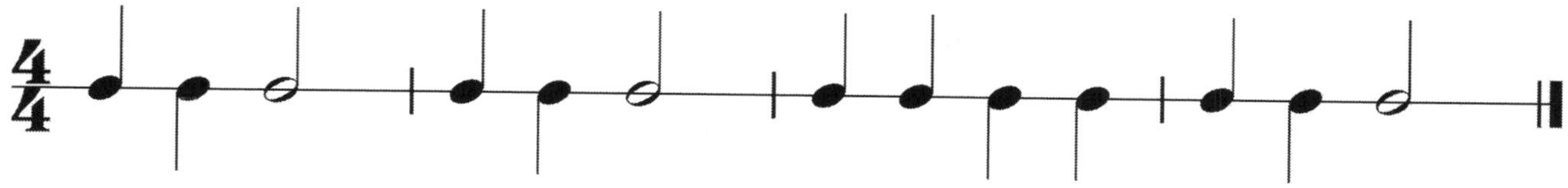

RHYTHM CHALLENGE 4

P	E	R	F	E	C	T

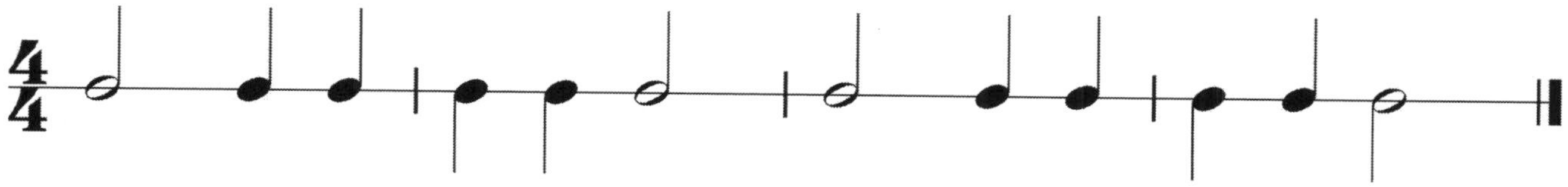

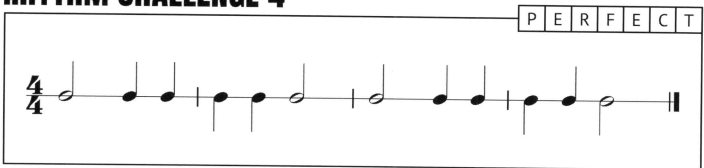

RHYTHM CHALLENGE 5

W	I	N	N	I	N	G

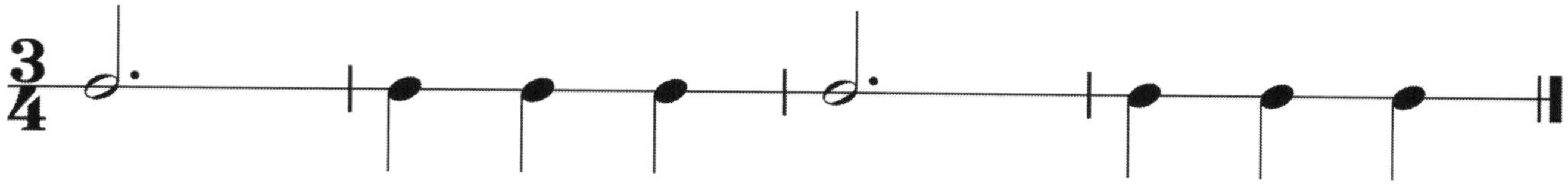

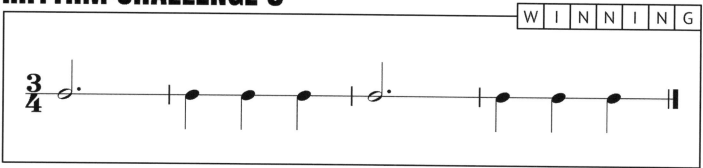

RHYTHM CHALLENGE 6

A	M	A	Z	I	N	G

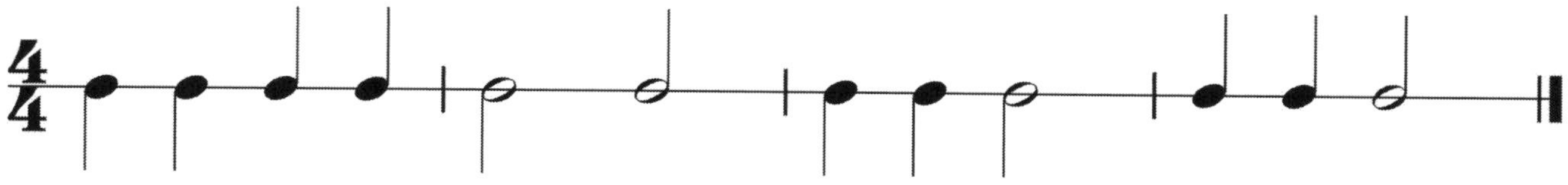

SET 07

UNIT 3

CHALLENGE SET

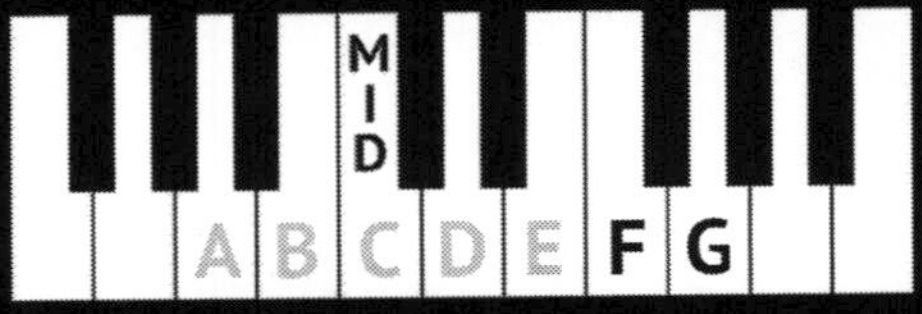

The following cross-staff exercises are intended for older beginners and students who want to test their skills.

BOUNCE BACK

A	W	E	S	O	M	E

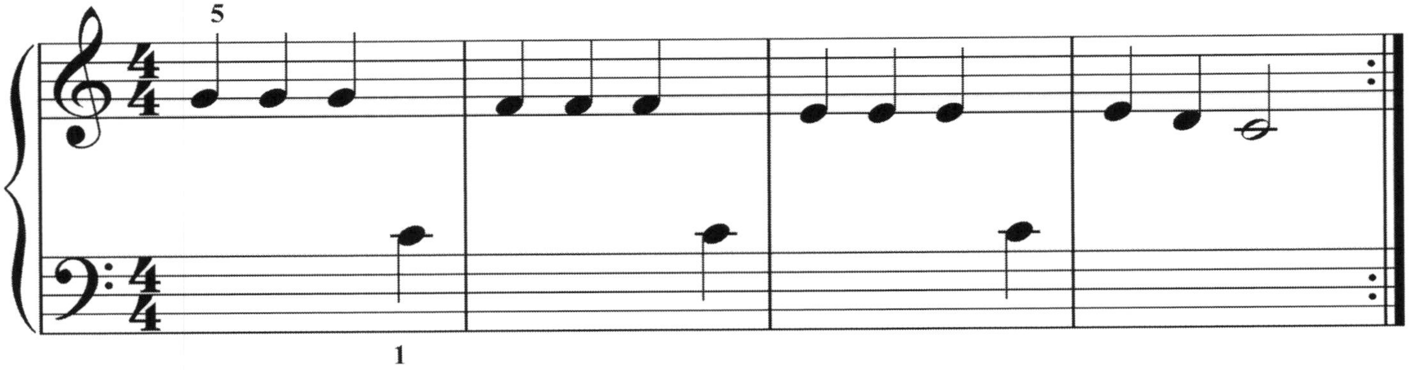

REBOUND

S	T	E	L	L	A	R

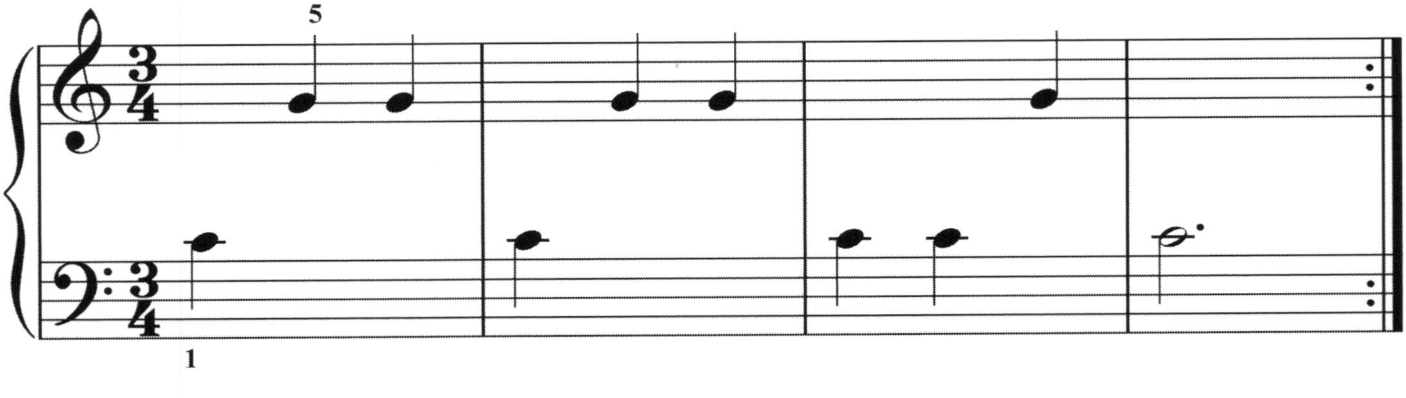

HOMEWARD BOUNCE

W I N N I N G

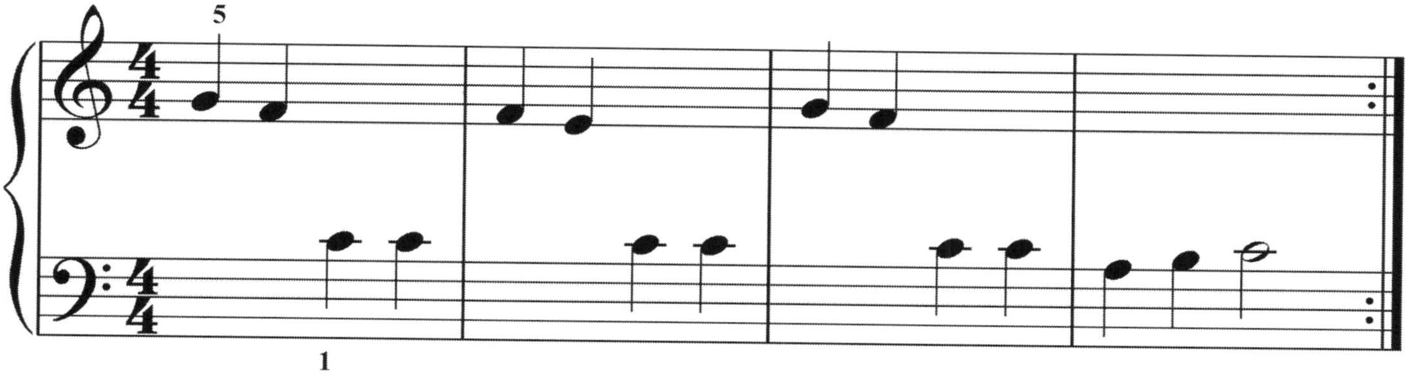

BOUND TOWN

P E R F E C T

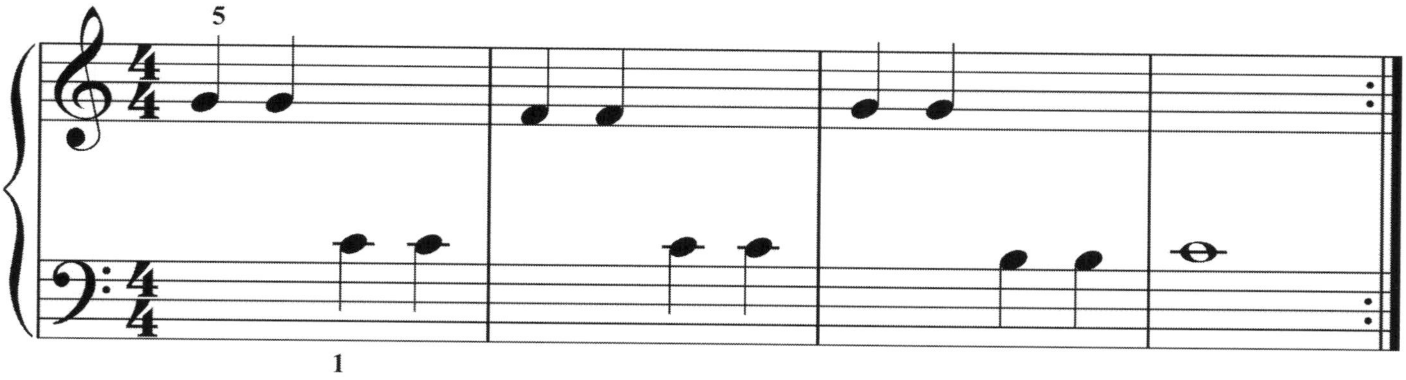

BOUNCE PASS

A M A Z I N G

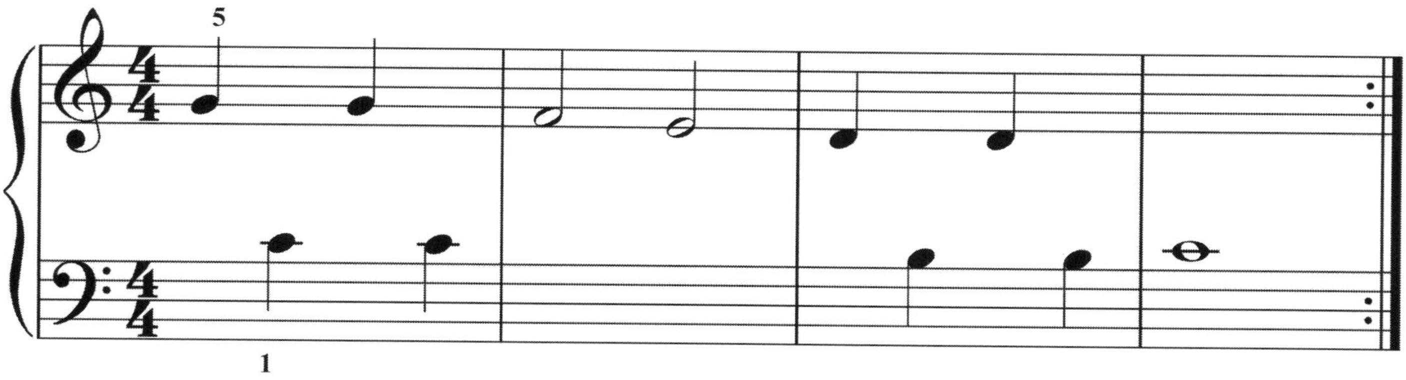

UNIT 4

AN INTRO

Let's get started! In each box,
draw a note that matches the first note.

F
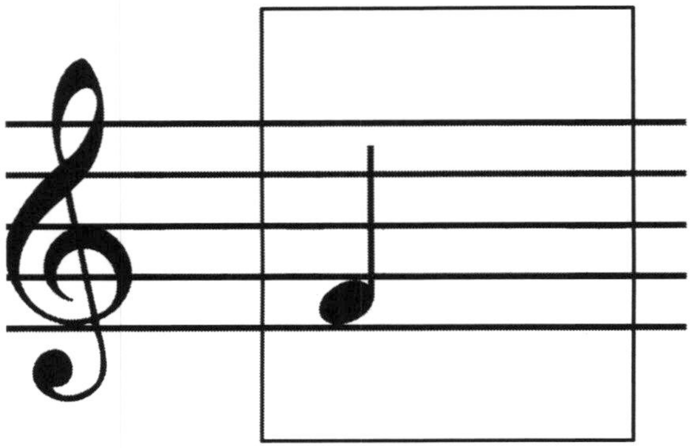

G
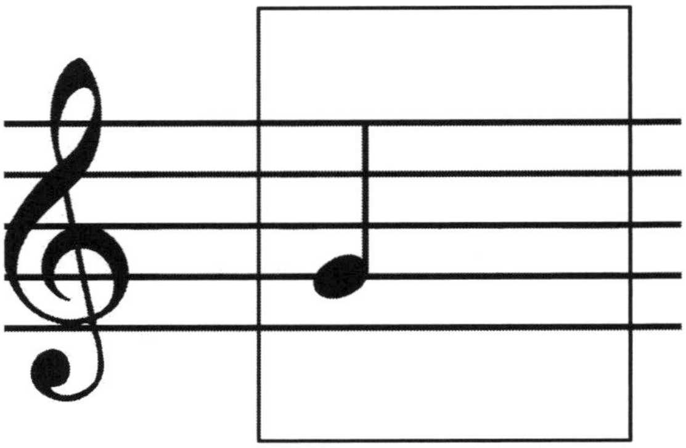

F
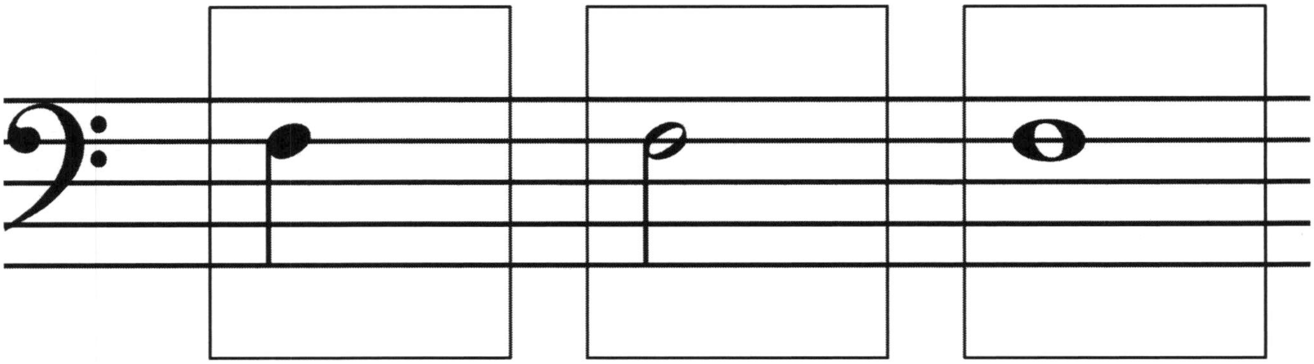

G
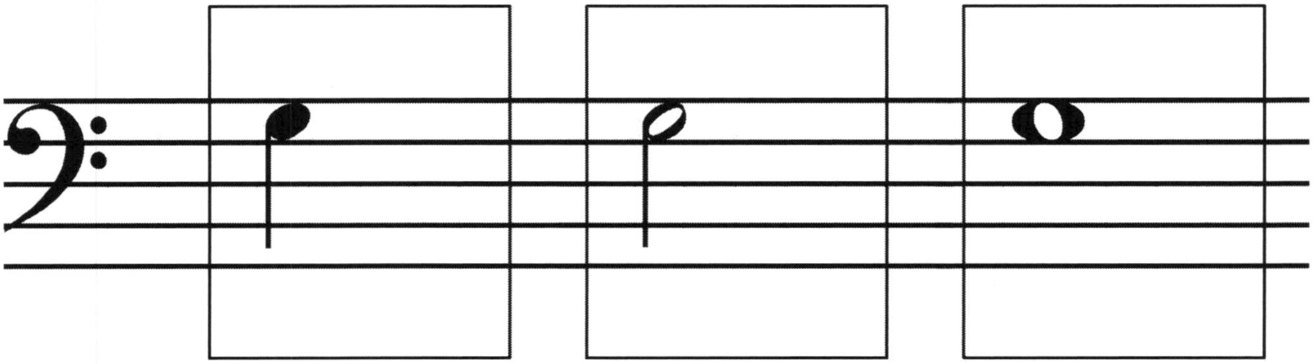

Color in one lettered box each time you practice a line of music.
After all of the boxes are colored, you will be one AWESOME piano player.

PRESS PLAY

A	W	E	S	O	M	E

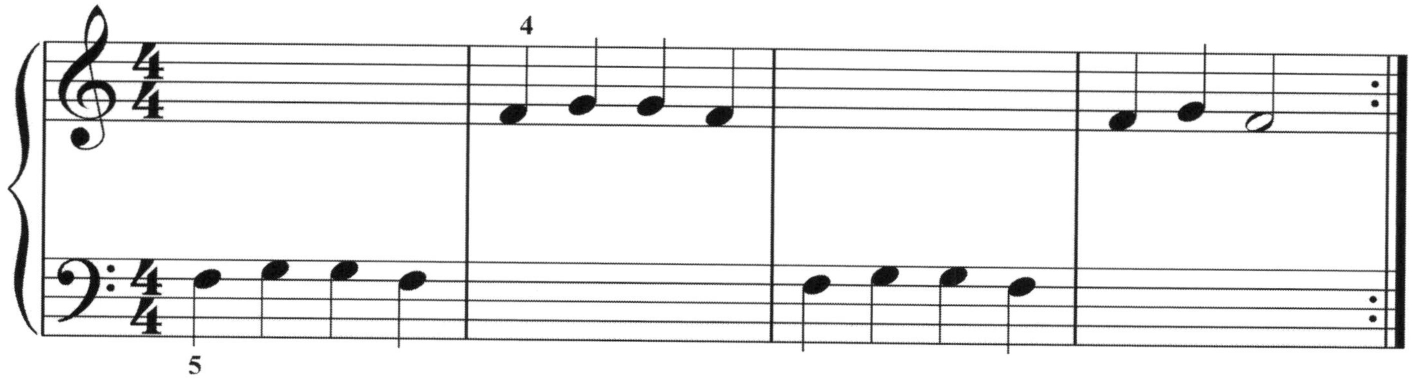

SIDE TO SIDE

P	E	R	F	E	C	T

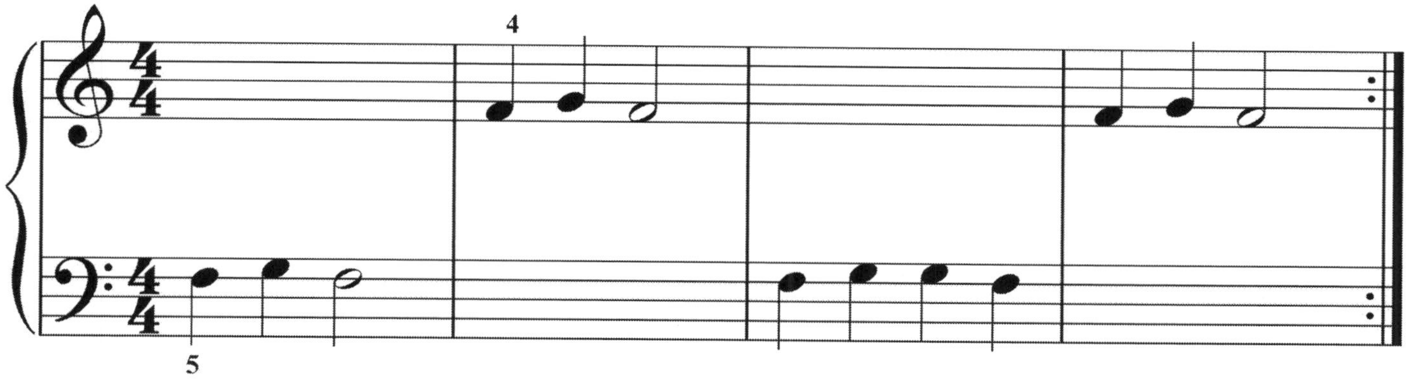

REVERSE FLY

A	M	A	Z	I	N	G

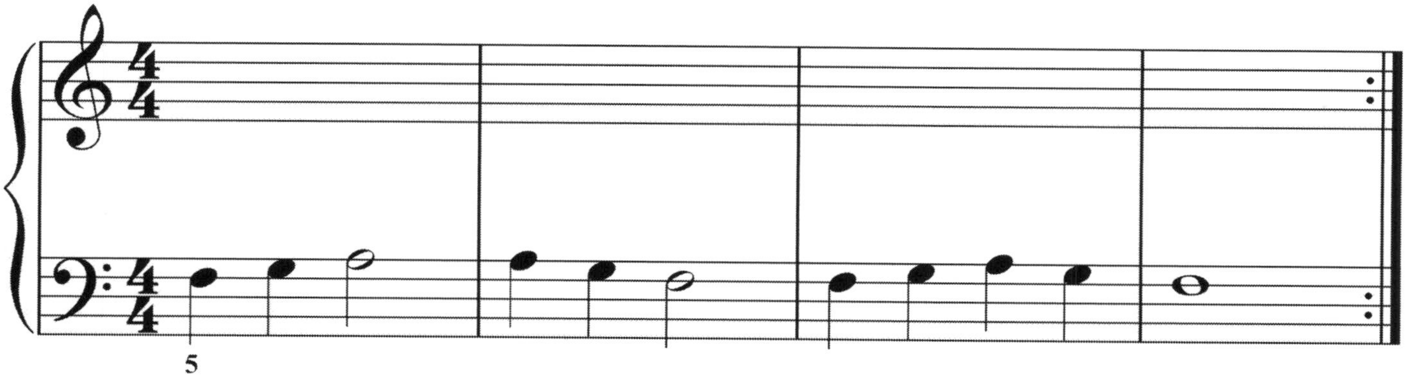

SET 01

Color in one lettered box each time you practice a line of music.
After all of the boxes are colored, you will be one AMAZING piano player.

PENDULUM

A	M	A	Z	I	N	G

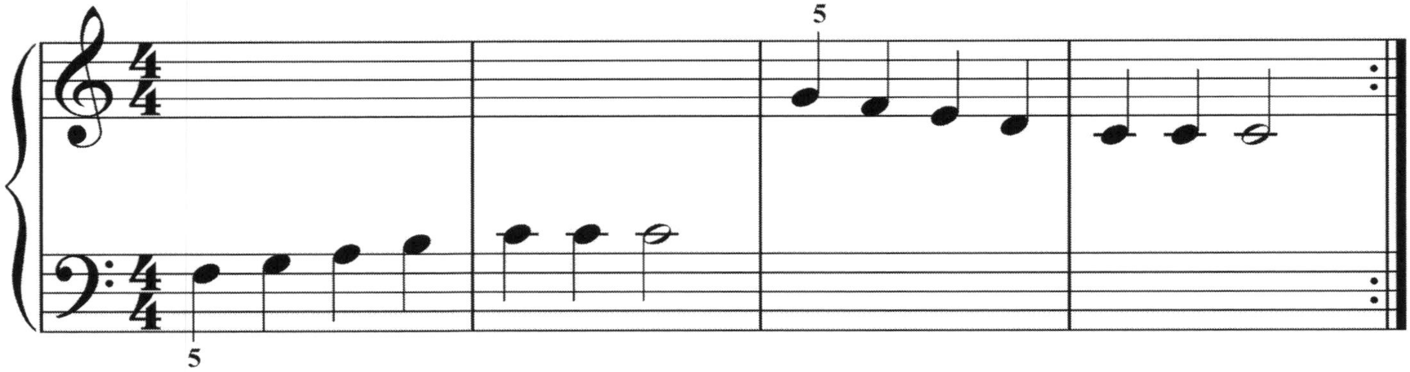

SPLISH SPLASH

S	T	E	L	L	A	R

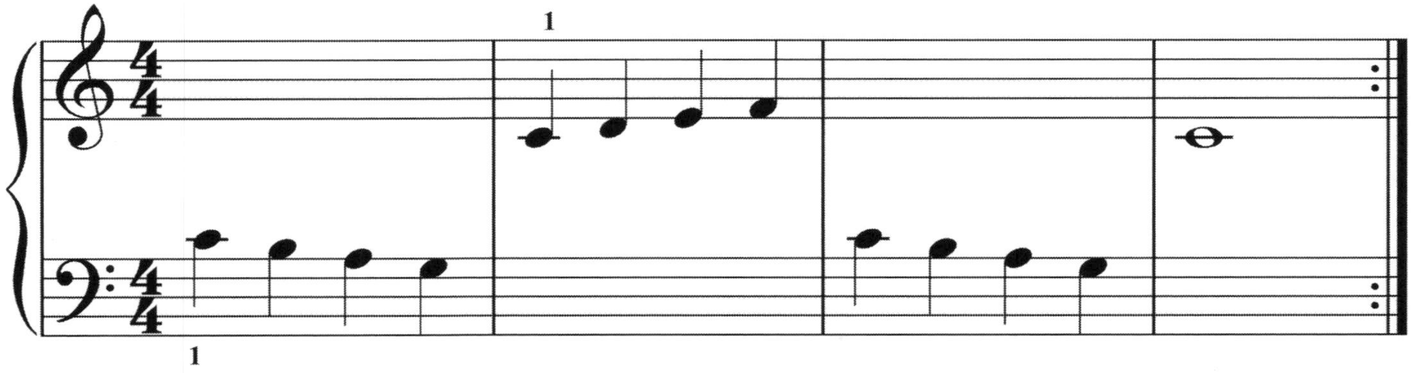

ROW FLOW

WINNING

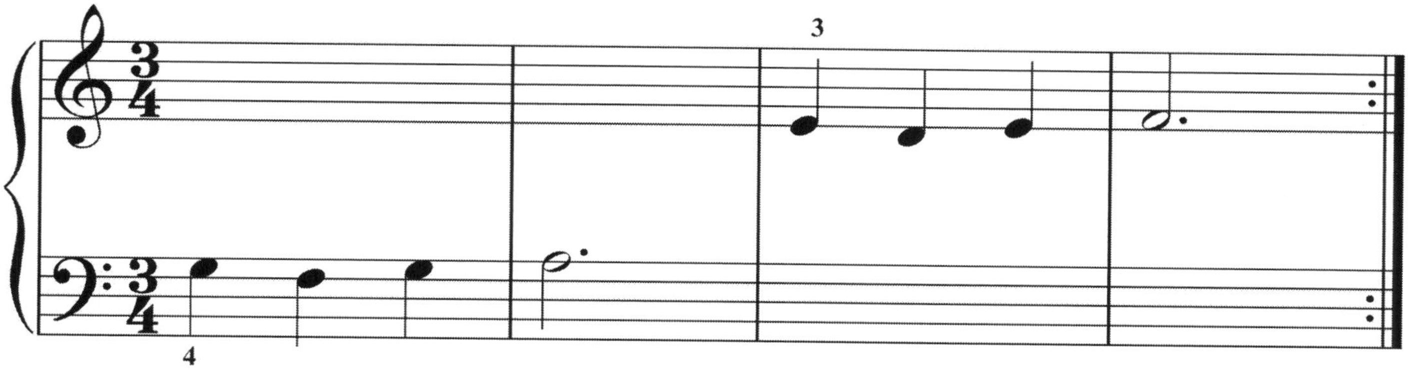

KICKBACK TRACK

PERFECT

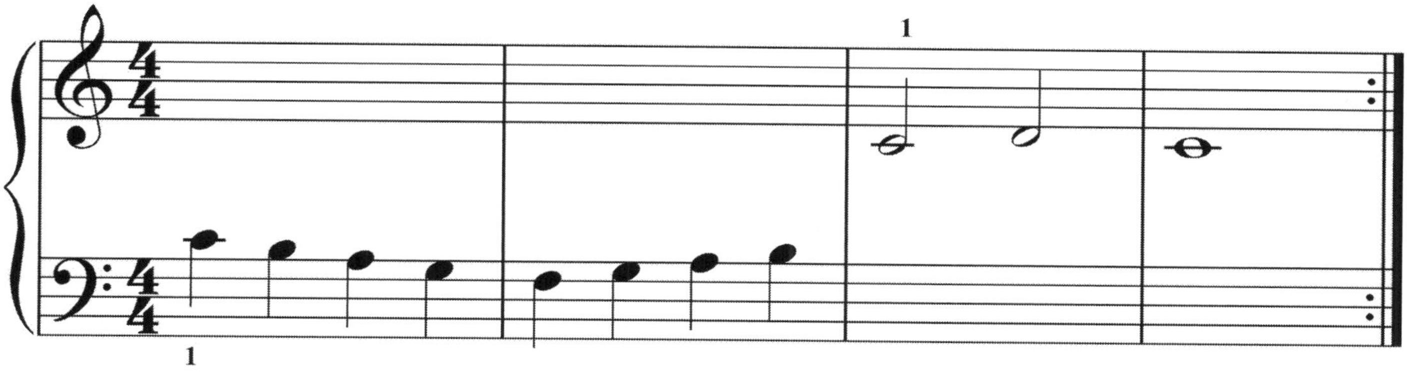

POWER PLAY

AWESOME

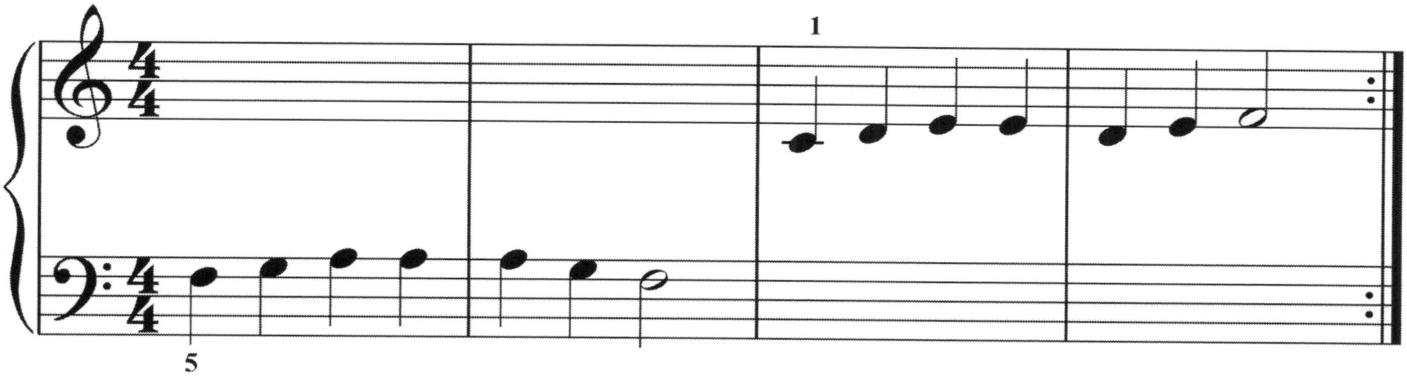

SET 02

Color in one lettered box each time you practice a line of music.
After all of the boxes are colored, you will be one STELLAR piano player.

CLIMB TIME

S T E L L A R

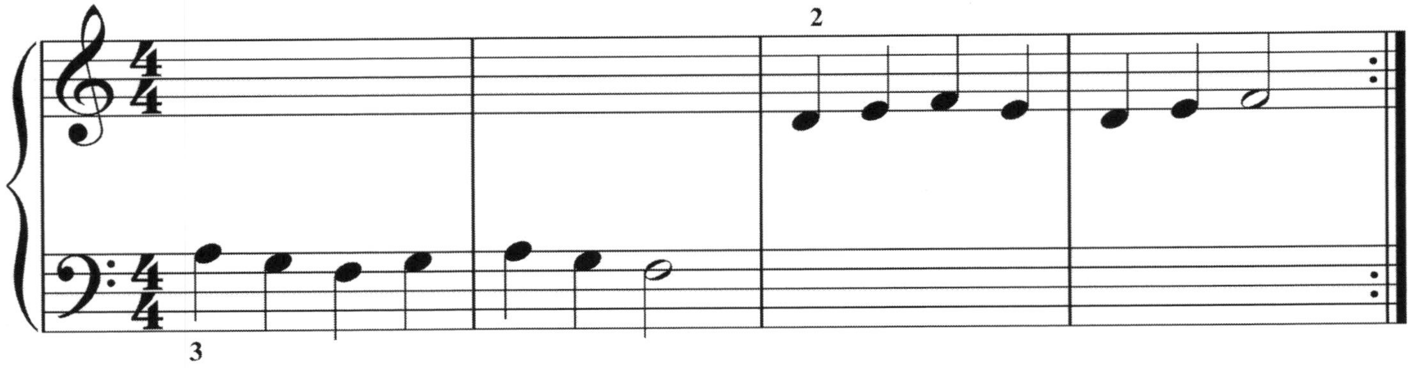

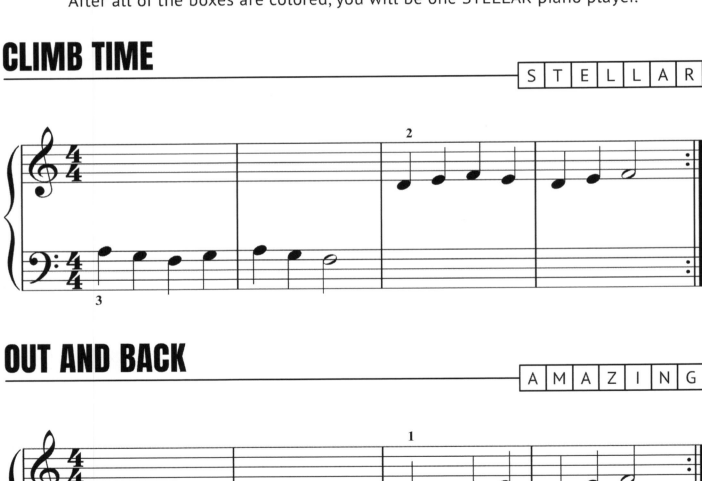

OUT AND BACK

A M A Z I N G

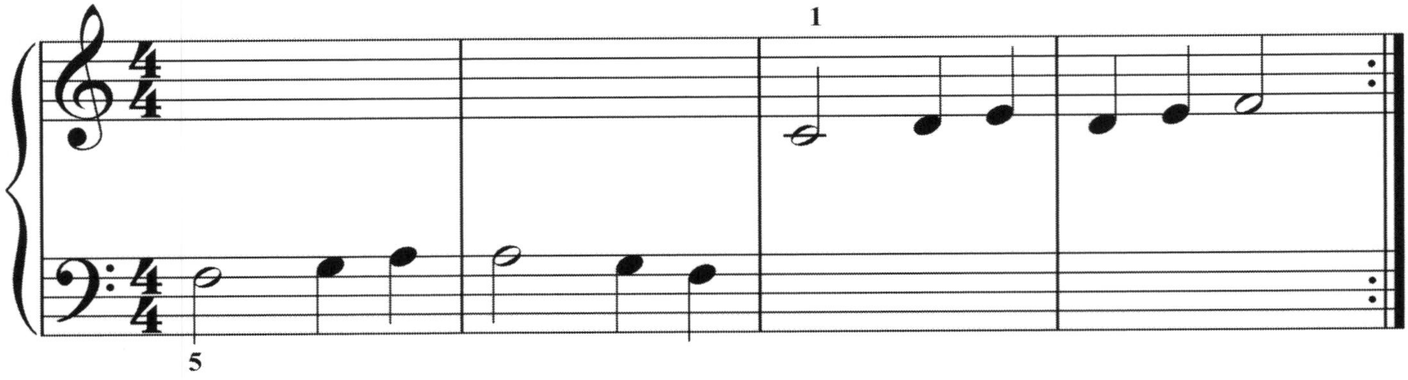

TOP HOP

W I N N I N G

BRIDGE DOWN

P E R F E C T

ROUNDHOUSE

A W E S O M E

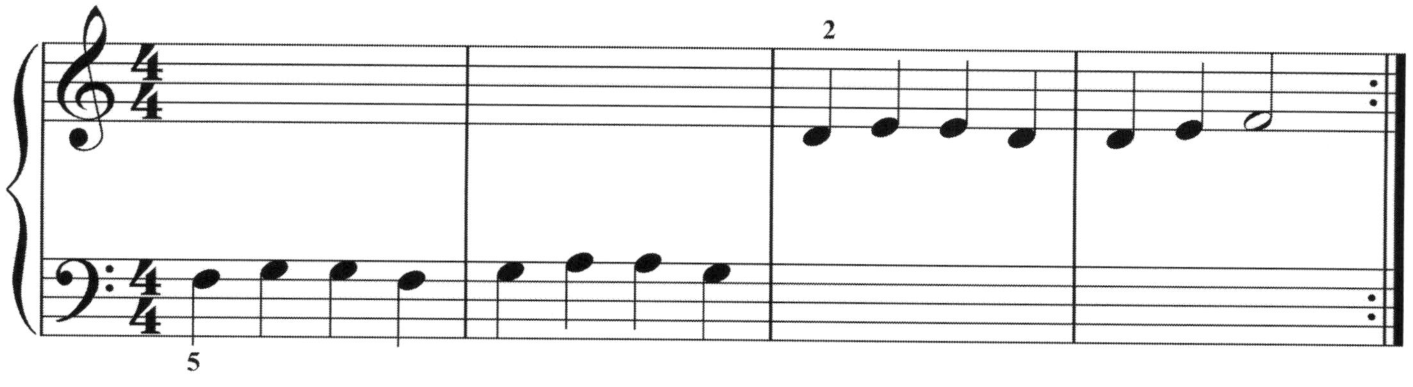

SET 03

UNIT 4

NEW!

SKIPPING EXERCISES

Color in one lettered box each time you practice a line of music.
After all of the boxes are colored, you will be one AWESOME piano player.

SHUFFLE SKIP

A	W	E	S	O	M	E

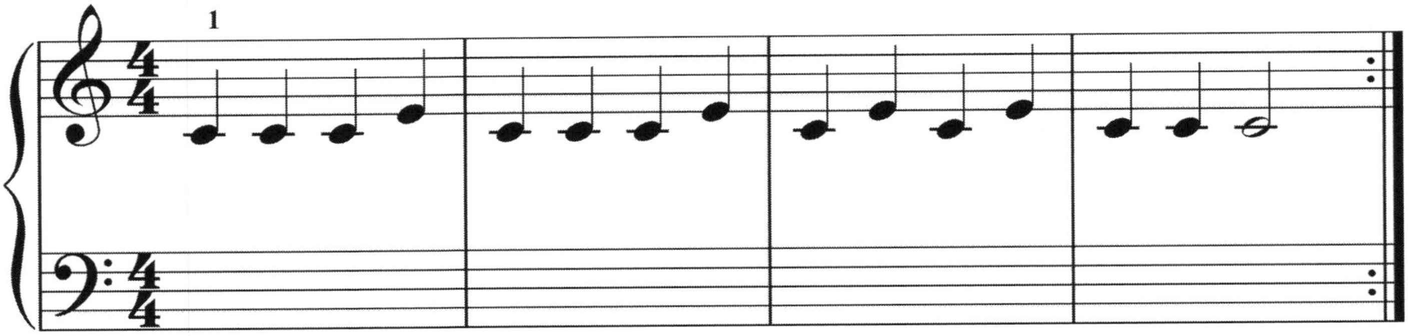

SCISSOR SKIP

A	M	A	Z	I	N	G

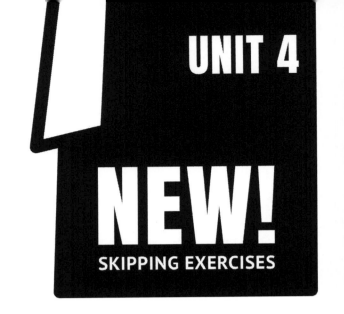

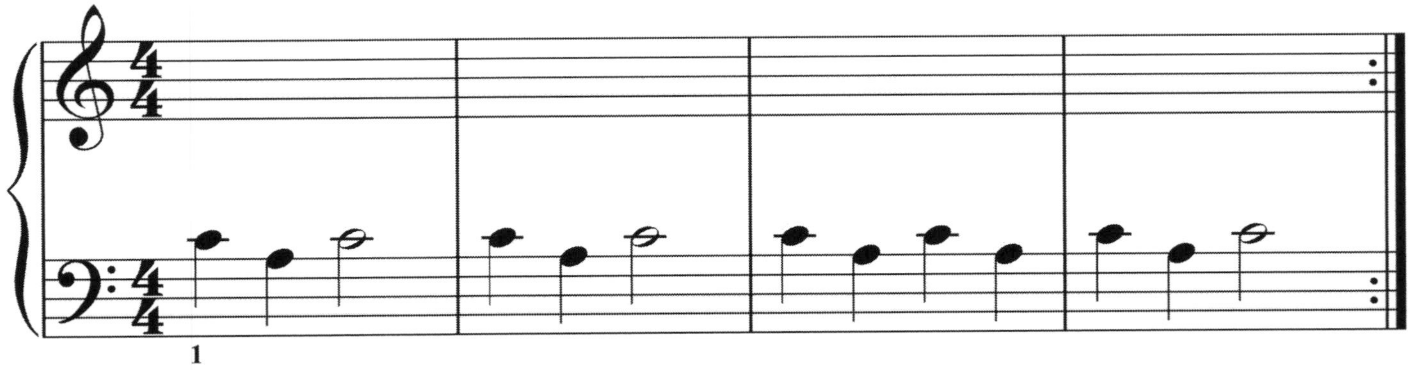

HIGH KNEES

W I N N I N G

DOUBLE UNDER

P E R F E C T

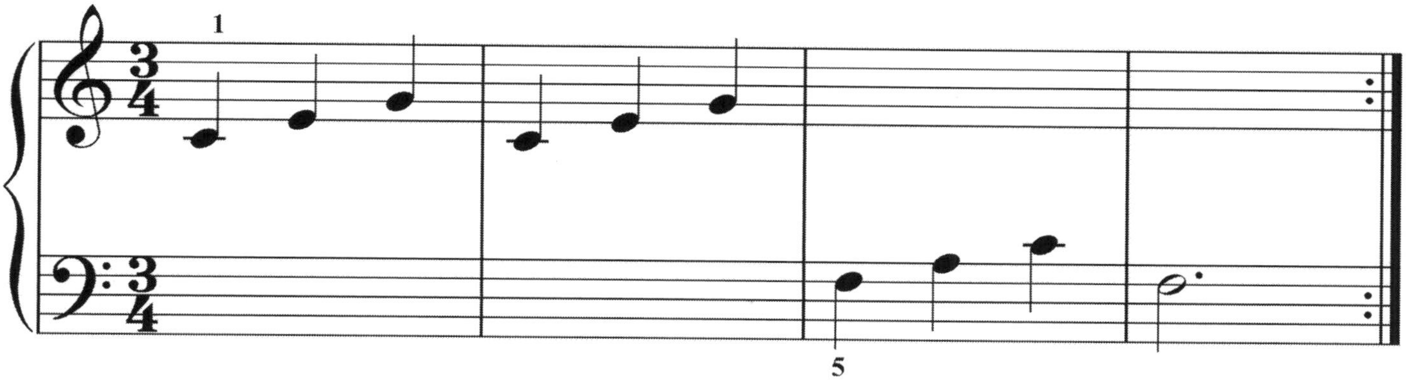

CRISS CROSS

S T E L L A R

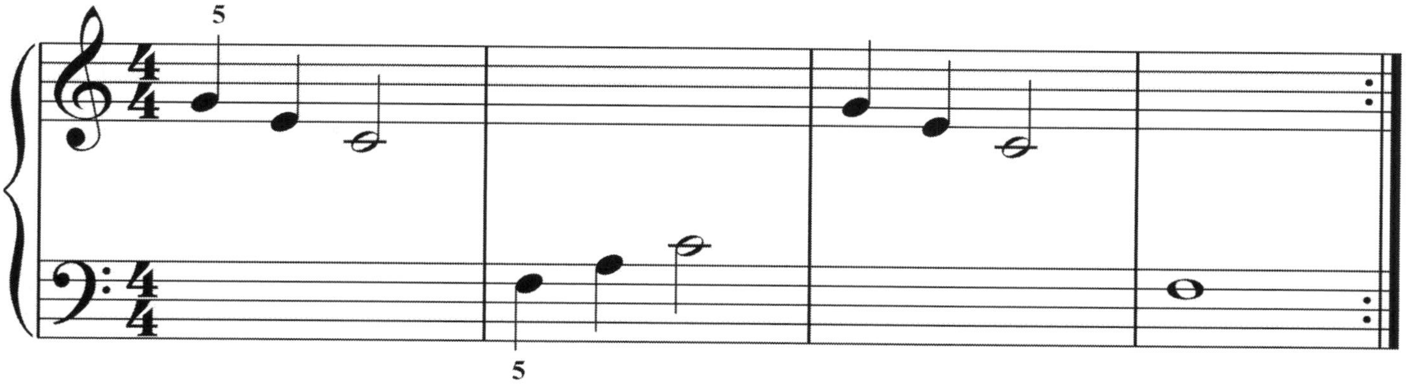

SET 04

UNIT 4

NEW!

SKIPPING CONTINUED

Color in one lettered box each time you practice a line of music.
After all of the boxes are colored, you will be one AMAZING piano player.

SKIER

A	M	A	Z	I	N	G

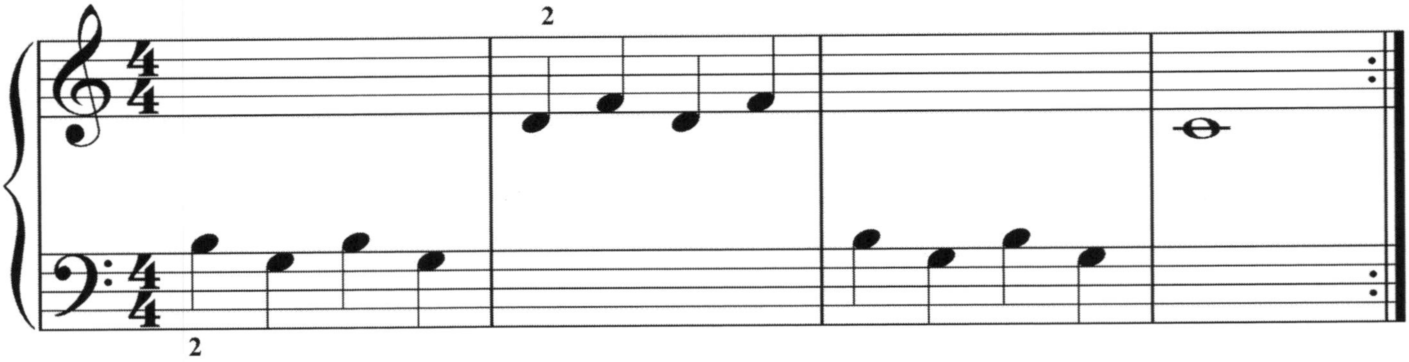

BELL HOP

A	W	E	S	O	M	E

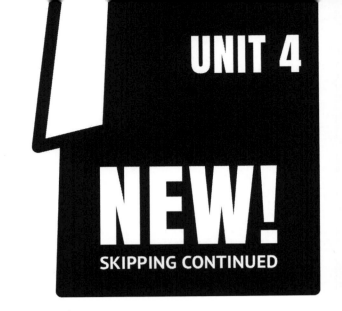

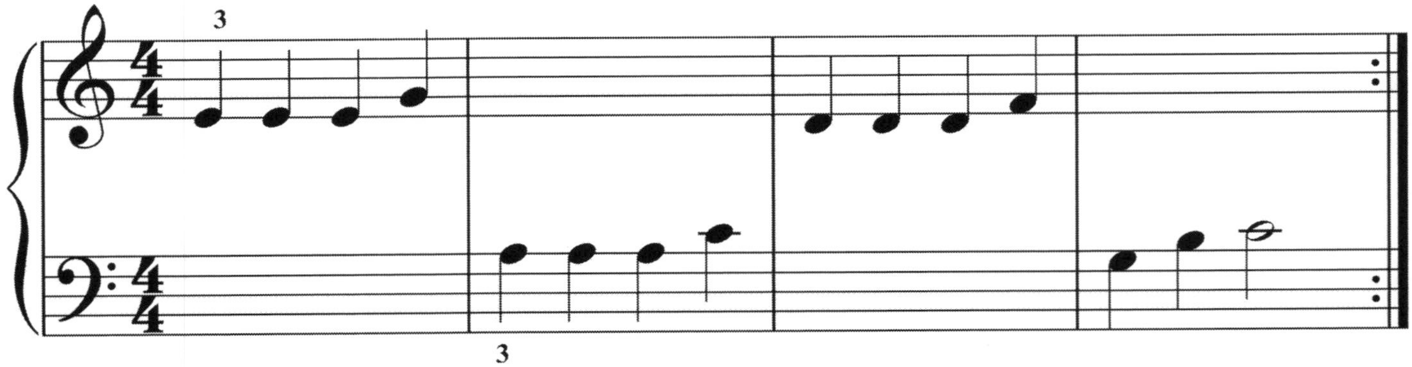

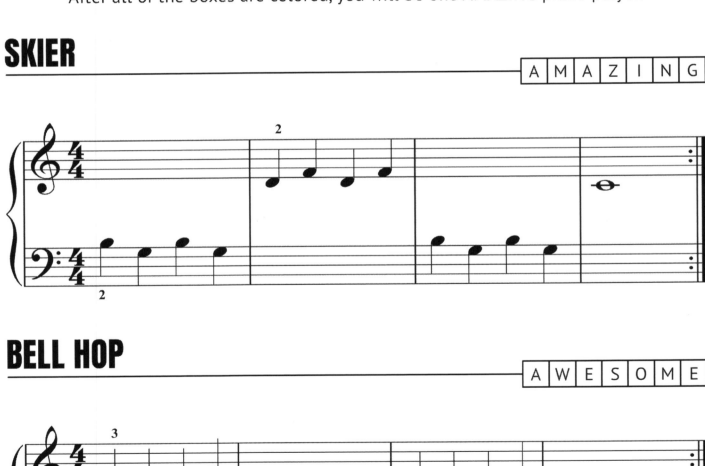

STRADDLE CROSS

WINNING

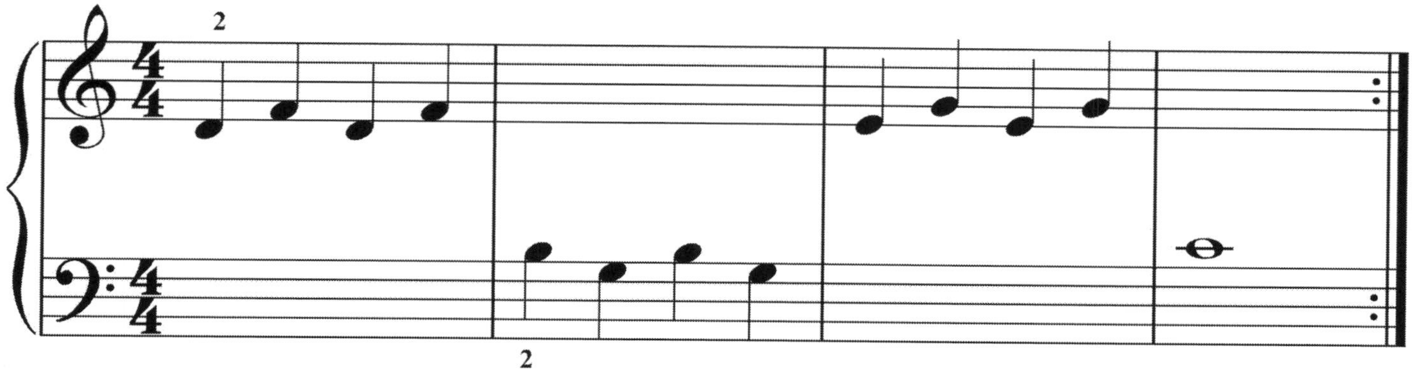

KICK SWING

PERFECT

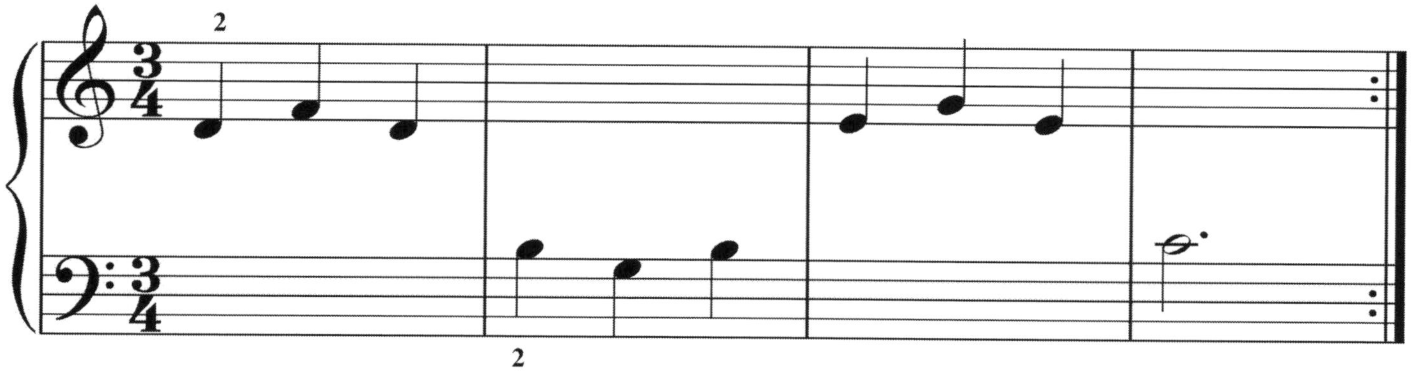

FULL TURN

STELLAR

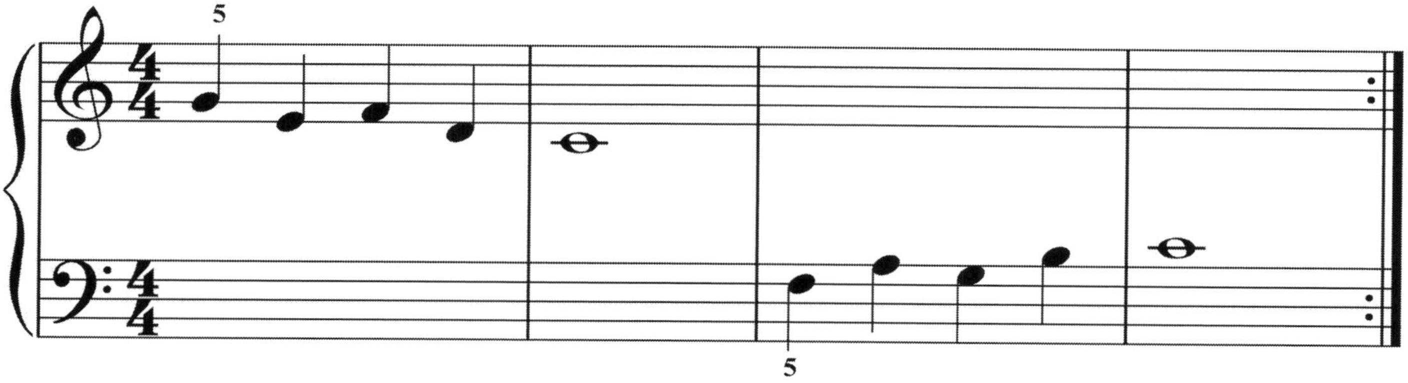

SIGHT READING ONE

SET 5 | PART 1

Look at Sight Reading One. Beginning at the START and ending at the FINISH, play the four measures that rest on the path. Use a colored crayon to draw a new four-measure path. Play again.

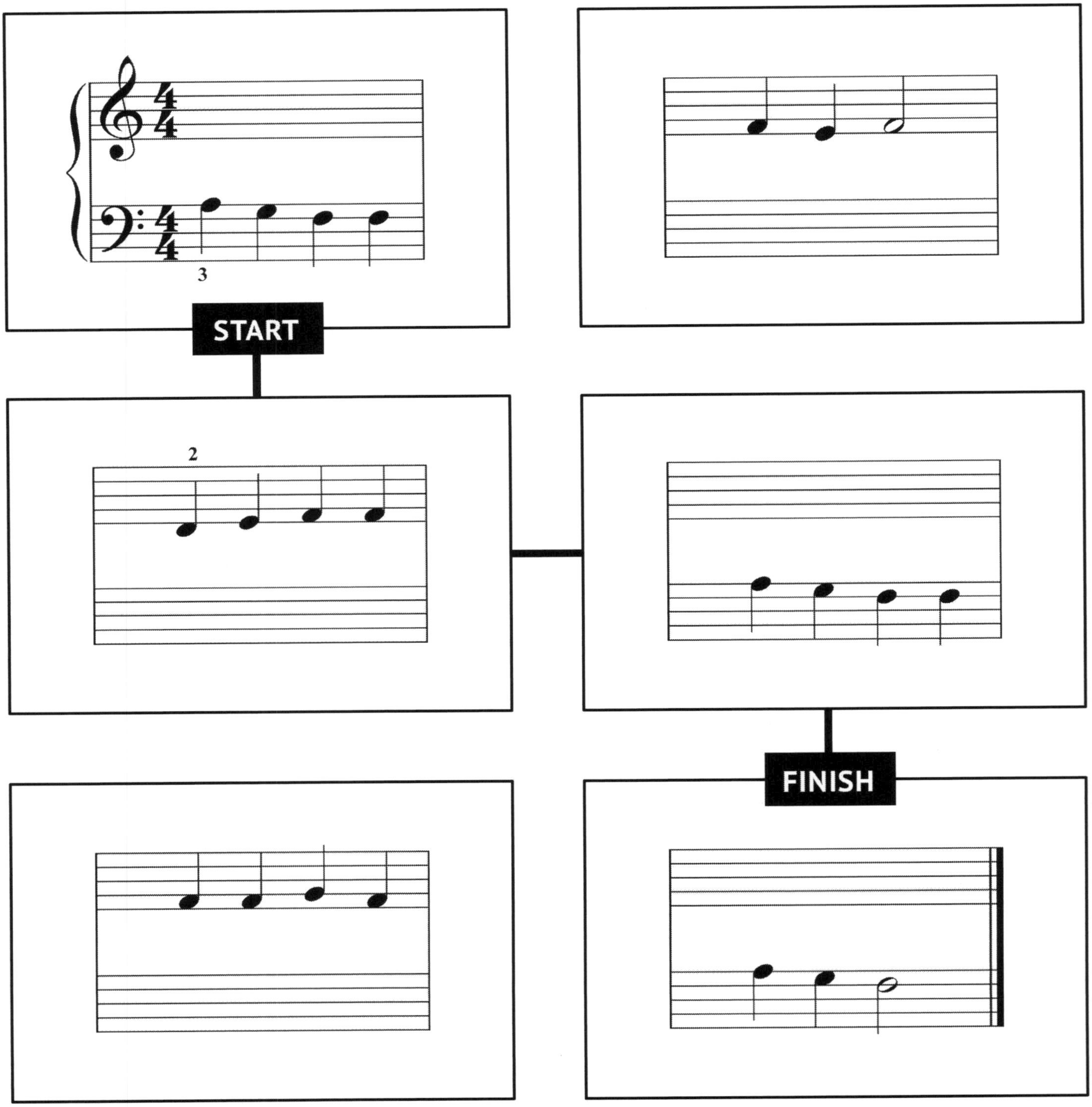

SET 5 | PART 2

Look at Sight Reading Two. Beginning at the START and ending at the FINISH, play the four measures that rest on the path. Use a colored crayon to draw a new four-measure path. Play again.

SIGHT READING TWO

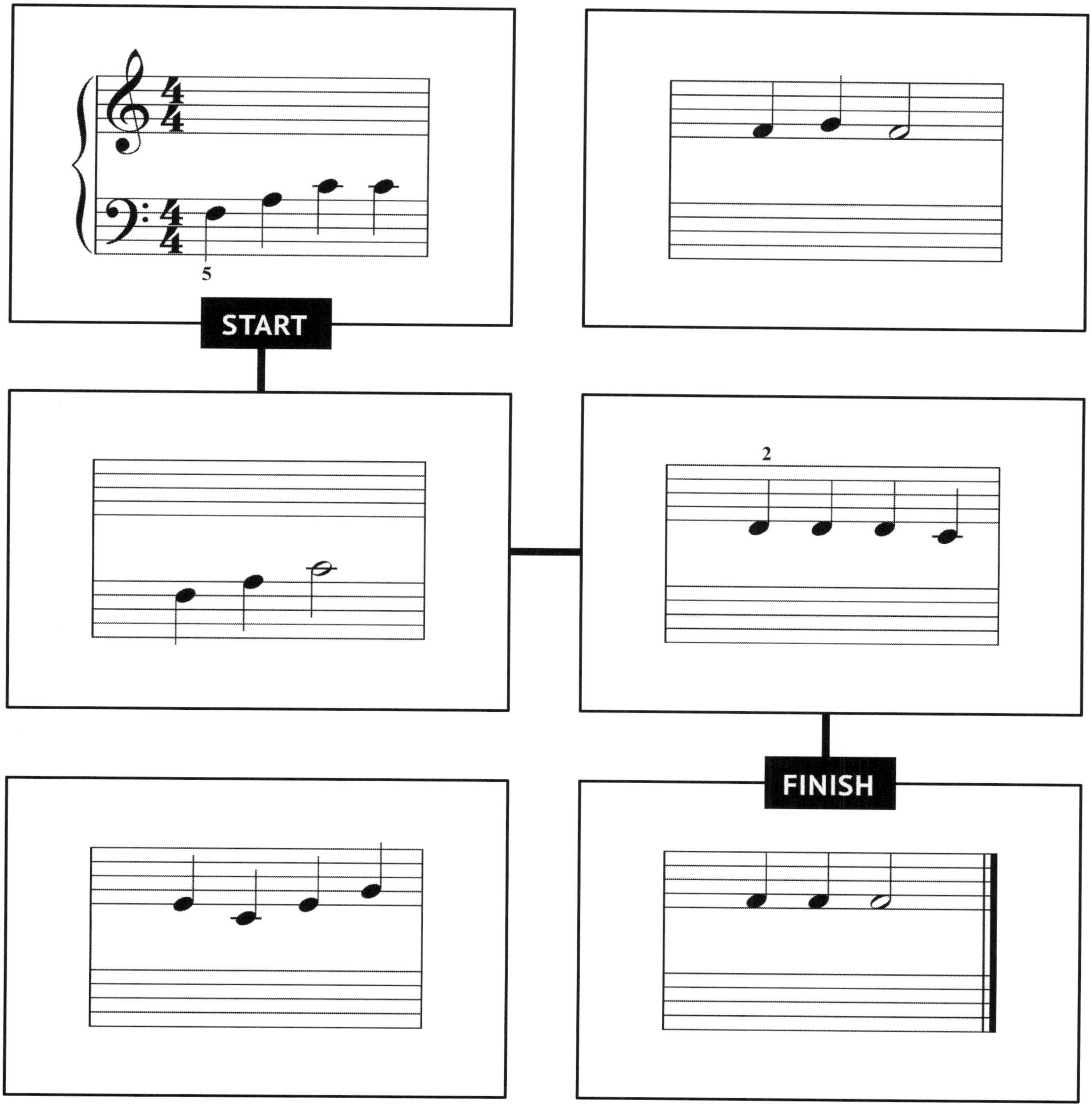

SET 06

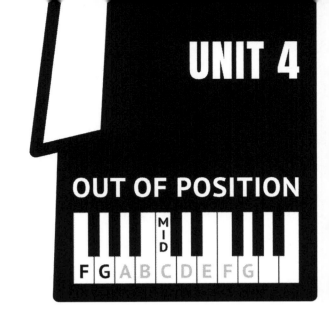

UNIT 4

OUT OF POSITION

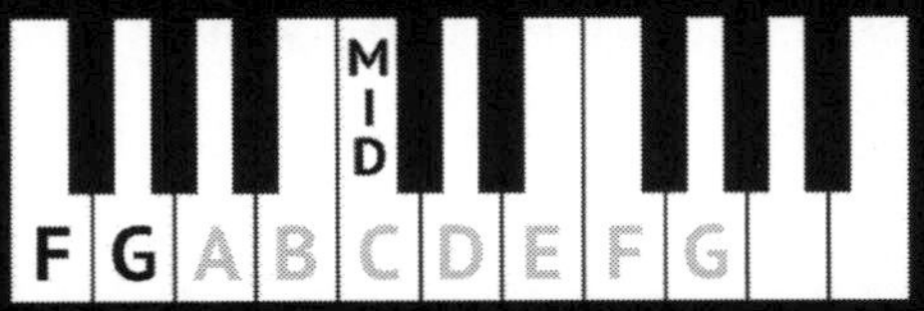

In the box above Exercise 1, write the name of the first note. Next, use the finger number to find your starting position. Repeat with Exercises 2 and 3.

MOVE AND GROOVE ☐

S	T	E	L	L	A	R

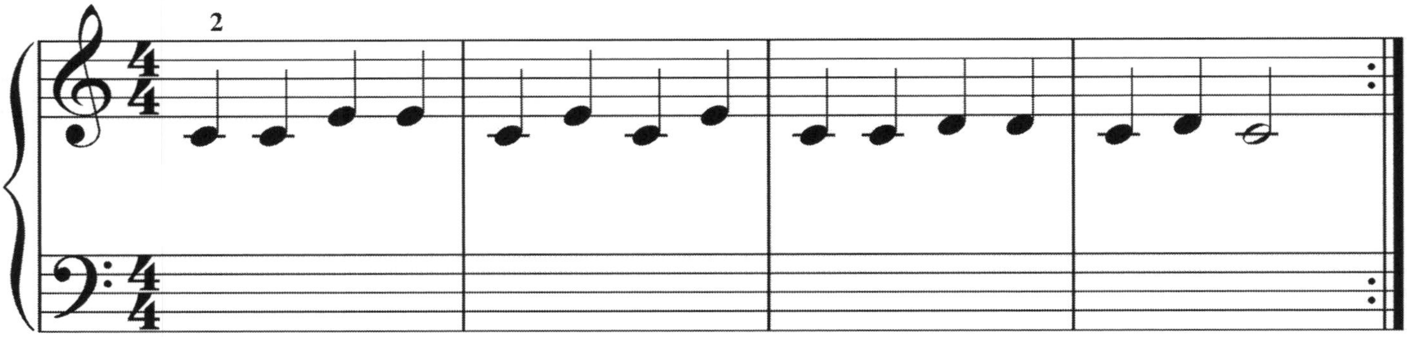

SPACE TRAVEL ☐

A	M	A	Z	I	N	G

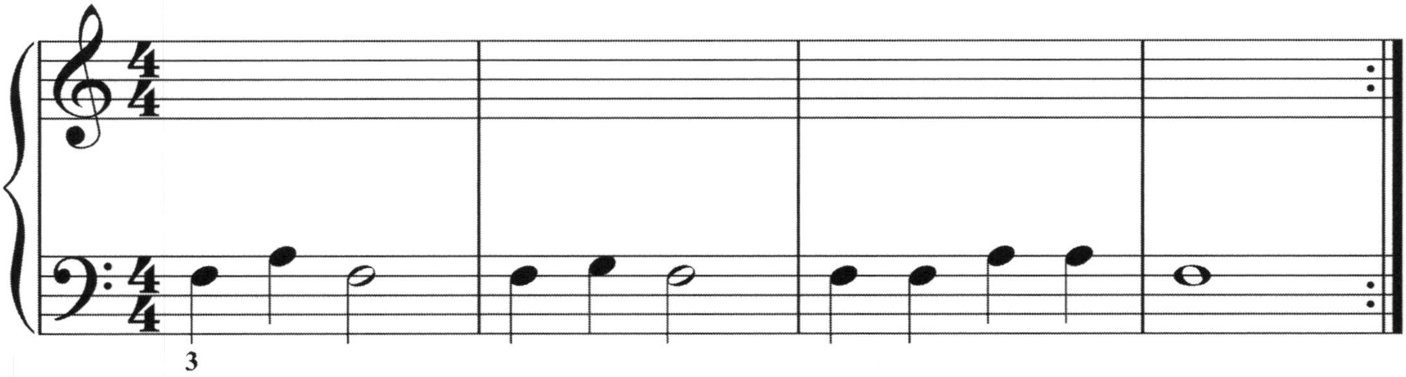

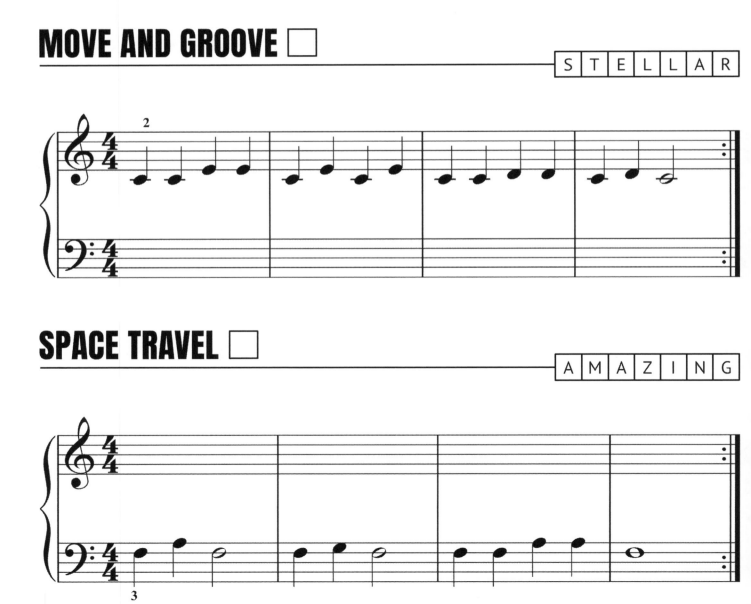

SHIFT WORK ☐

W I N N I N G

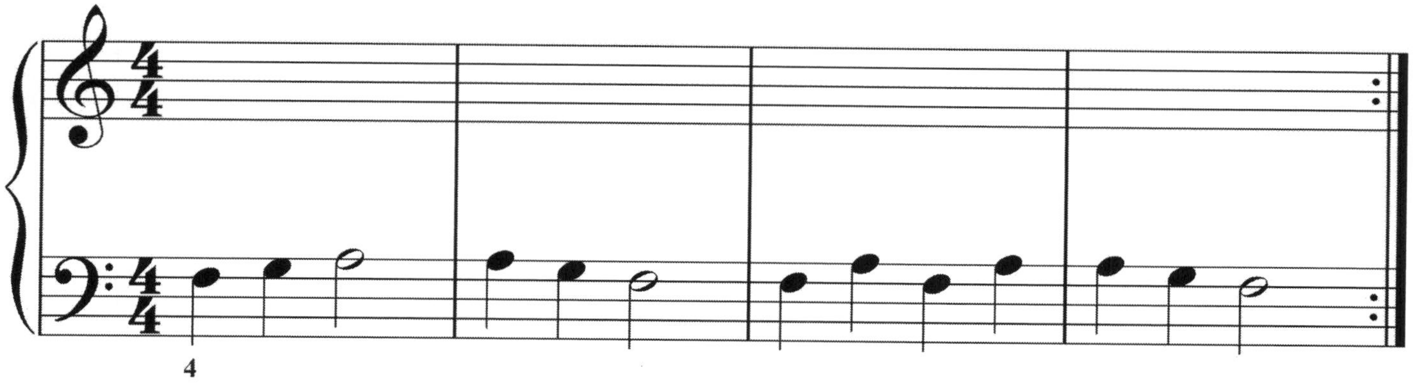

CHALLENGE PIECE 1

P E R F E C T

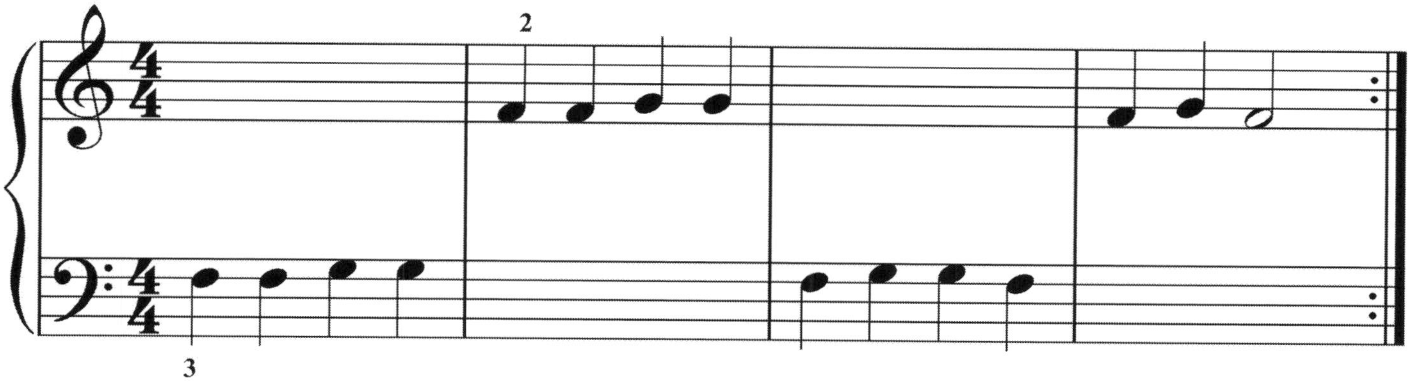

CHALLENGE PIECE 2

A W E S O M E

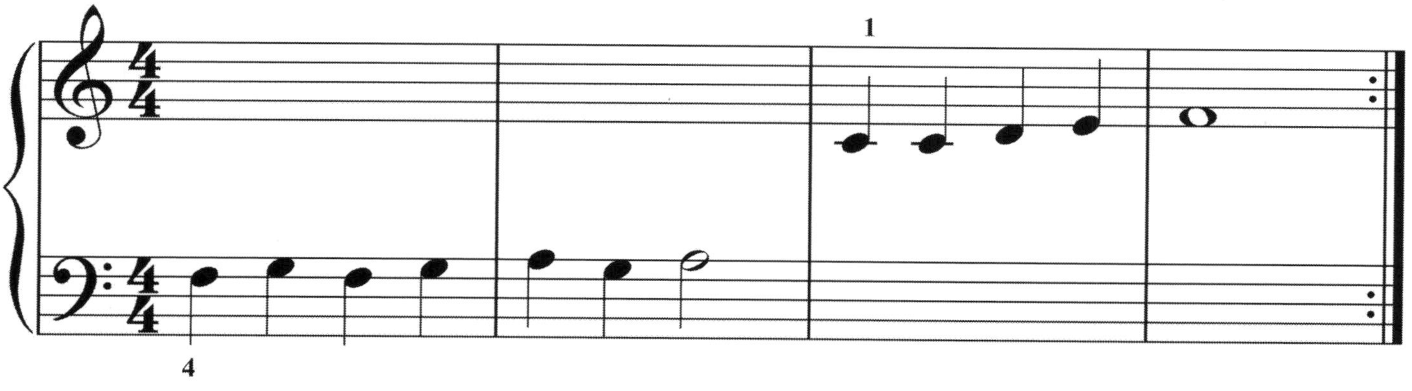

SET 07

UNIT 4

RHYTHM

Look at the first line of rhythm below. Stem-down notes are performed by tapping both hands on your lap. Stem-up notes are performed by clapping your hands together. After performing the first rhythm, complete the remaining exercises.

RHYTHM CHALLENGE 1

A	W	E	S	O	M	E

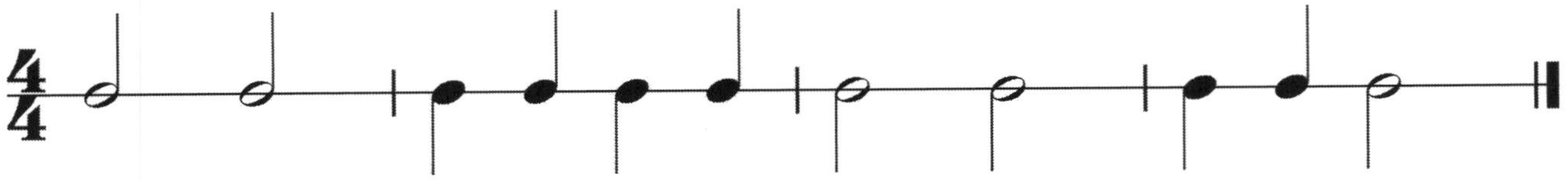

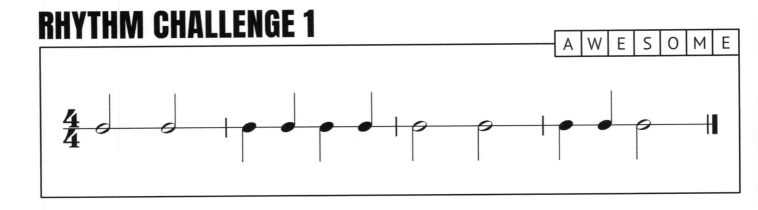

RHYTHM CHALLENGE 2

S	T	E	L	L	A	R

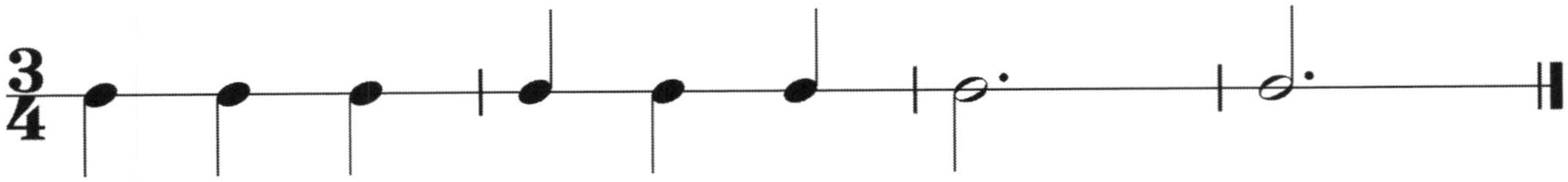

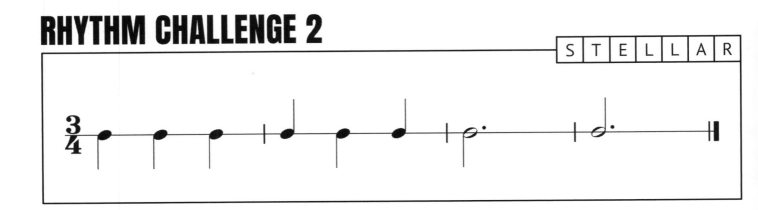

RHYTHM CHALLENGE 3

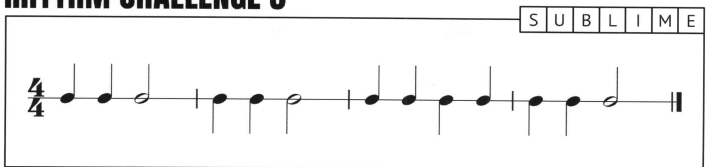

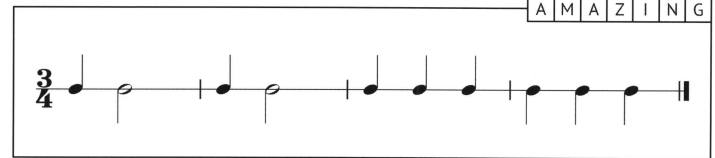

S U B L I M E

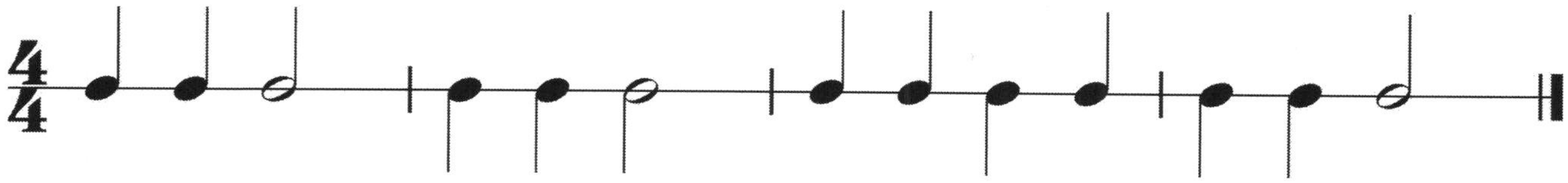

RHYTHM CHALLENGE 4

P E R F E C T

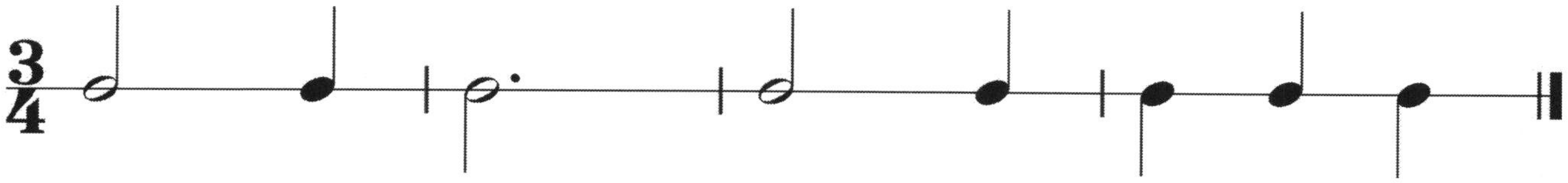

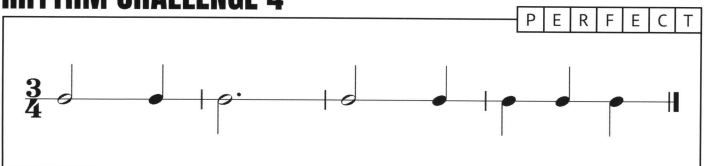

RHYTHM CHALLENGE 5

W I N N I N G

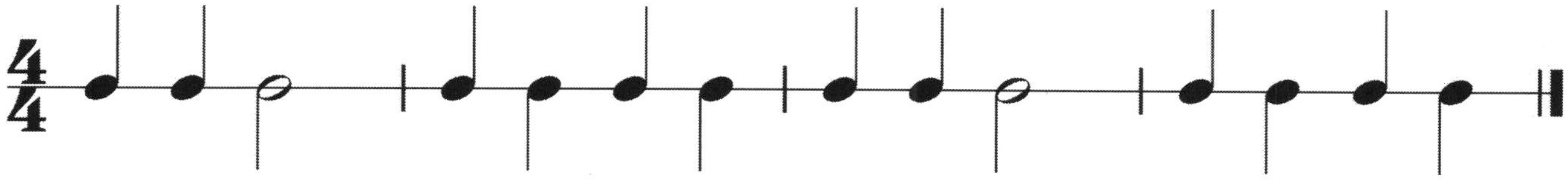

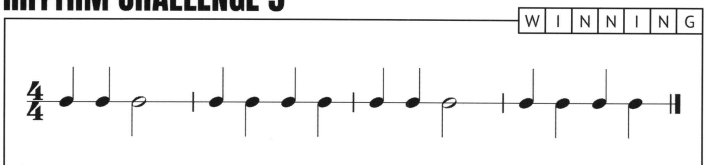

RHYTHM CHALLENGE 6

A M A Z I N G

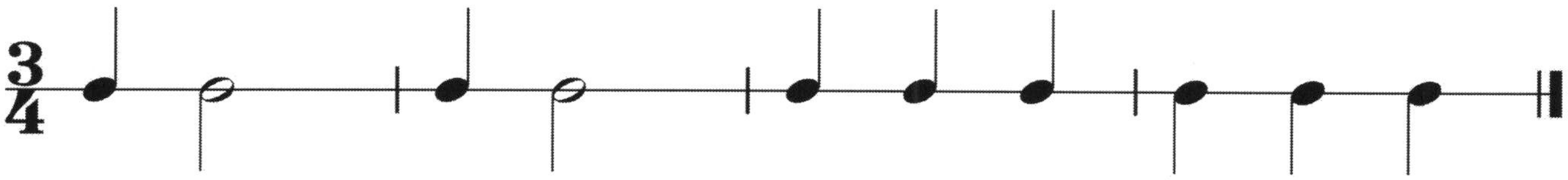

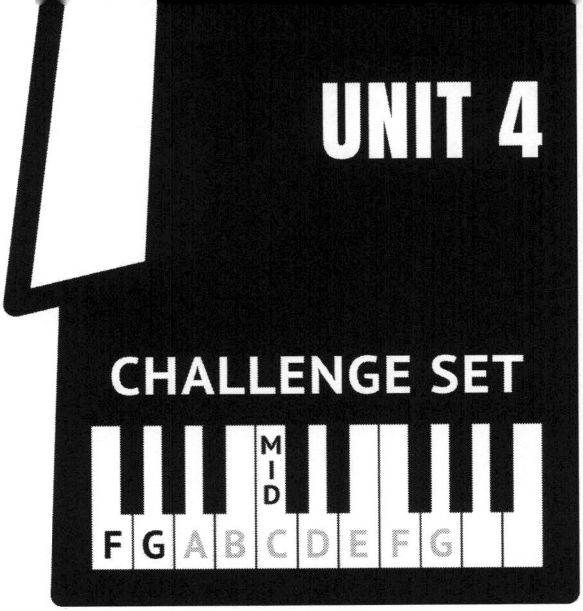

The following cross-staff exercises are intended for older beginners and students who want to test their skills.

BOUNCE BACK

A W E S O M E

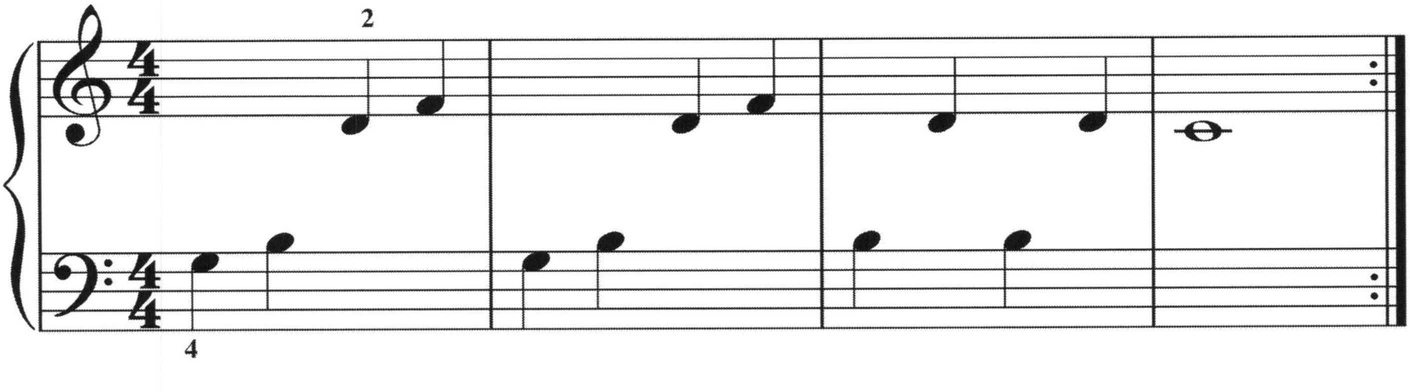

REBOUND

S T E L L A R

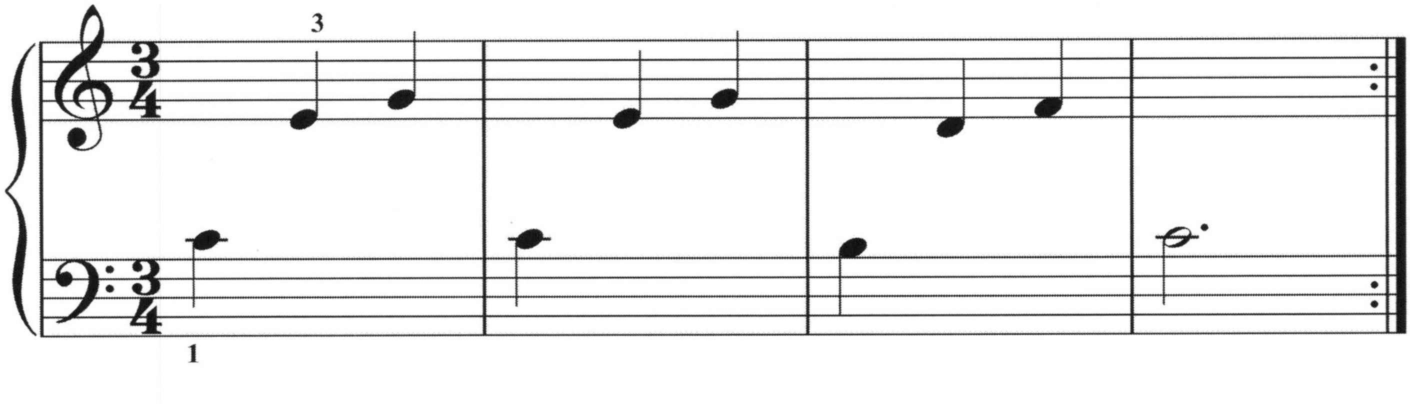

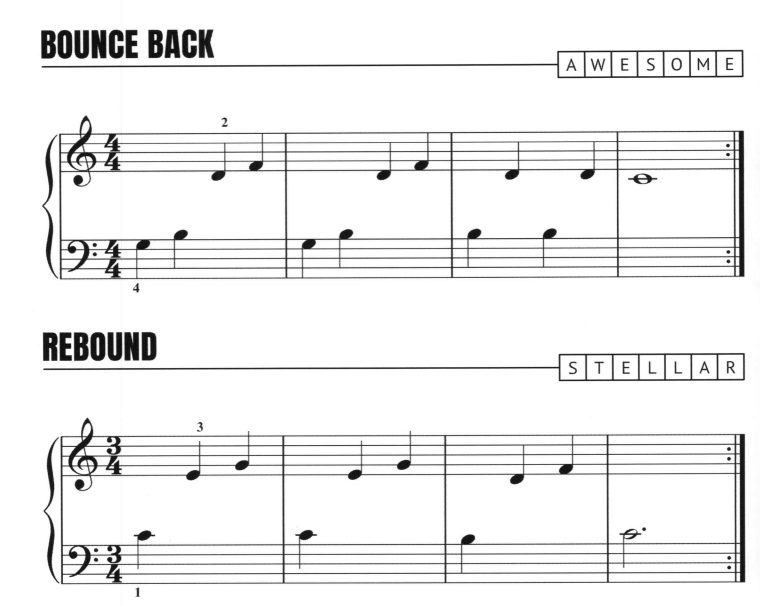

HOMEWARD BOUNCE

W I N N I N G

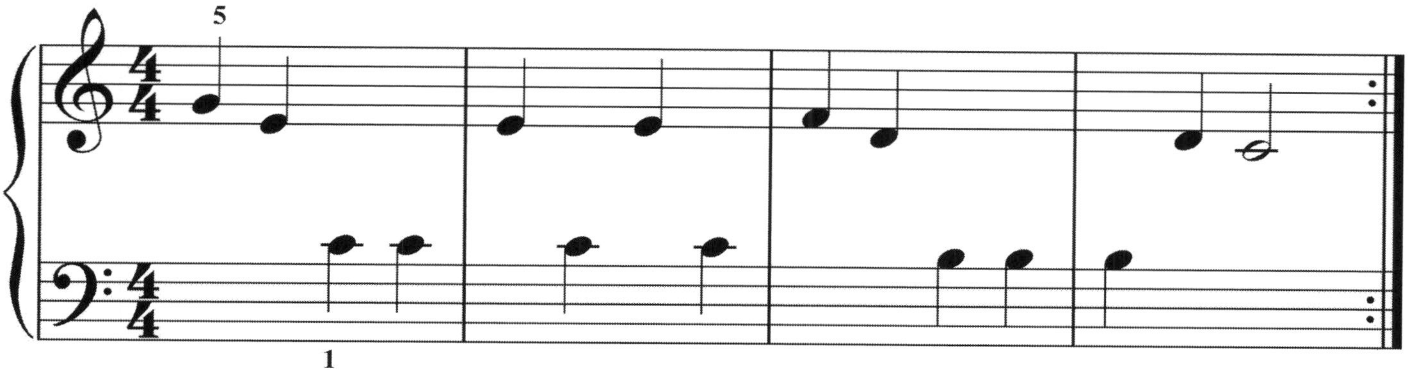

BOUND TOWN

P E R F E C T

BOUNCE PASS

A M A Z I N G

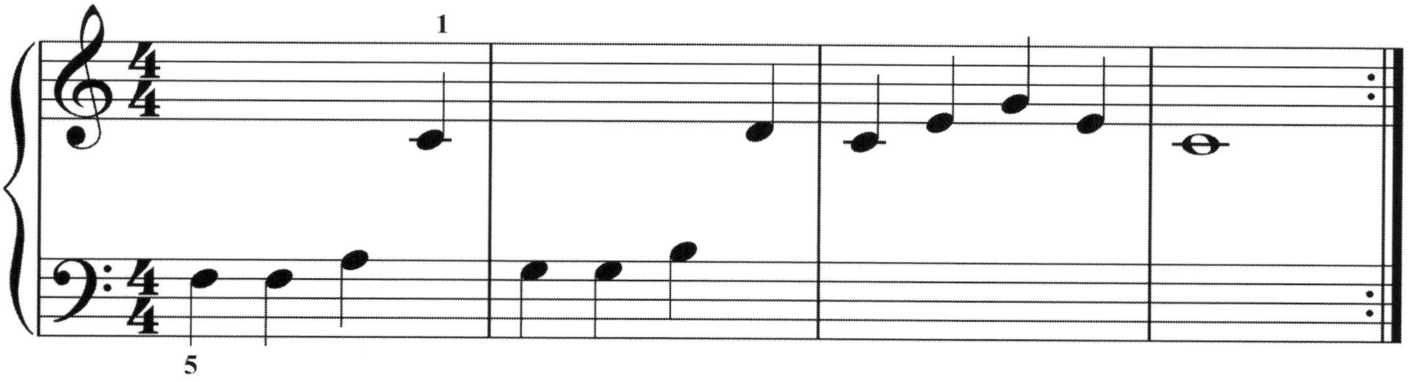

AN INTRO

Let's get started! In each box,
draw a note that matches the first note.

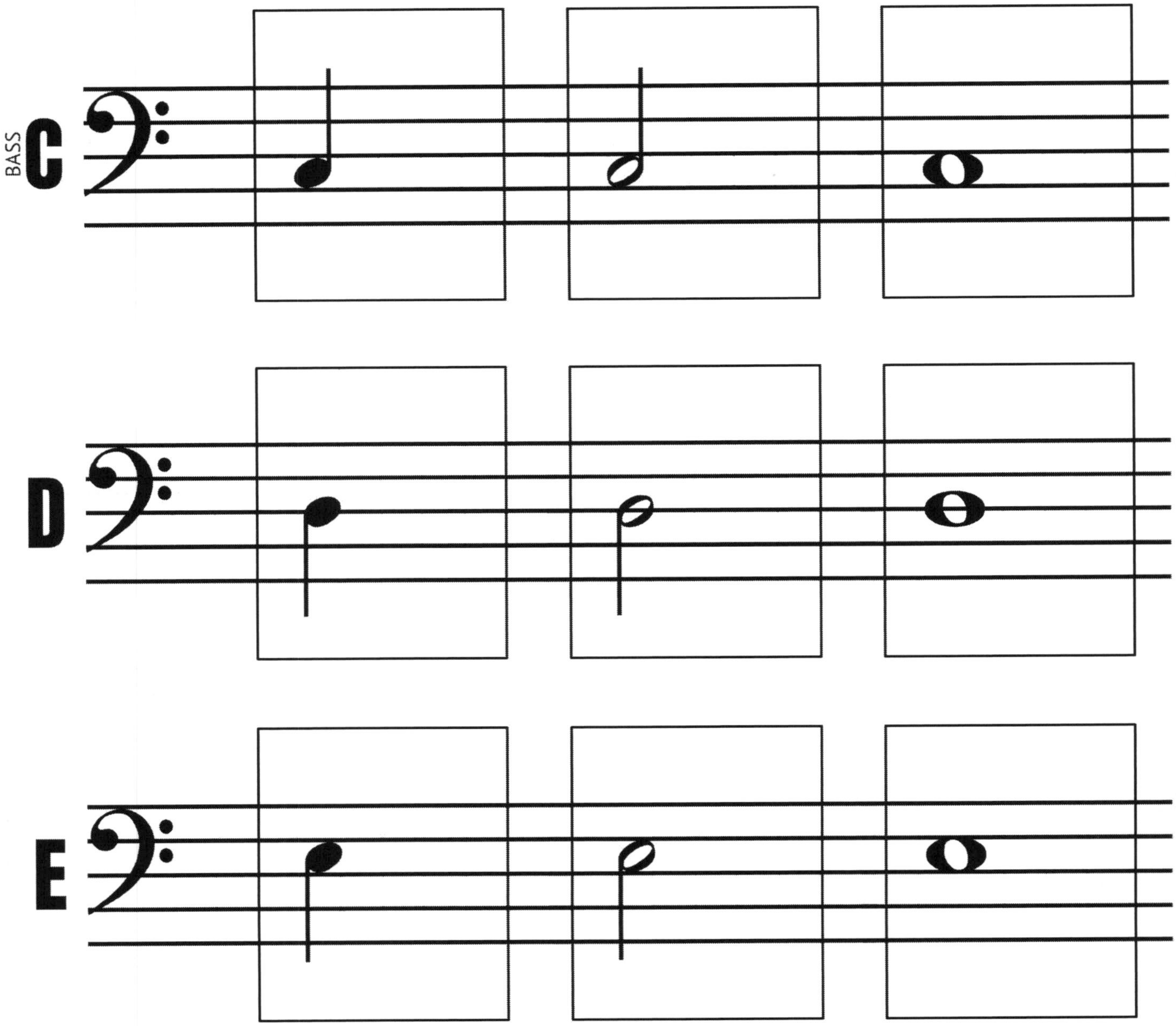

Color in one lettered box each time you practice a line of music.
After all of the boxes are colored, you will be one AWESOME piano player.

PRESS PLAY

A	W	E	S	O	M	E

SIDE TO SIDE

P	E	R	F	E	C	T

STEP-UPS

A	M	A	Z	I	N	G

SET 01

Color in one lettered box each time you practice a line of music.
After all of the boxes are colored, you will be one AMAZING piano player.

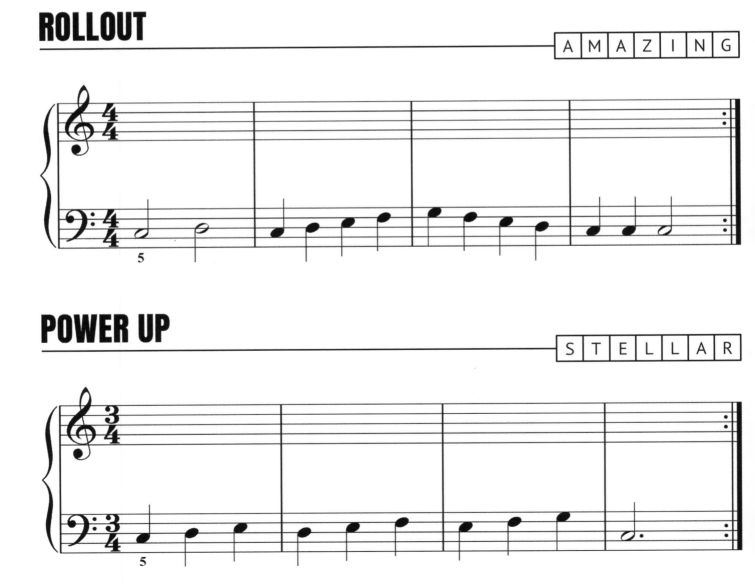

ROLLOUT

A	M	A	Z	I	N	G

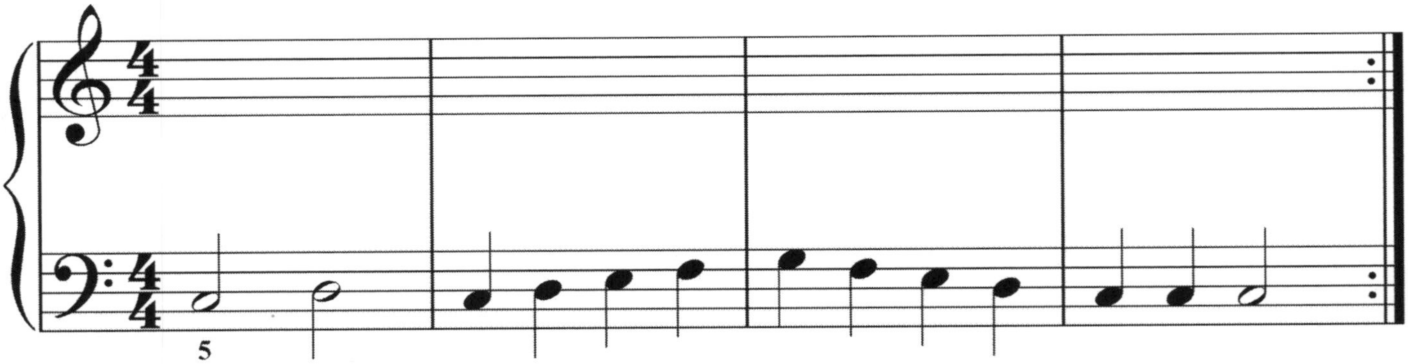

POWER UP

S	T	E	L	L	A	R

PRESS PLAY

W I N N I N G

KICKBACK TRACK

P E R F E C T

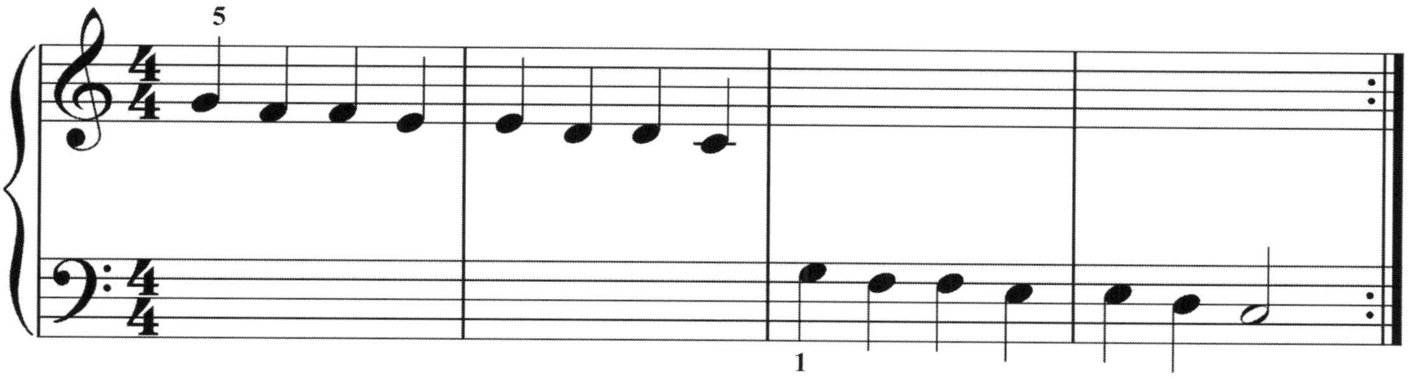

REVERSE FLY

A W E S O M E

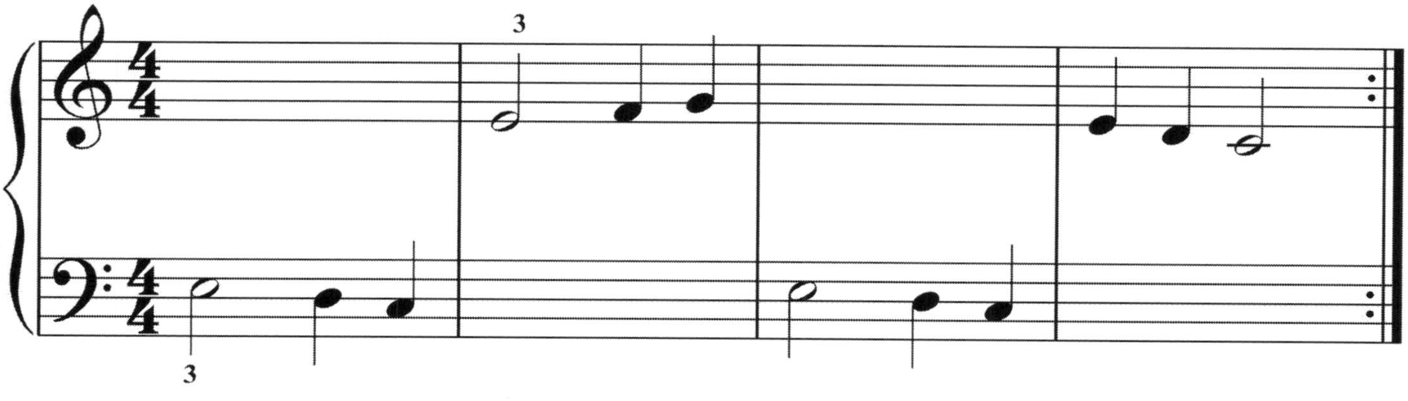

SET 02

Color in one lettered box each time you practice a line of music.
After all of the boxes are colored, you will be one STELLAR piano player.

CLIMB TIME

S T E L L A R

HURDLE HOPS

A M A Z I N G

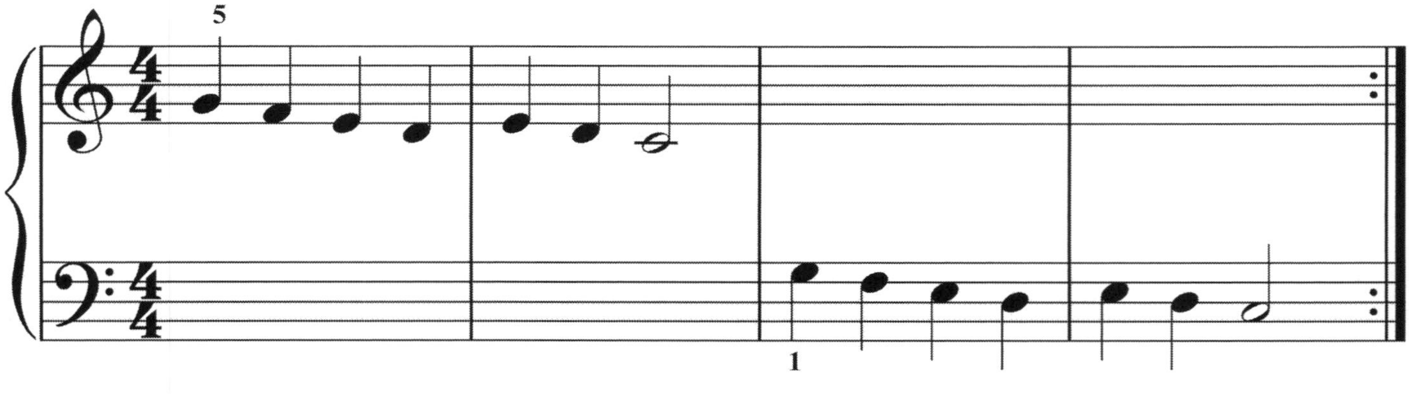

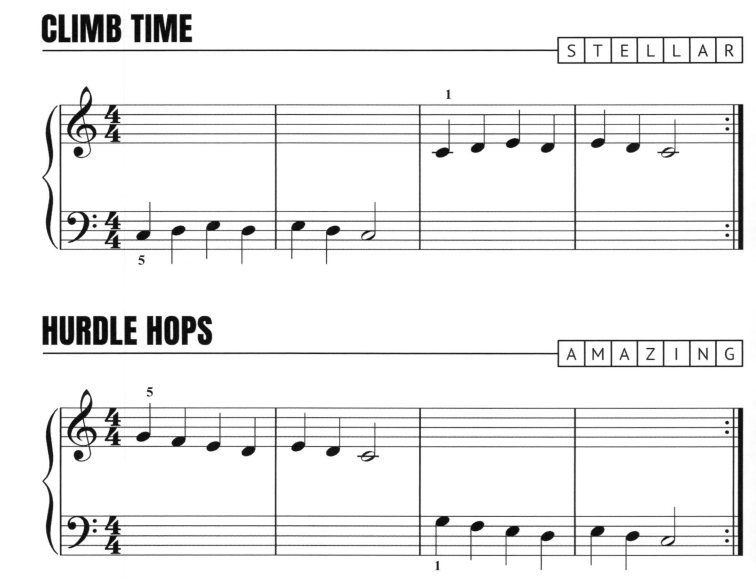

WOODCHOP

W	I	N	N	I	N	G

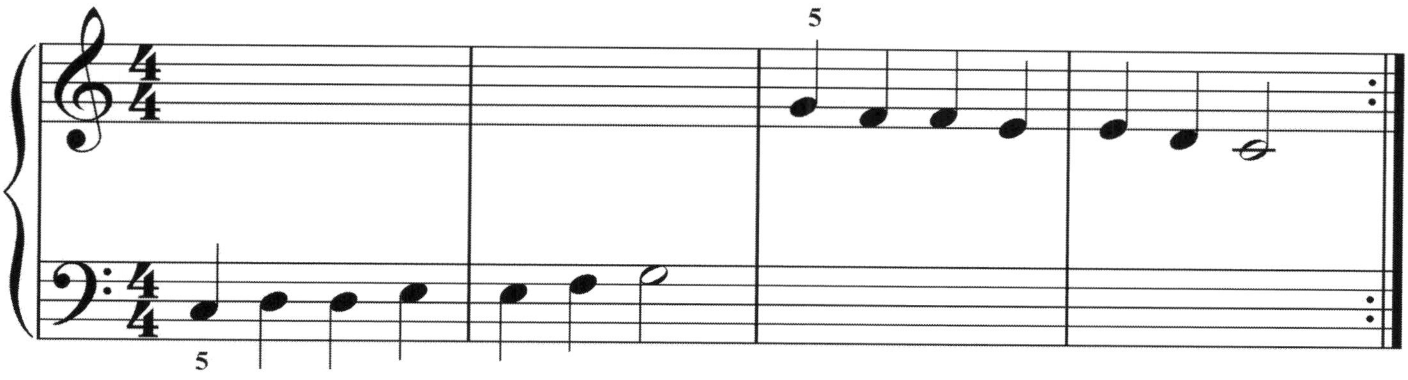

LADDER STACK

P	E	R	F	E	C	T

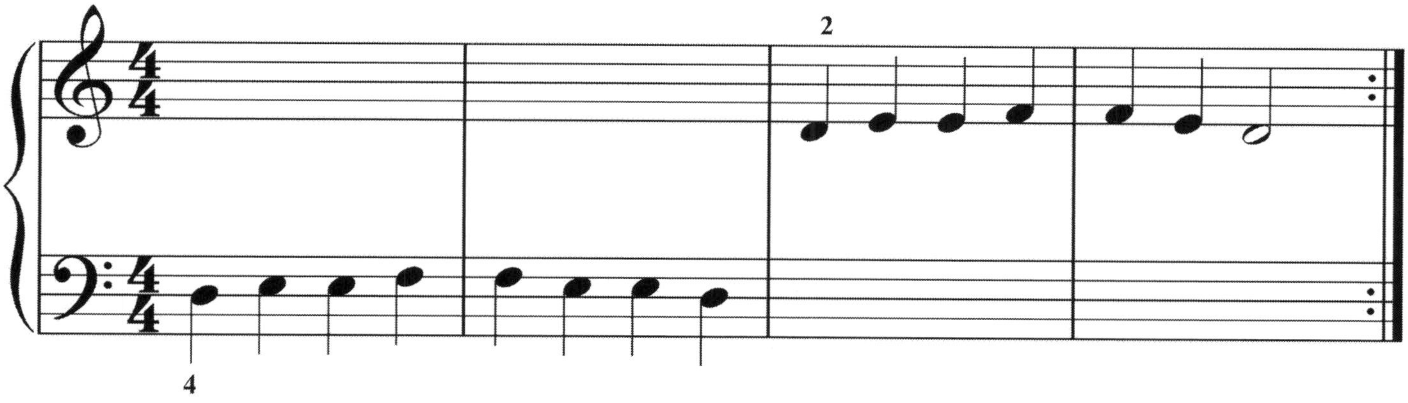

DOUBLE NO TROUBLE

A	W	E	S	O	M	E

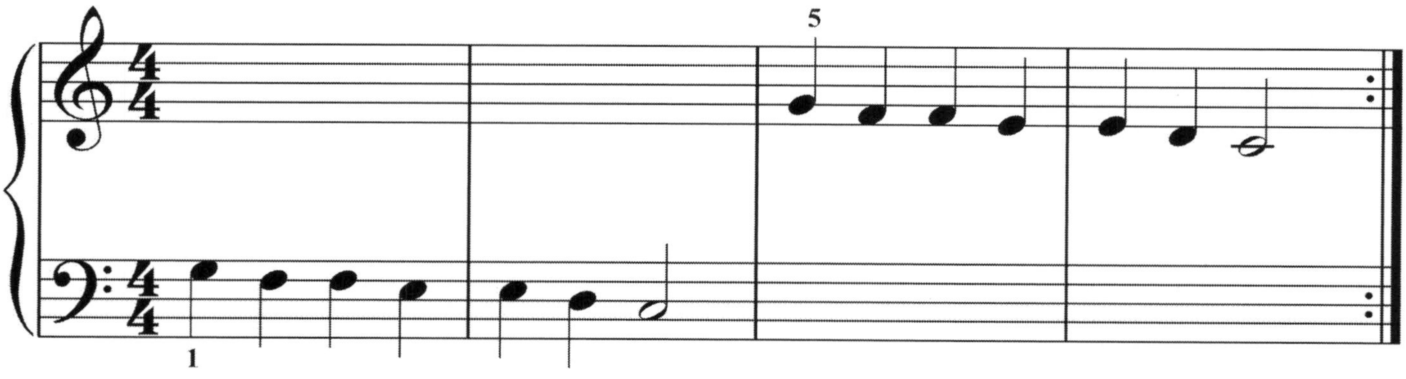

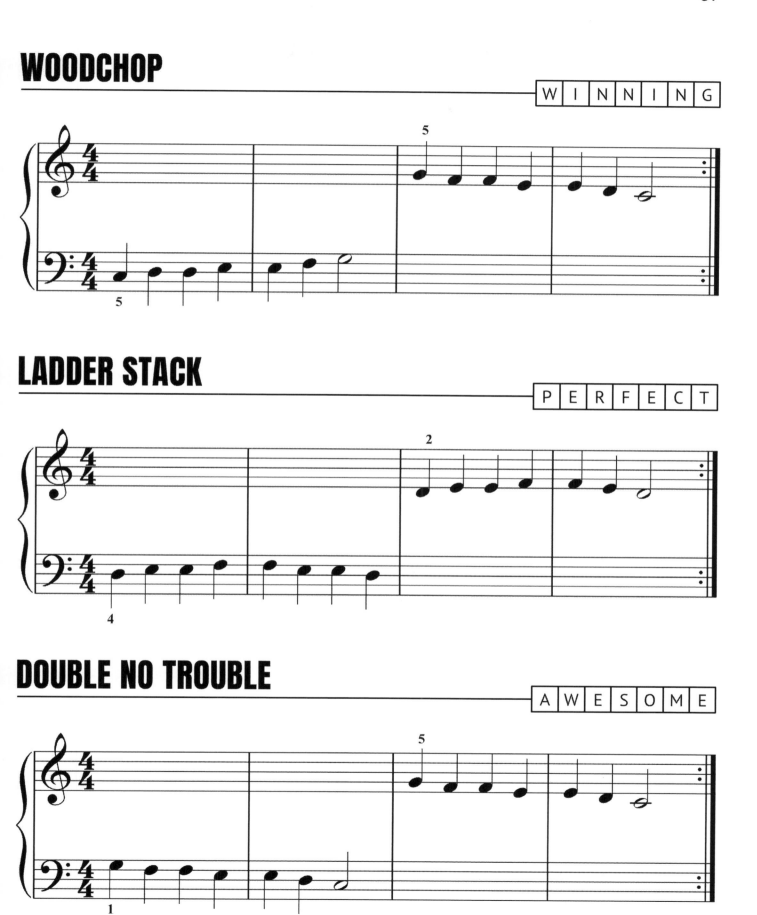

SET 03

Color in one lettered box each time you practice a line of music.
After all of the boxes are colored, you will be one AWESOME piano player.

SHUFFLE SKIP

A	W	E	S	O	M	E

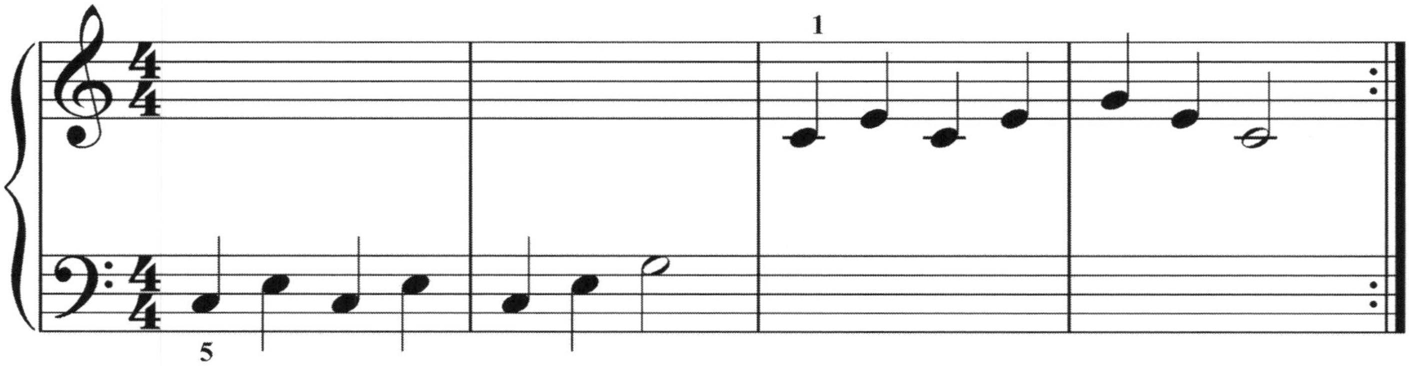

SCISSOR SKIP

A	M	A	Z	I	N	G

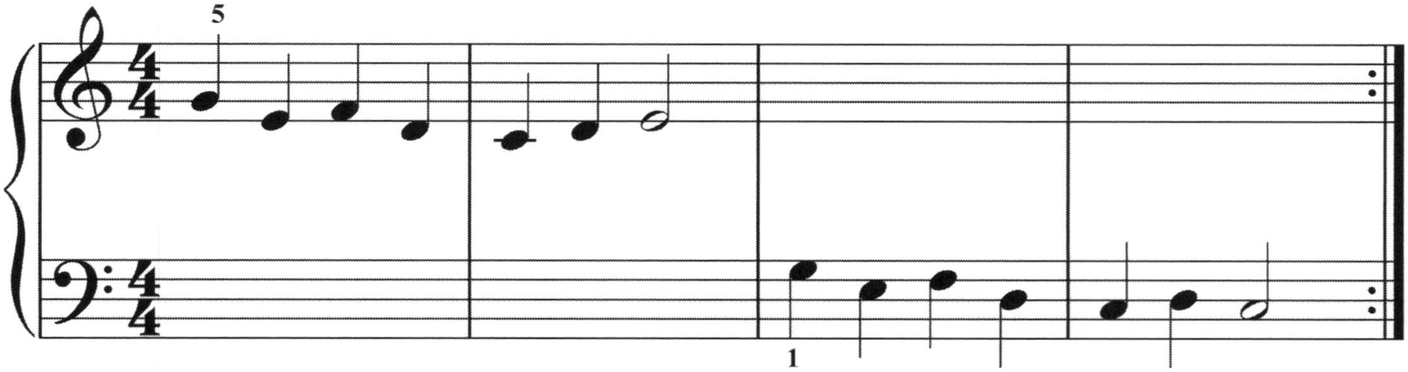

HIGH KNEES

W	I	N	N	I	N	G

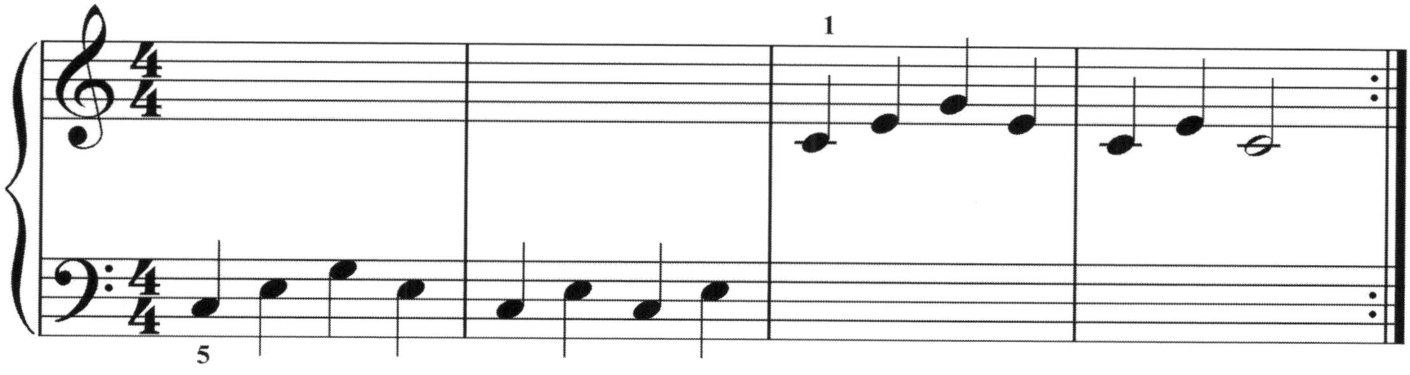

DOUBLE UNDER

P	E	R	F	E	C	T

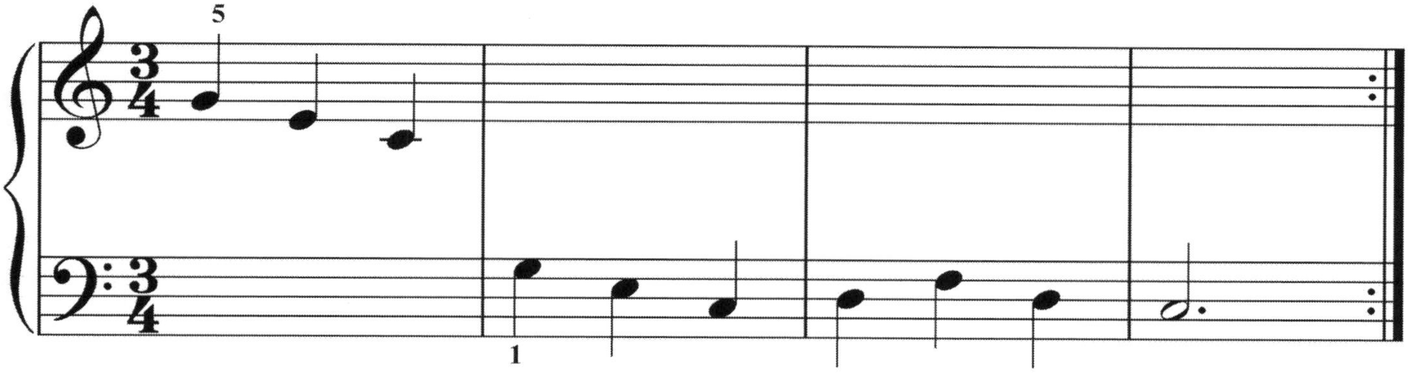

CRISS CROSS

S	T	E	L	L	A	R

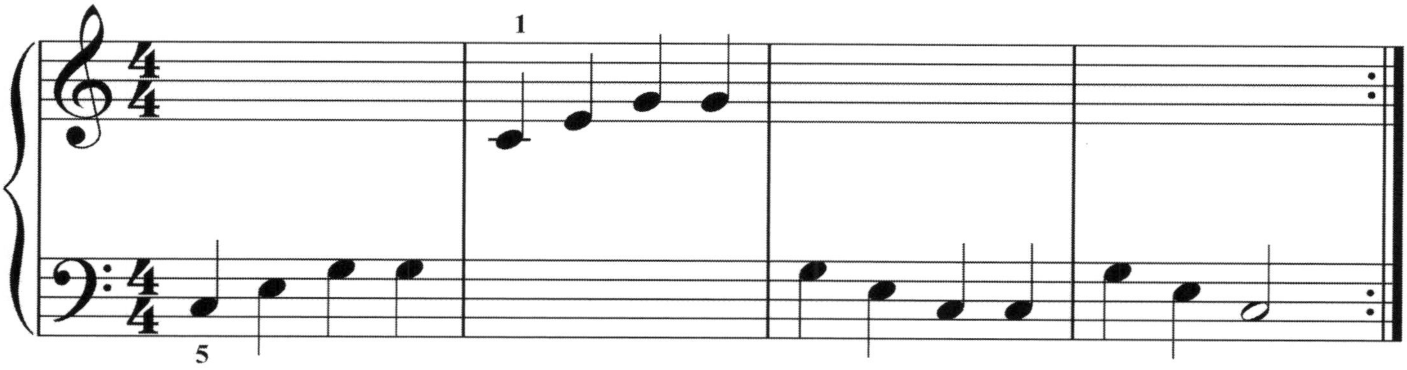

SET 04

Color in one lettered box each time you practice a line of music.
After all of the boxes are colored, you will be one PERFECT piano player.

STRADDLE CROSS

P	E	R	F	E	C	T

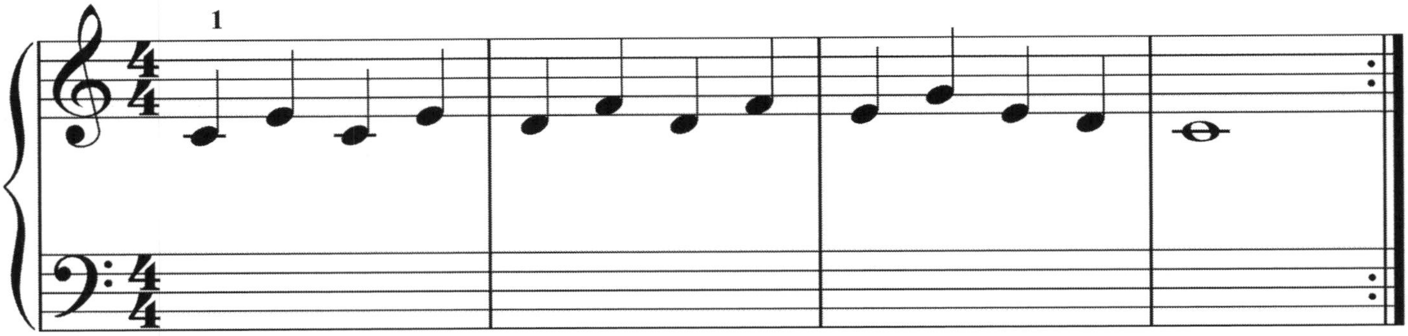

SKIER

A	M	A	Z	I	N	G

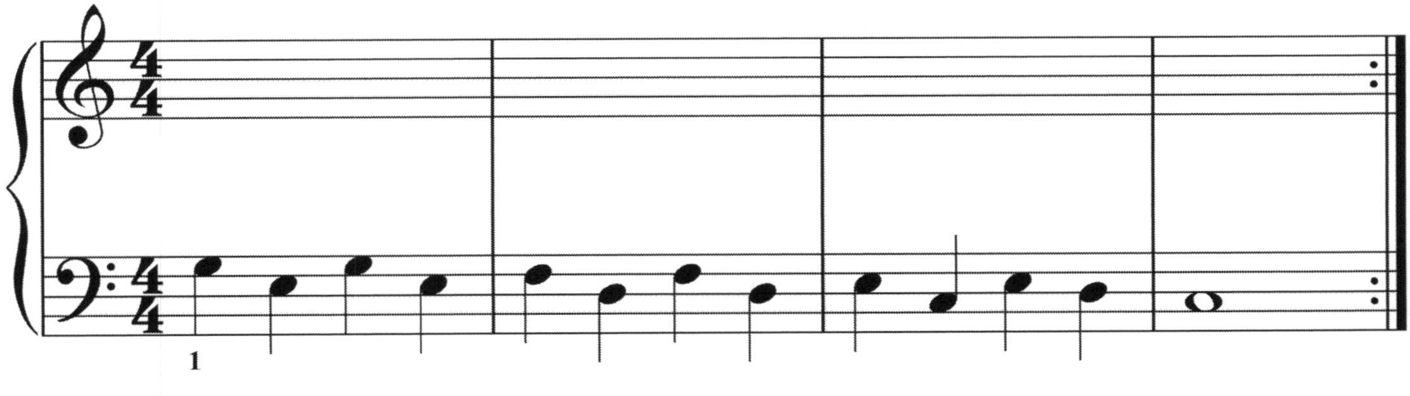

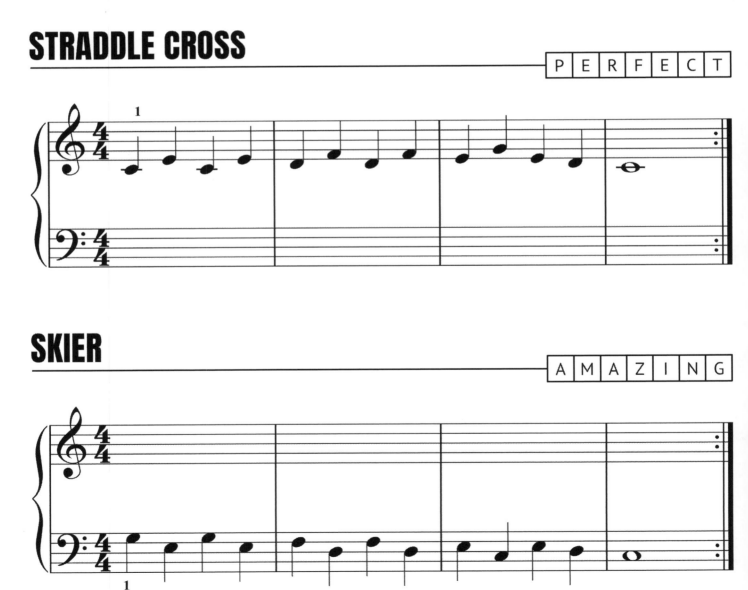

BELL HOP

W I N N I N G

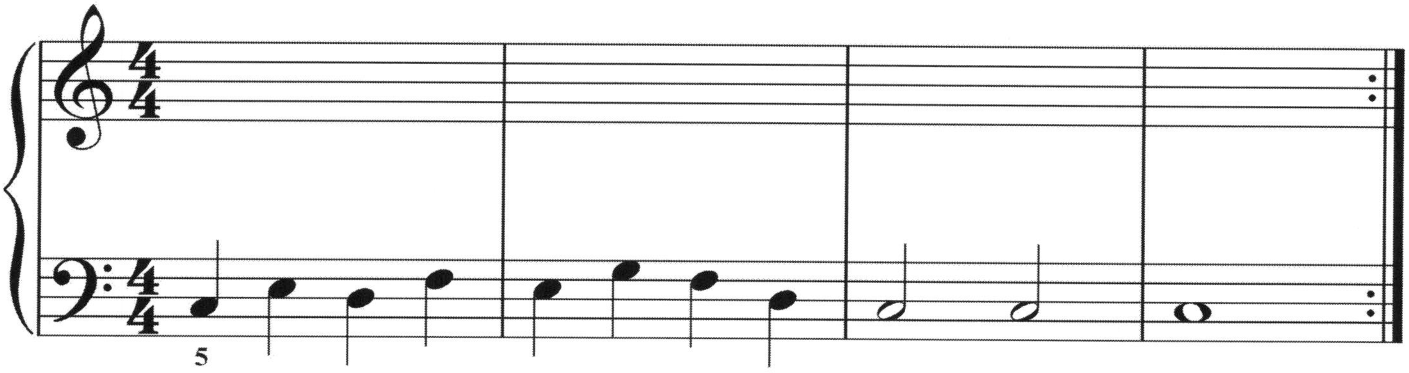

SIDE SWING

A W E S O M E

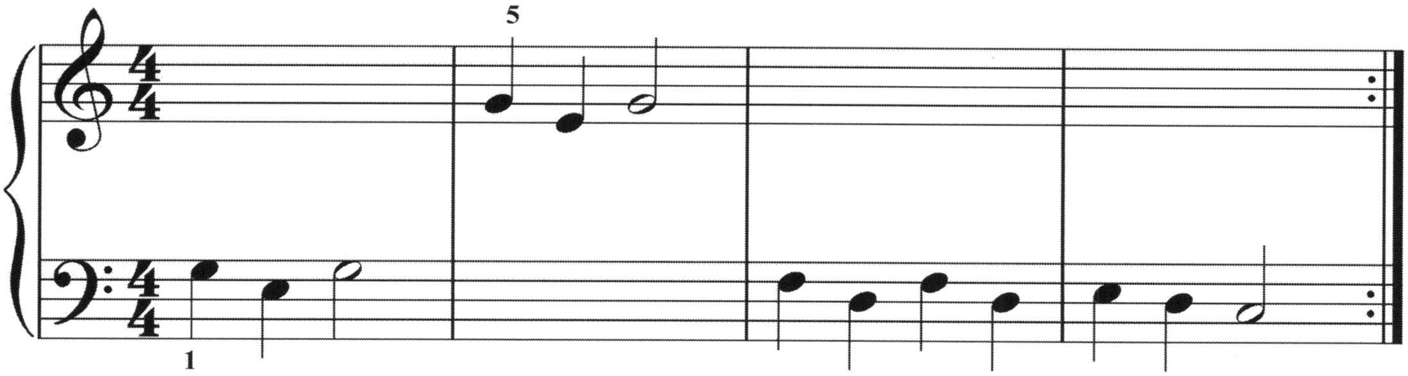

FULL TURN

S T E L L A R

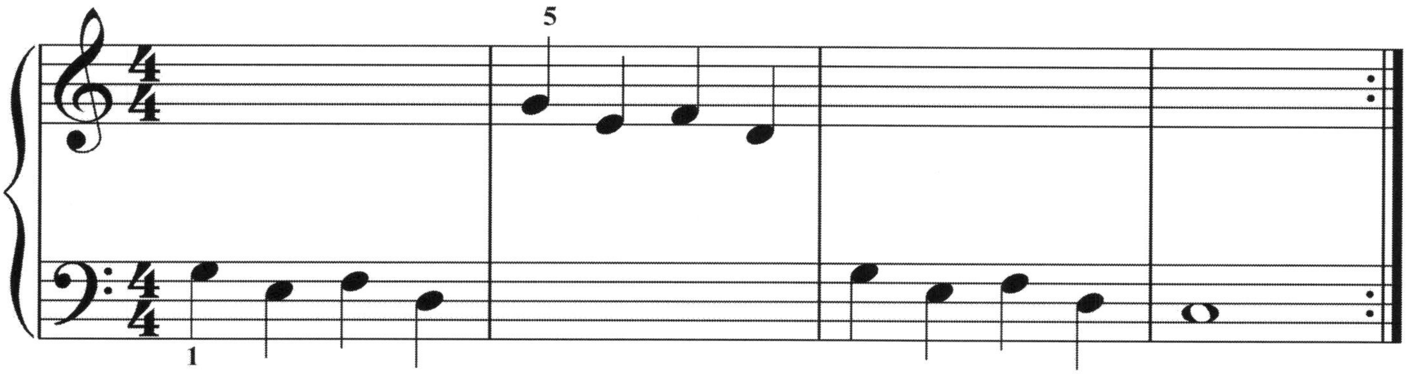

SIGHT READING ONE

SET 5 | PART 1

Look at Sight Reading One. Beginning at the START and ending at the FINISH, play the four measures that rest on the path. Use a colored crayon to draw a new four-measure path. Play again.

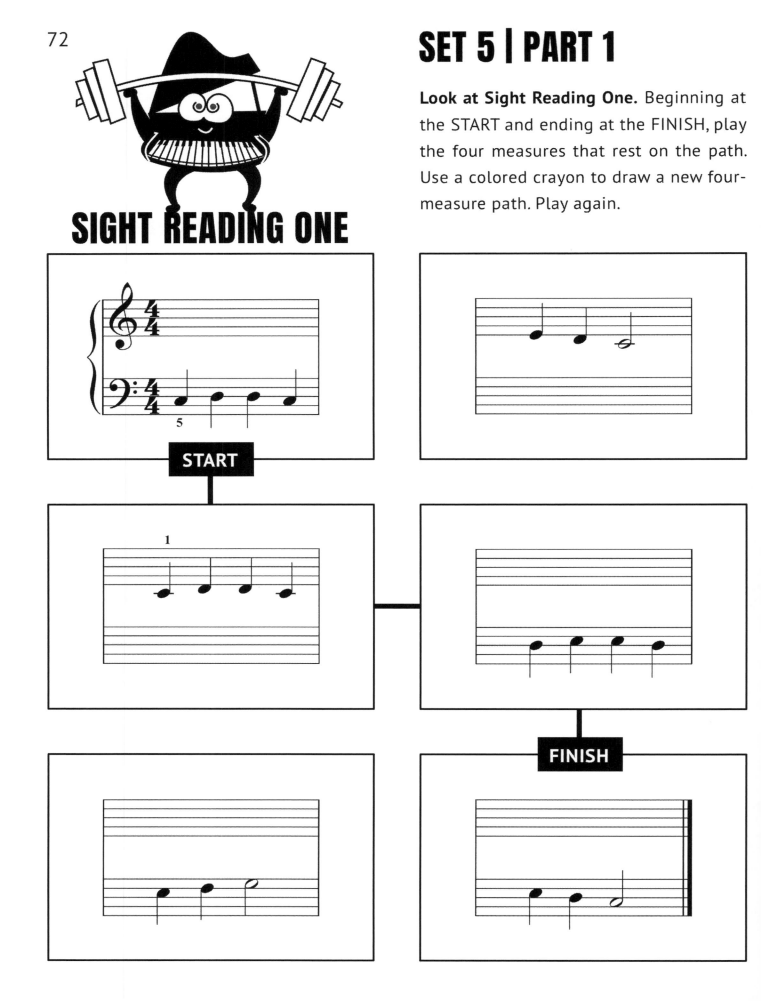

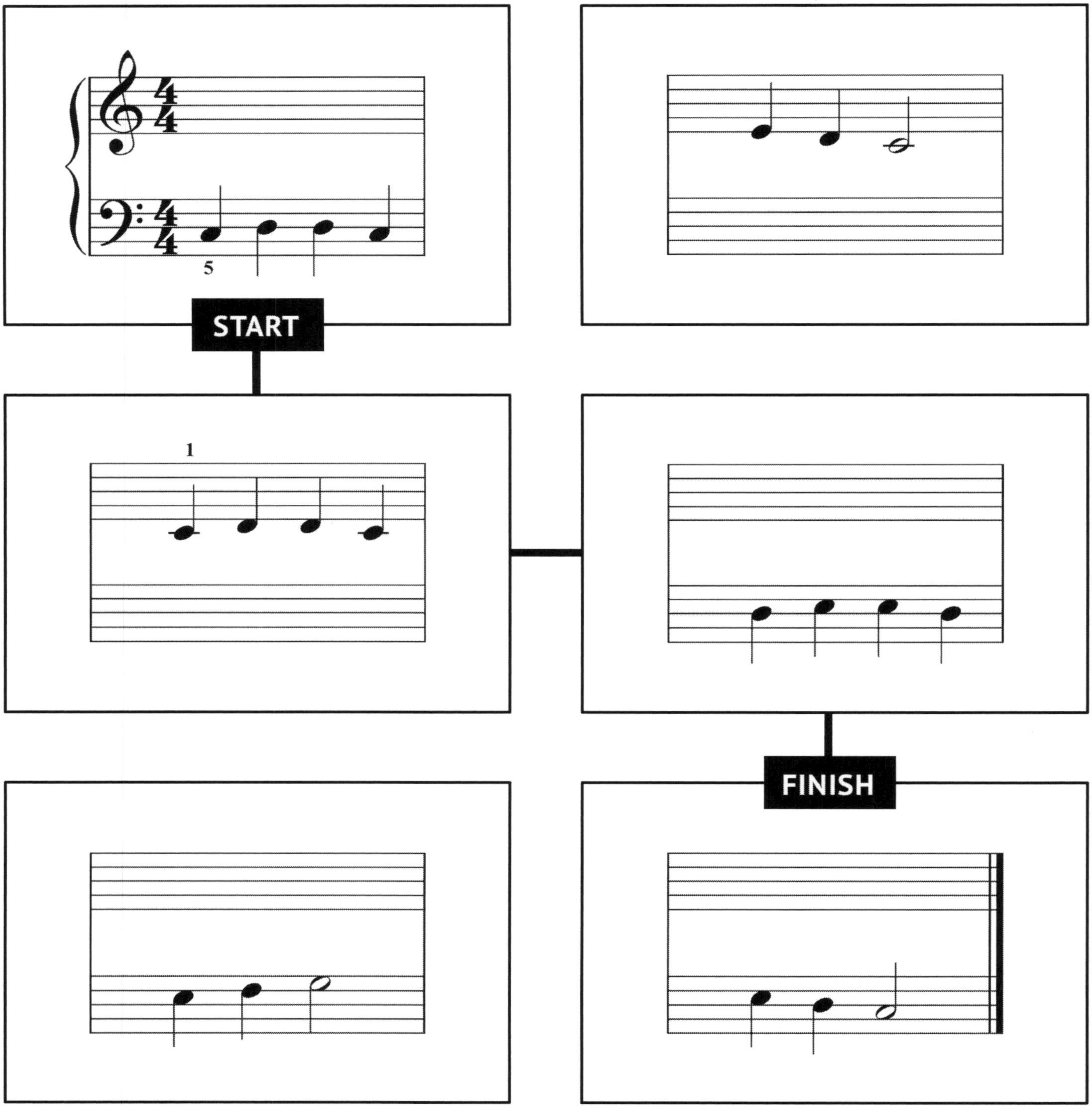

SET 5 | PART 2

Look at Sight Reading Two. Beginning at the START and ending at the FINISH, play the four measures that rest on the path. Use a colored crayon to draw a new four-measure path. Play again.

SIGHT READING TWO

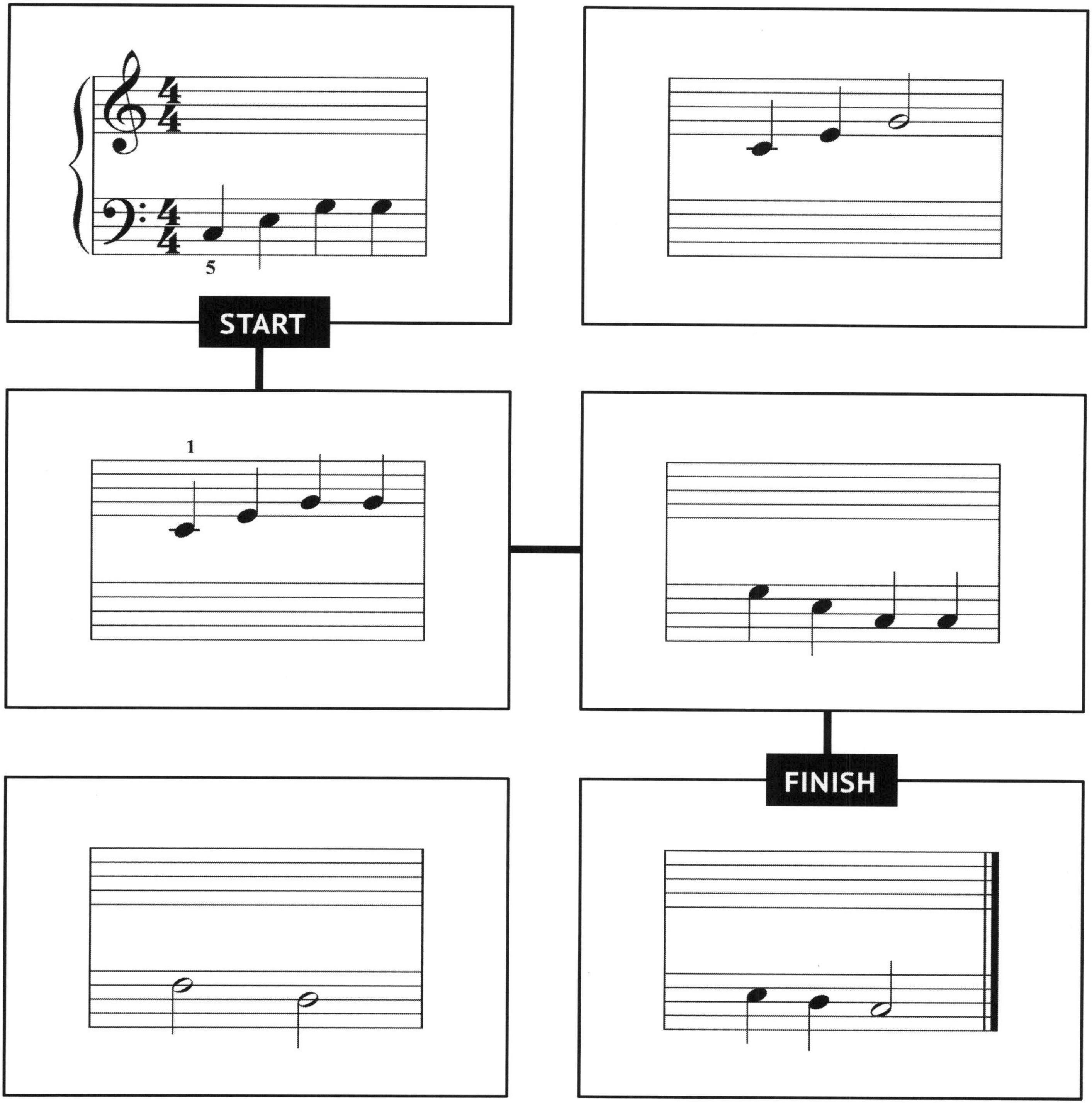

SET 06

UNIT 5

OUT OF POSITION

In the box above Exercise 1, write the name of the first note. Next, use the finger number to find your starting position. Repeat with Exercises 2 and 3.

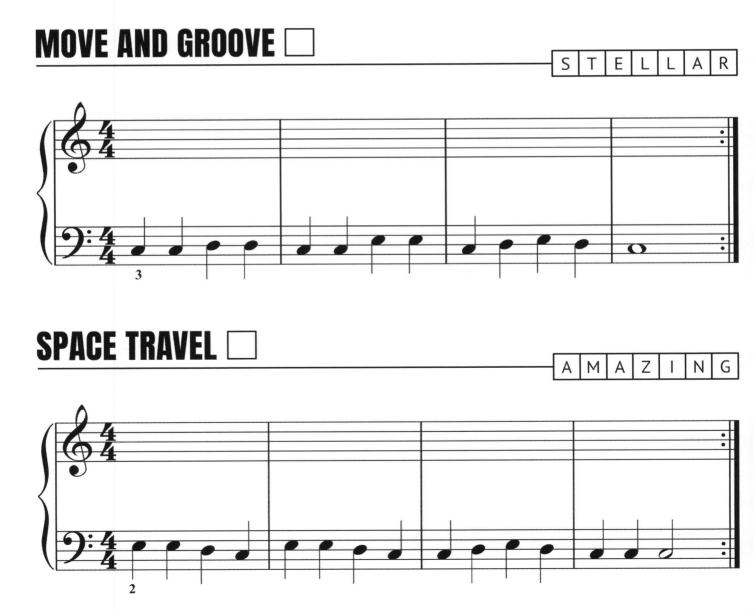

MOVE AND GROOVE ☐

S T E L L A R

SPACE TRAVEL ☐

A M A Z I N G

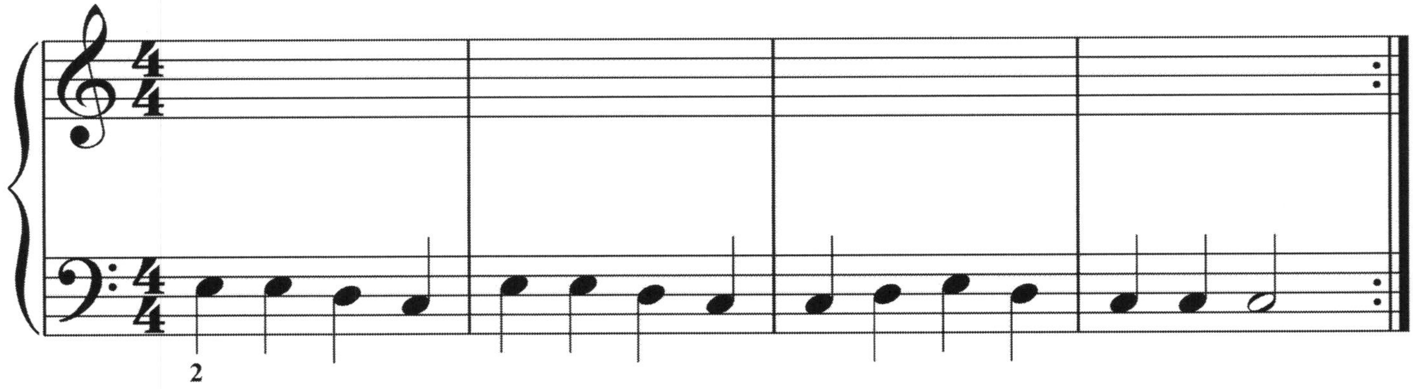

SHIFT WORK ☐

W I N N I N G

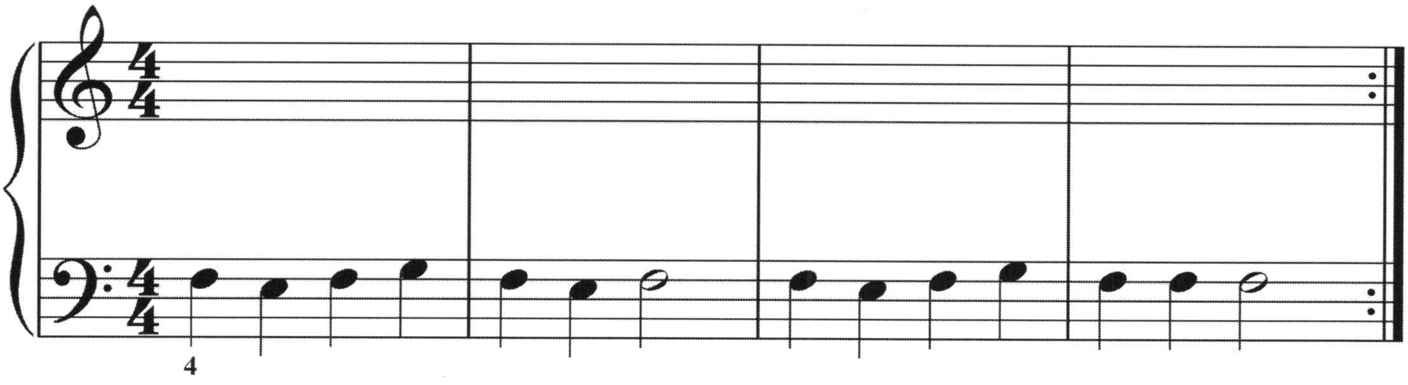

CHALLENGE PIECE 1

P E R F E C T

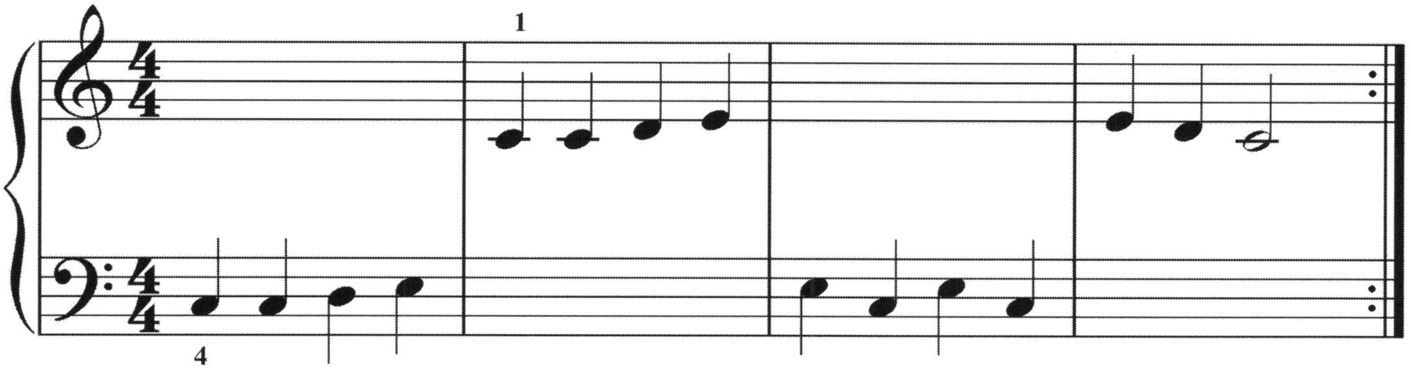

CHALLENGE PIECE 2

A W E S O M E

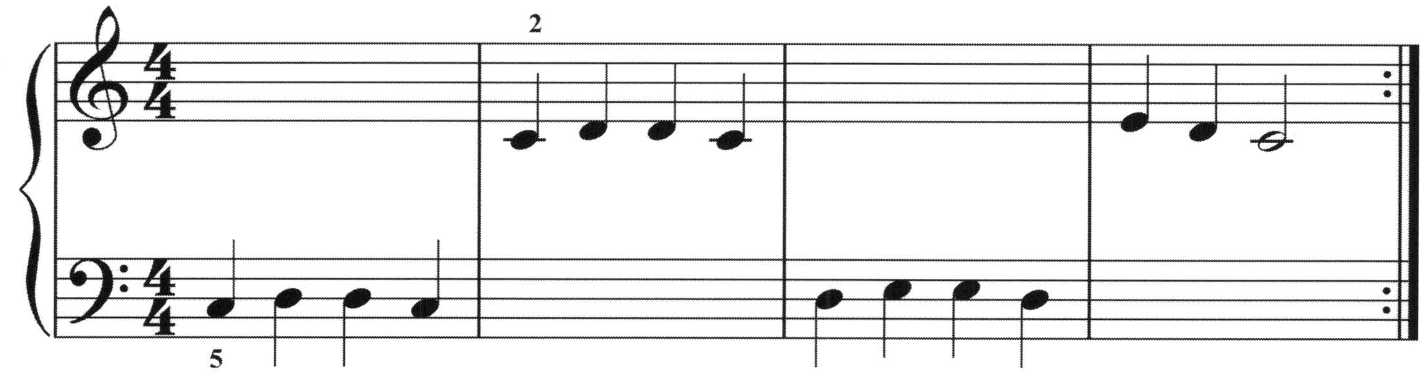

SET 07

UNIT 5

NEW!

QUARTER REST

Look at the first line of rhythm below. Stem-down notes are performed by tapping both hands on your lap. Stem-up notes are performed by clapping your hands together. After performing the first rhythm, complete the remaining exercises.

RHYTHM CHALLENGE 1

A W E S O M E

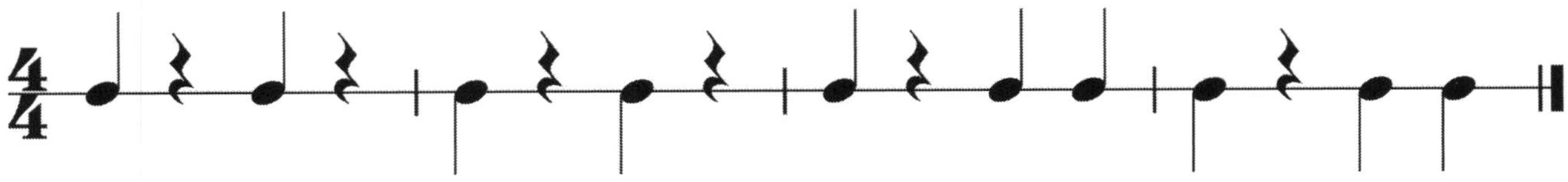

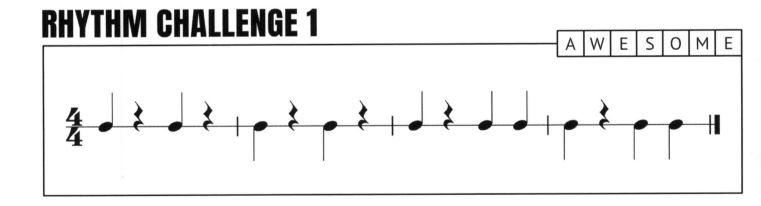

RHYTHM CHALLENGE 2

S T E L L A R

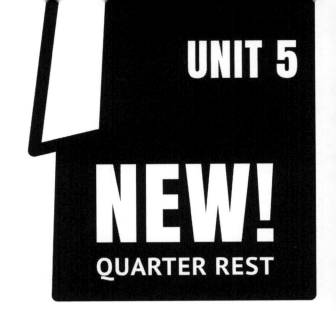

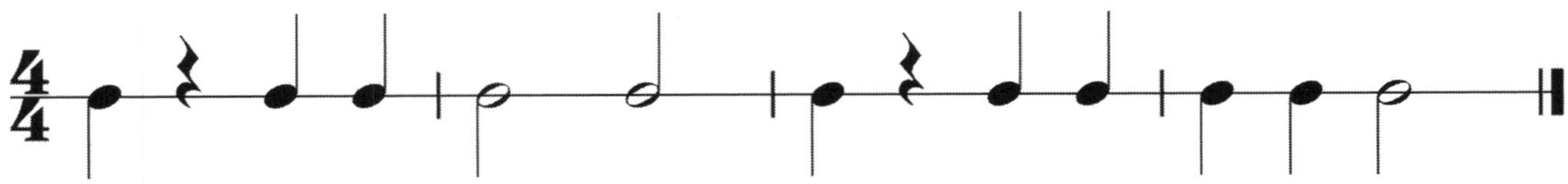

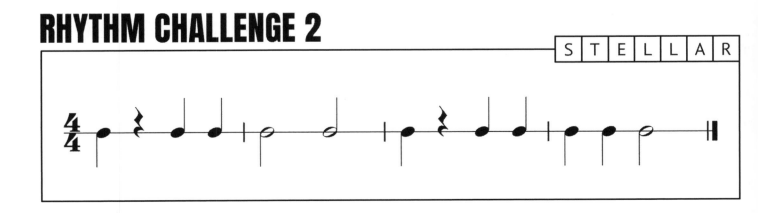

RHYTHM CHALLENGE 3

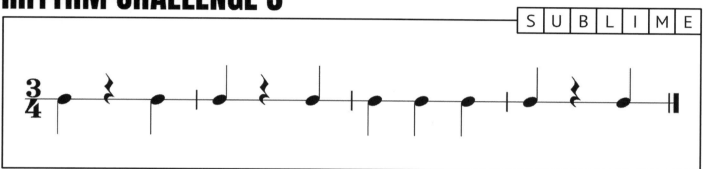

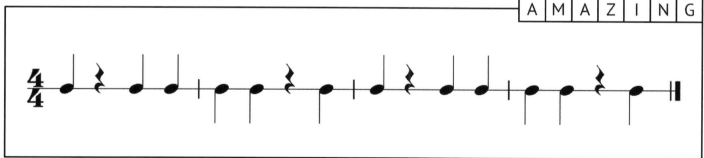

S	U	B	L	I	M	E

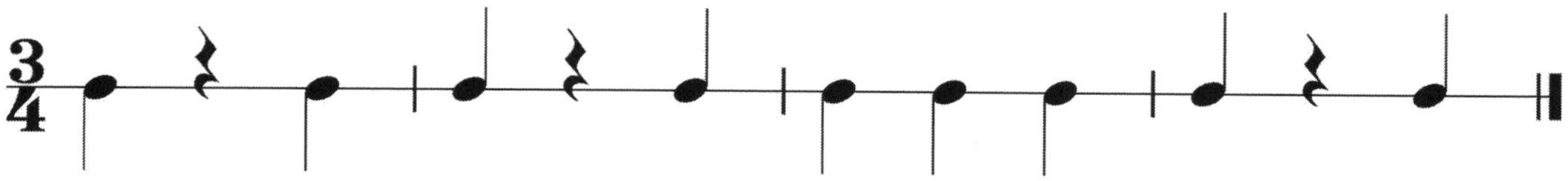

RHYTHM CHALLENGE 4

P	E	R	F	E	C	T

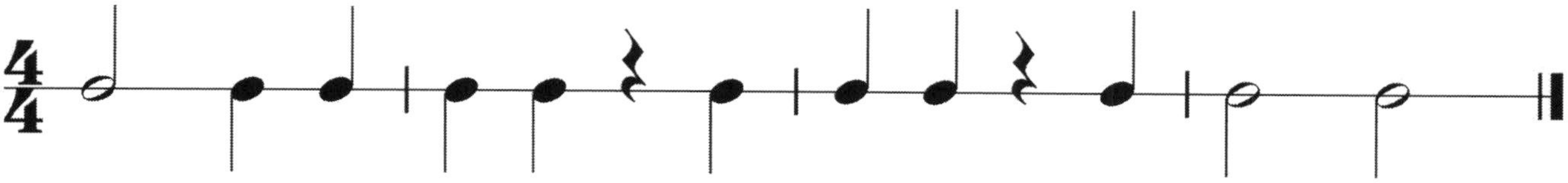

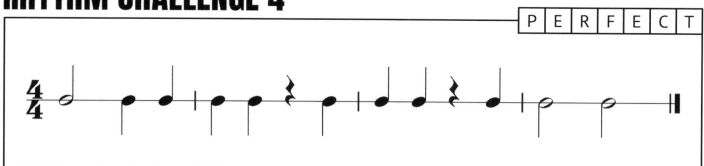

RHYTHM CHALLENGE 5

W	I	N	N	I	N	G

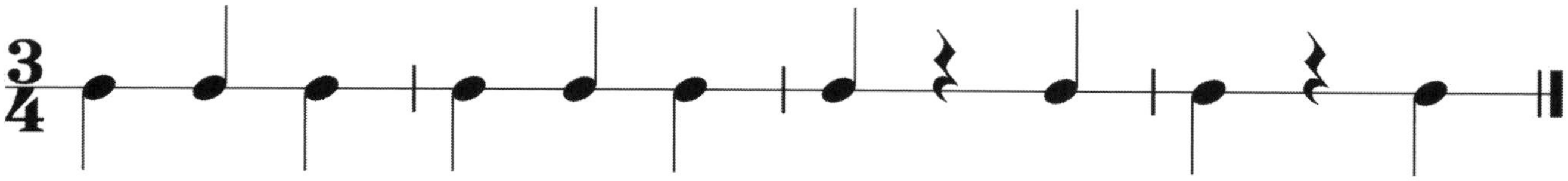

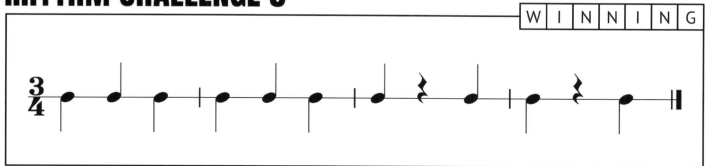

RHYTHM CHALLENGE 6

A	M	A	Z	I	N	G

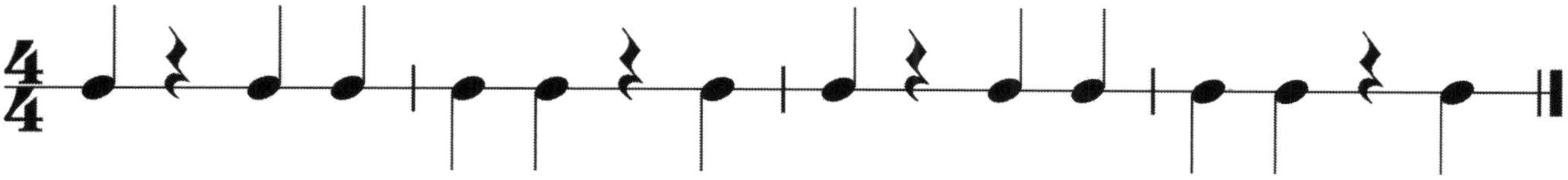

SET 08

UNIT 5

NEW!

QUARTER REST

Color in one lettered box each time you practice a line of music.
After all of the boxes are colored, you will be one AWESOME piano player.

SPROCKET ROCKET

A	W	E	S	O	M	E

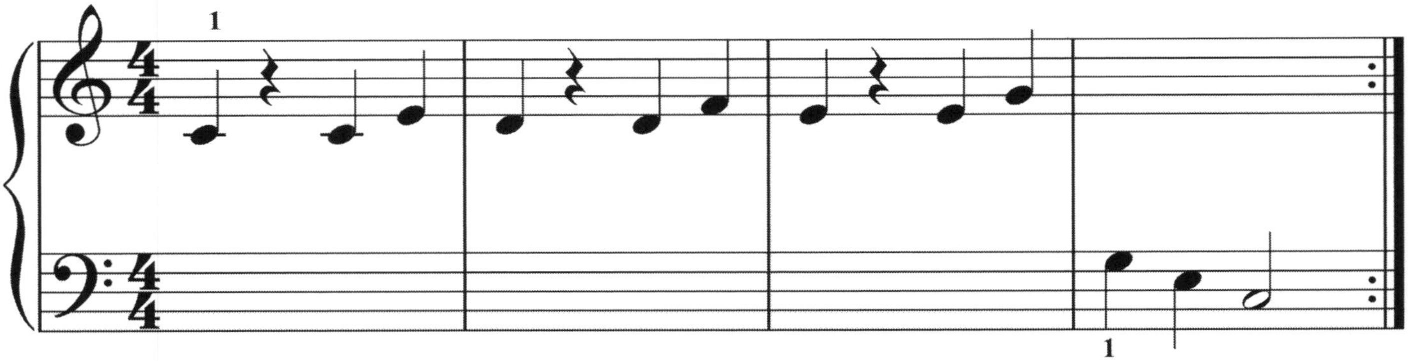

SADDLE UP

A	M	A	Z	I	N	G

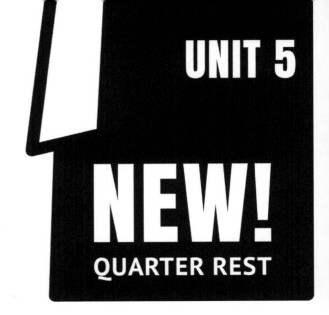

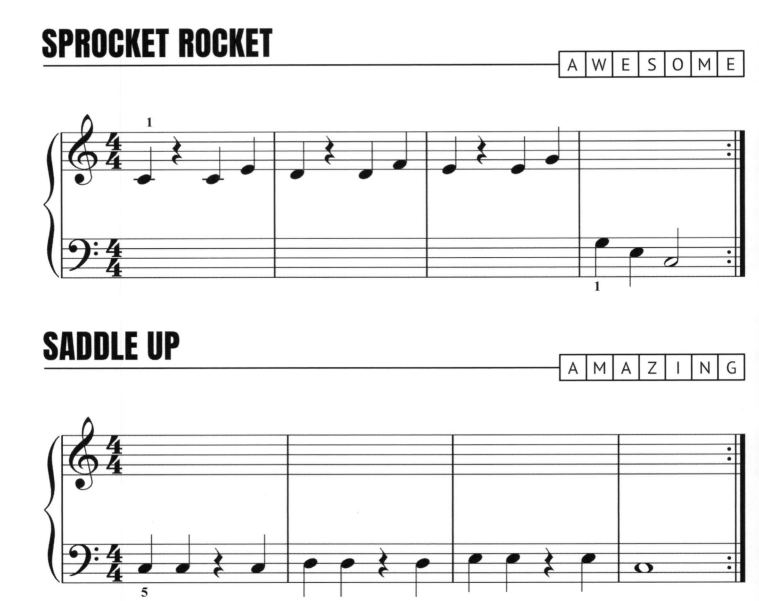

HIGH GEAR

W I N N I N G

HOP AND HOVER

P E R F E C T

PEDAL POWER

S T E L L A R

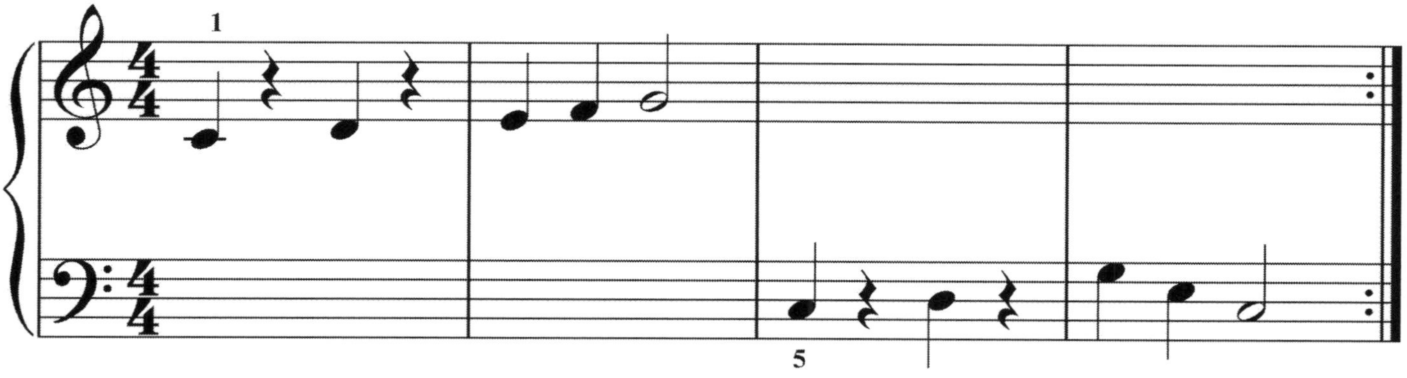

SET 09

UNIT 5

CHALLENGE SET

The following cross-staff exercises are intended for older beginners and students who want to test their skills.

BOUNCE BACK

A W E S O M E

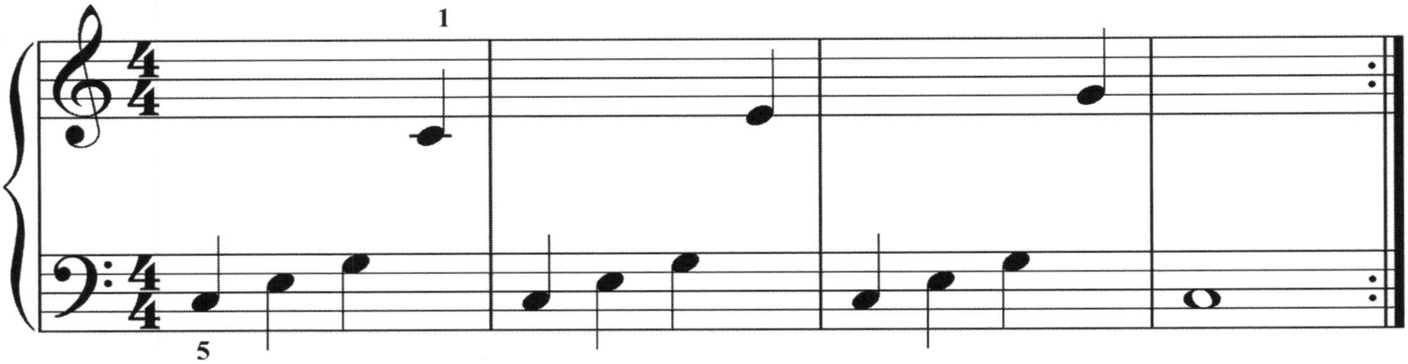

REBOUND

S T E L L A R

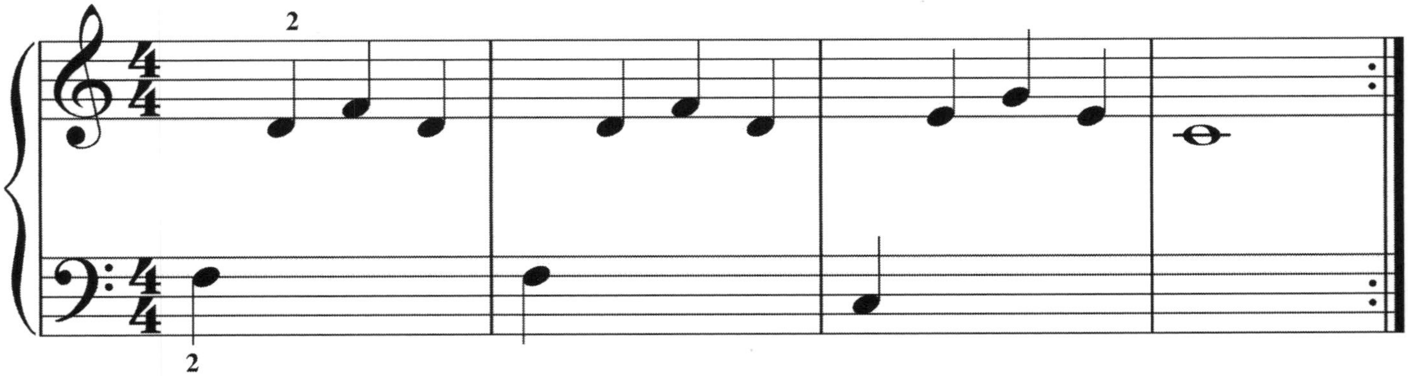

HOMEWARD BOUNCE

W	I	N	N	I	N	G

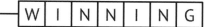

BOUND TOWN

P	E	R	F	E	C	T

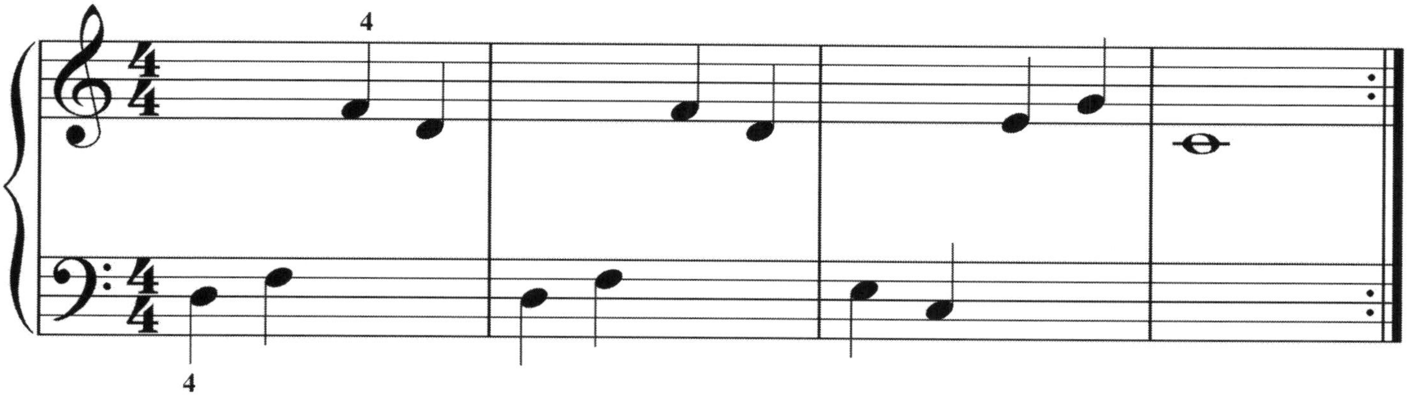

BOUNCE PASS

A	M	A	Z	I	N	G

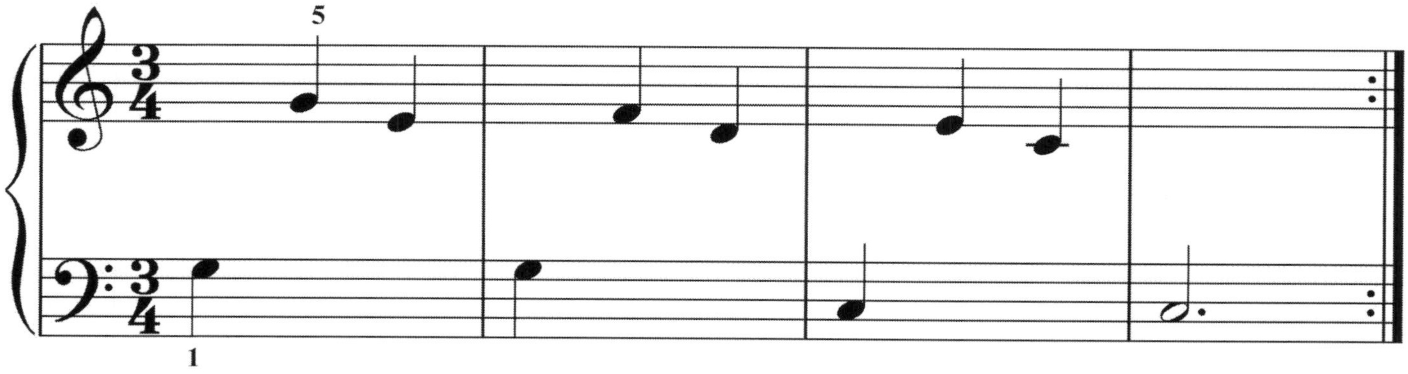

HANDS TOGETHER

It's better to exercise with a buddy. Let's start playing hands together. The exercises on the following pages will help you practice playing in parallel motion and contrary motion and with held fifths and held whole notes.

Color in one lettered box each time you practice a line of music.
After all of the boxes are colored, you will be one AWESOME piano player.

PRESS PLAY

A W E S O M E

DOWNTOWN

P E R F E C T

SKIP-UPS

A M A Z I N G

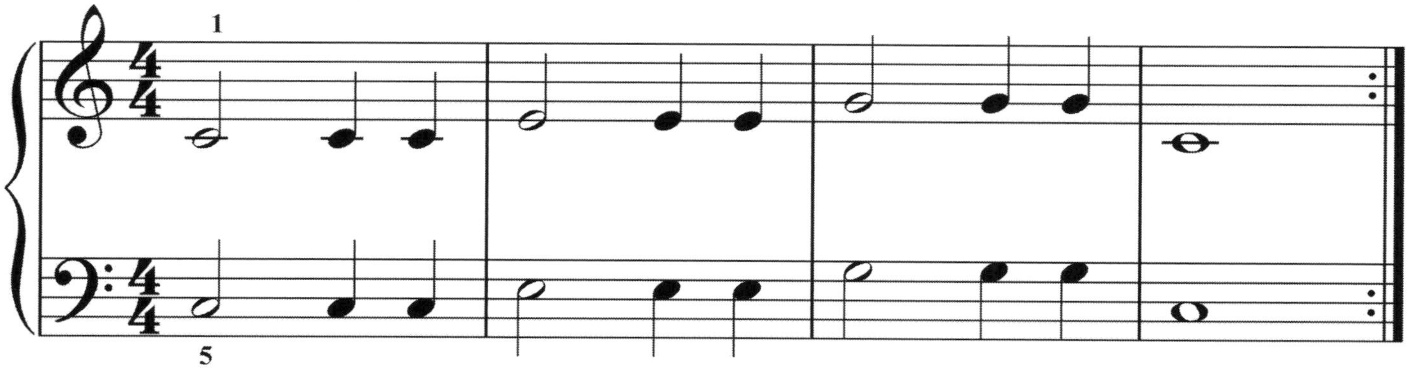

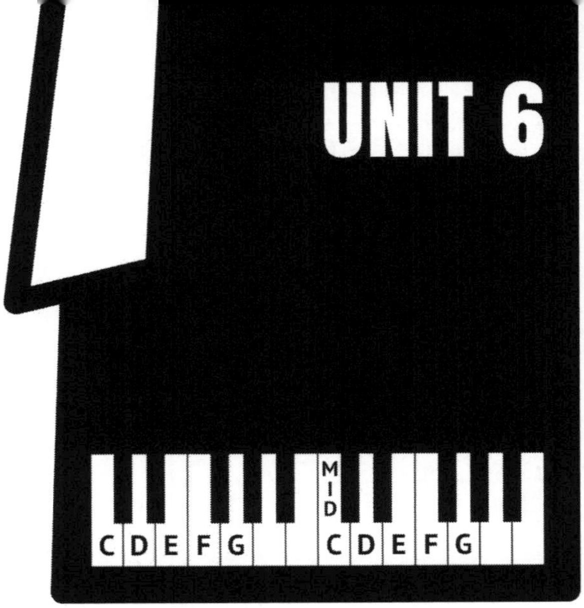

SET 01

Color in one lettered box each time you practice a line of music.
After all of the boxes are colored, you will be one AMAZING piano player.

CRUNCH TIME

A	M	A	Z	I	N	G

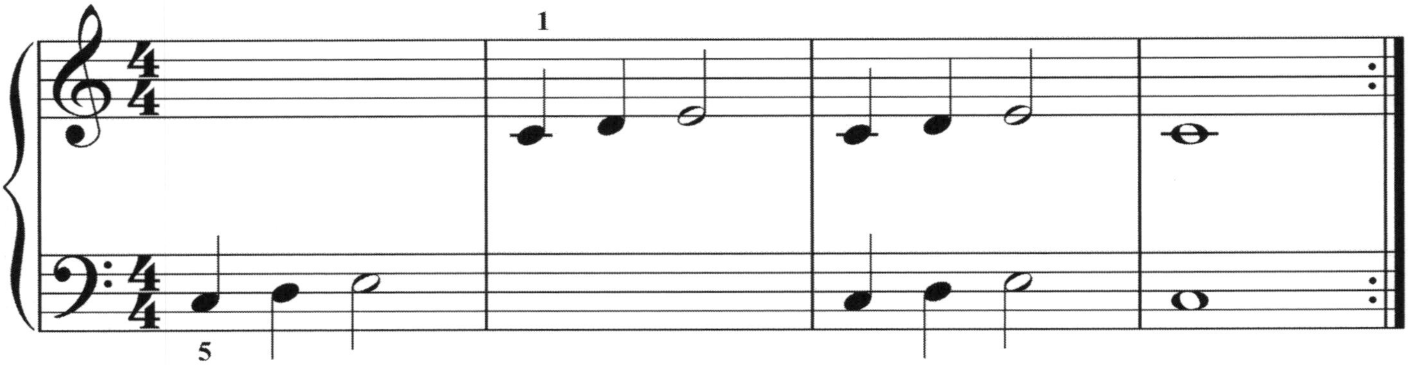

CURL WHIRL

S	T	E	L	L	A	R

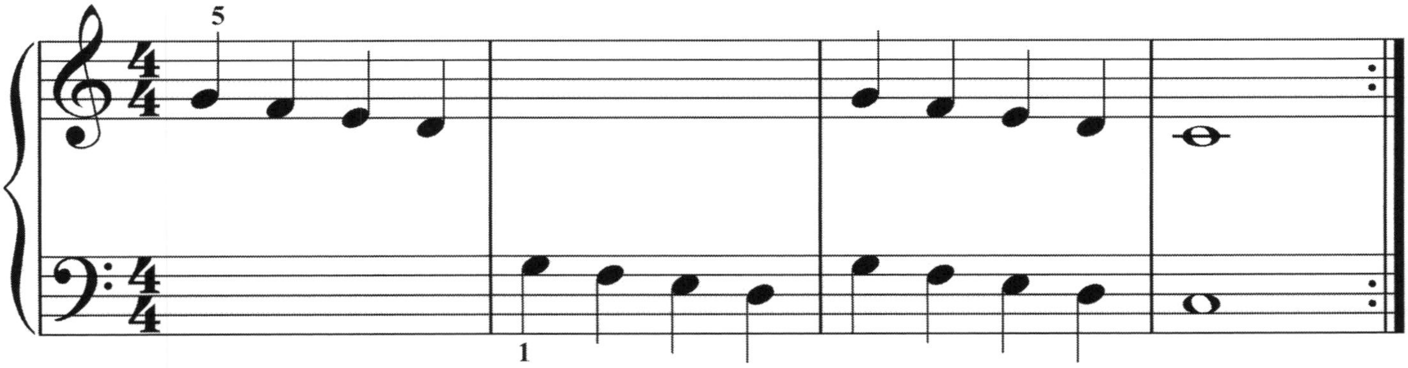

POWER PLAY

W	I	N	N	I	N	G

KICKBACK TRACK

P	E	R	F	E	C	T

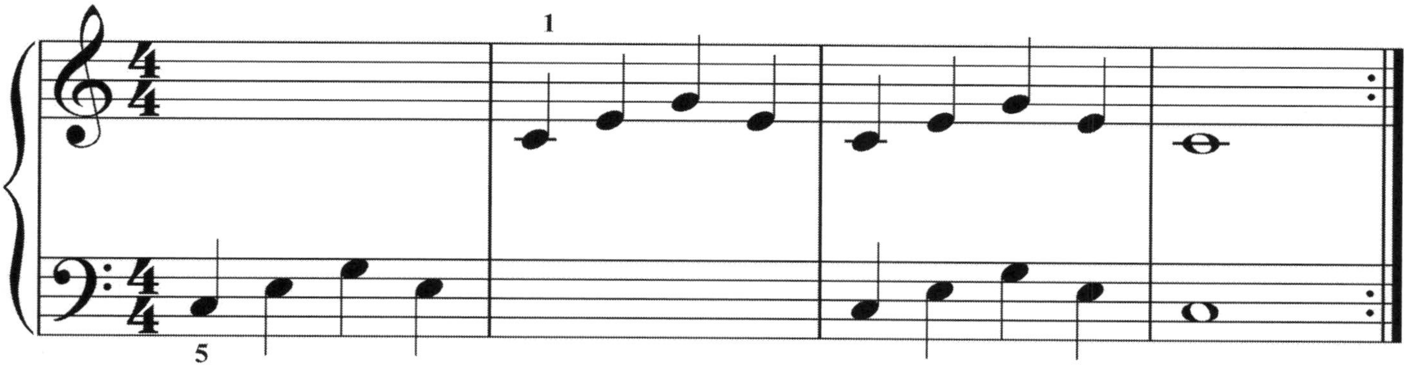

BENCH PRESS

A	W	E	S	O	M	E

SET 02

Color in one lettered box each time you practice a line of music.
After all of the boxes are colored, you will be one PERFECT piano player.

LADDER STACK

P	E	R	F	E	C	T

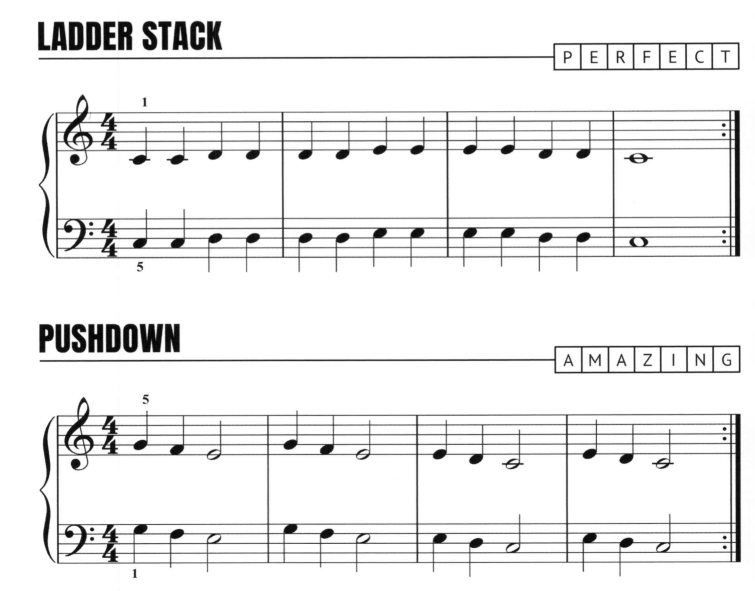

PUSHDOWN

A	M	A	Z	I	N	G

CLIMB TIME

W I N N I N G

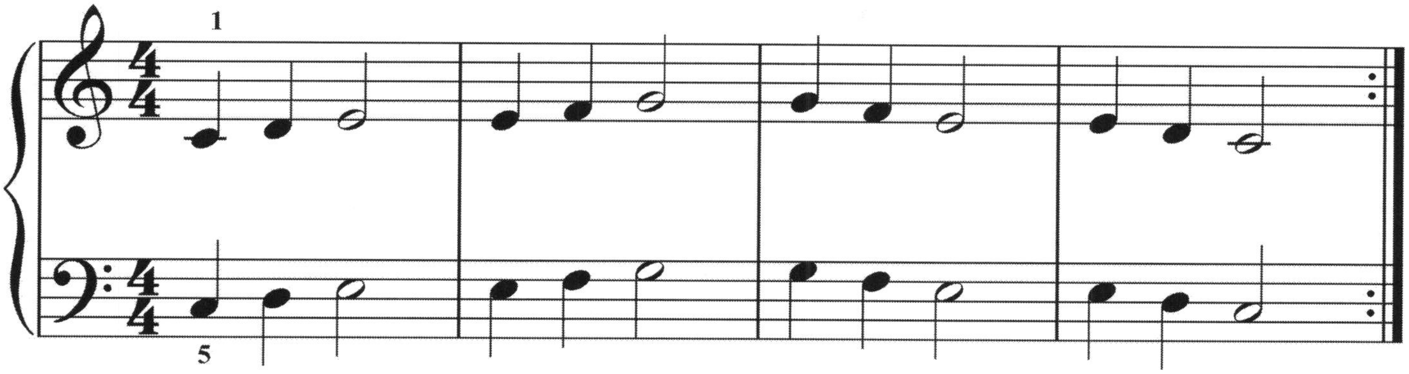

ROLLOUT

A W E S O M E

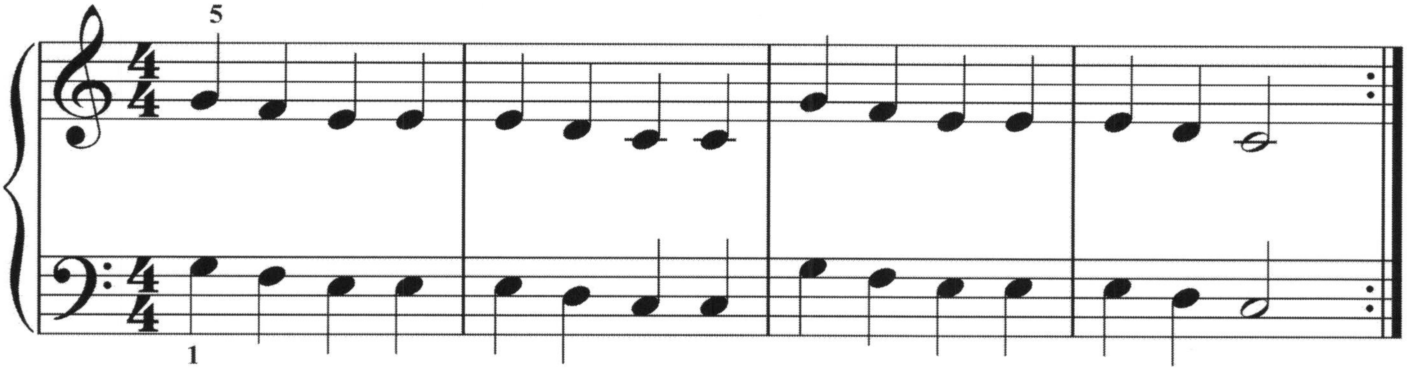

REVERSE FLY

S T E L L A R

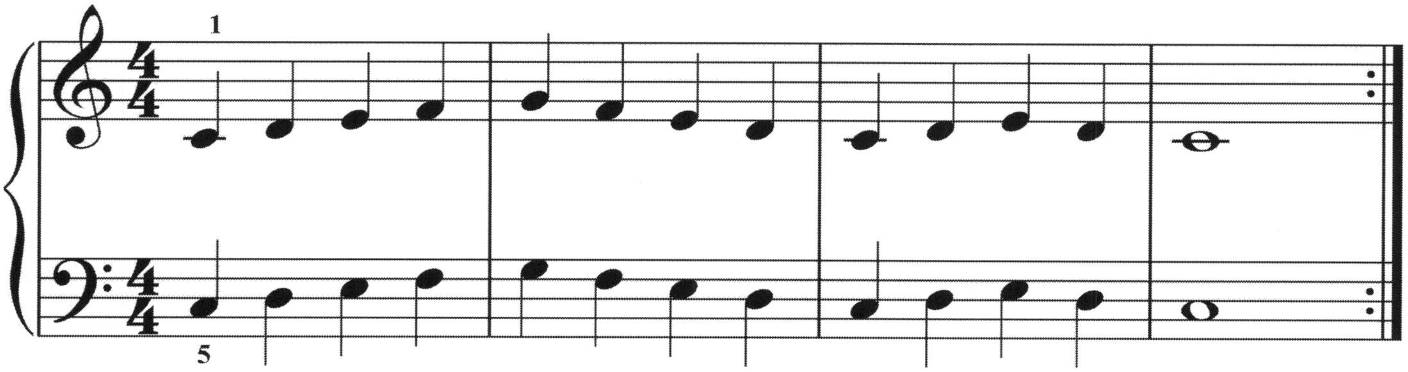

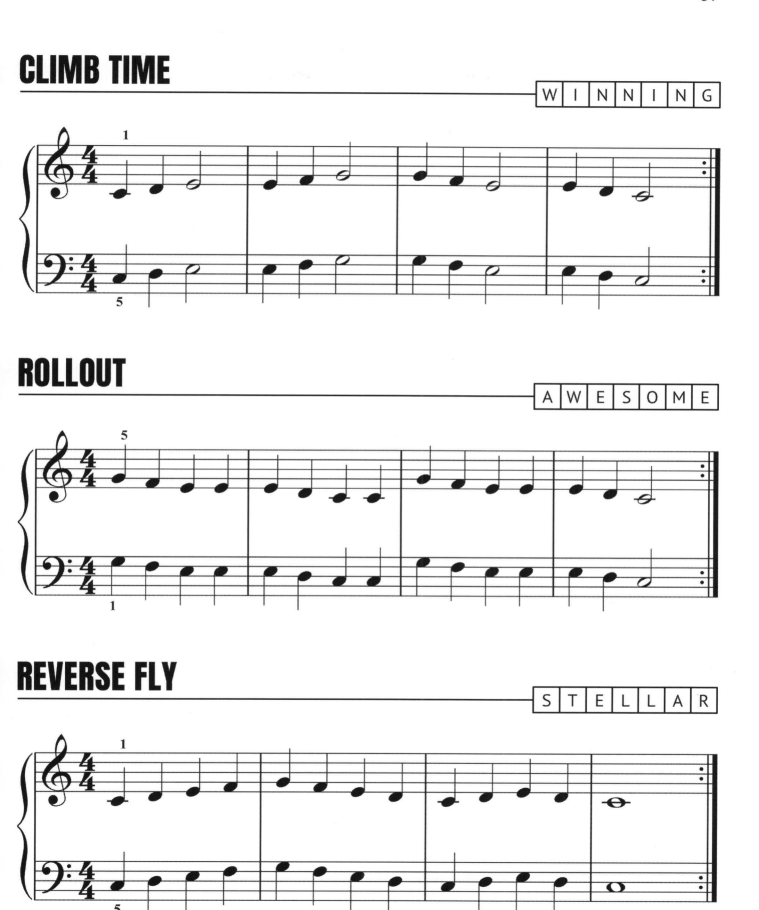

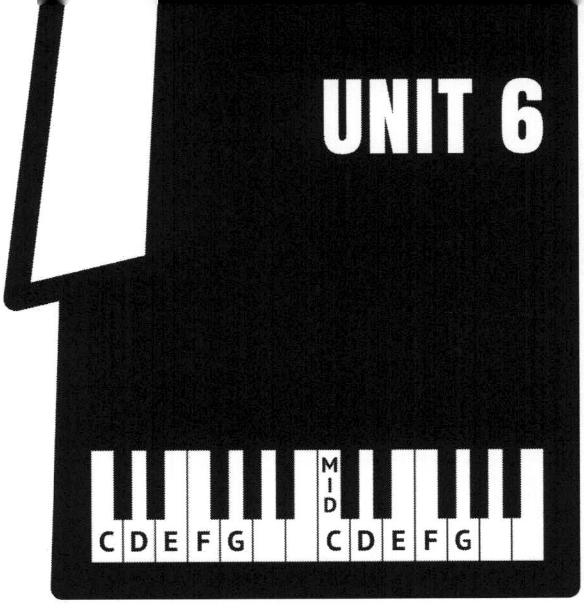

SET 03

Color in one lettered box each time you practice a line of music.
After all of the boxes are colored, you will be one STELLAR piano player.

SHUFFLE SKIP

S	T	E	L	L	A	R

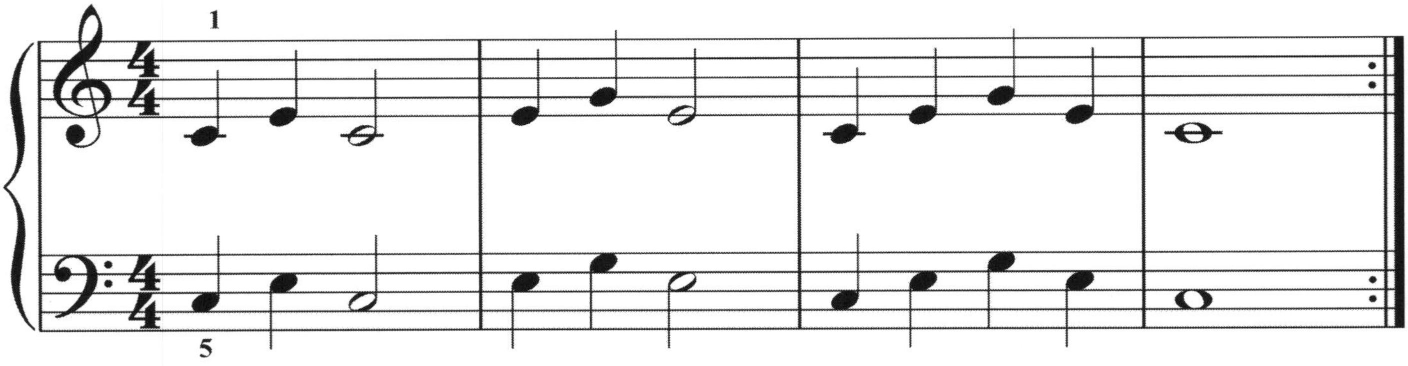

SCISSOR SKIP

A	M	A	Z	I	N	G

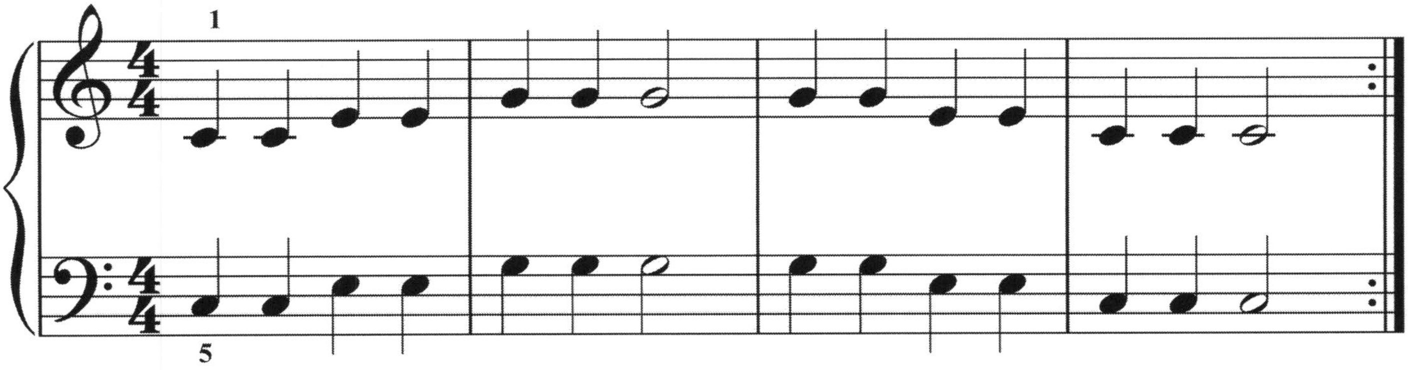

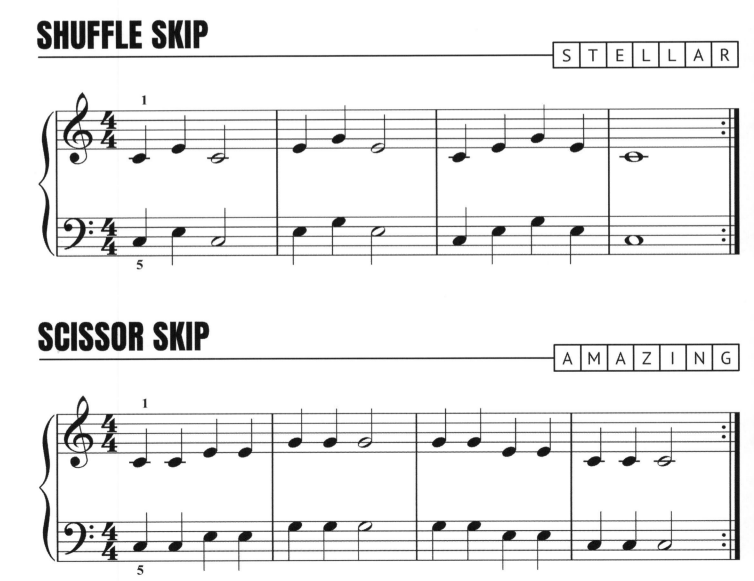

HIGH KNEES

W I N N I N G

DOUBLE UNDER

P E R F E C T

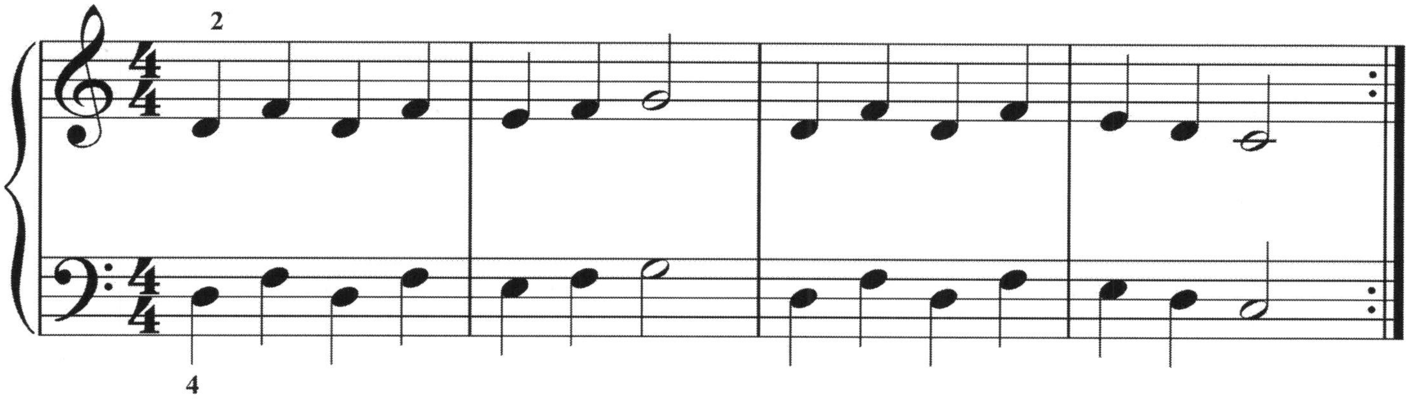

CRISS CROSS

A W E S O M E

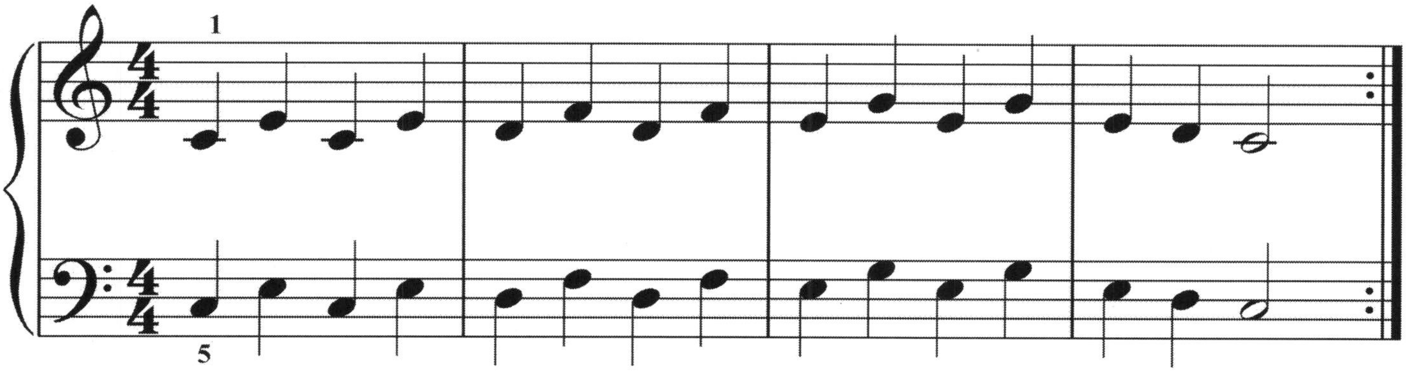

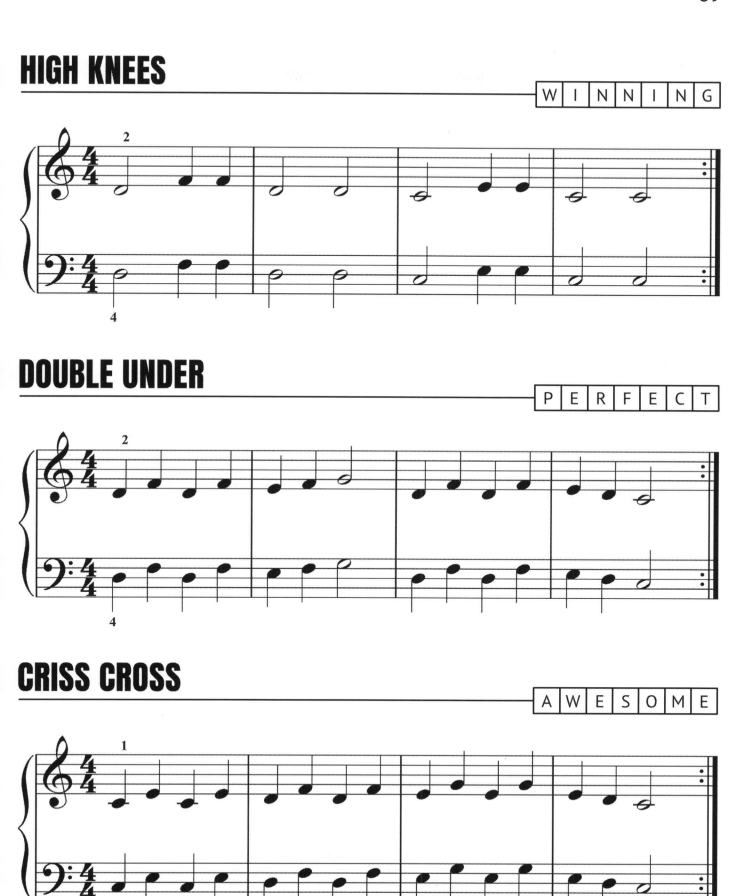

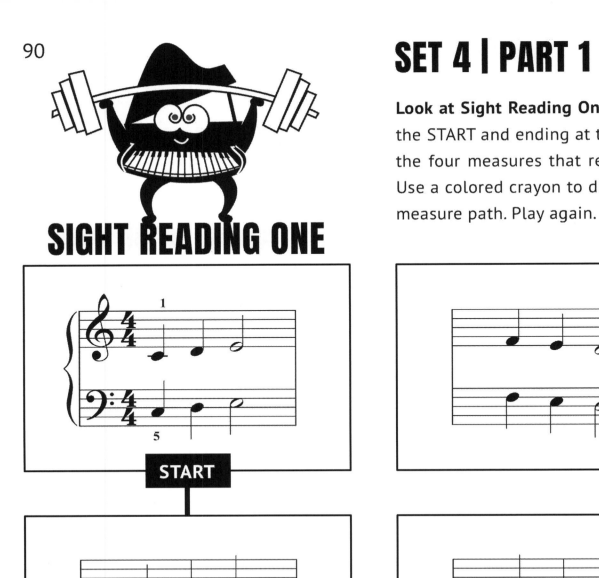

SET 4 | PART 1

Look at Sight Reading One. Beginning at the START and ending at the FINISH, play the four measures that rest on the path. Use a colored crayon to draw a new four-measure path. Play again.

SIGHT READING ONE

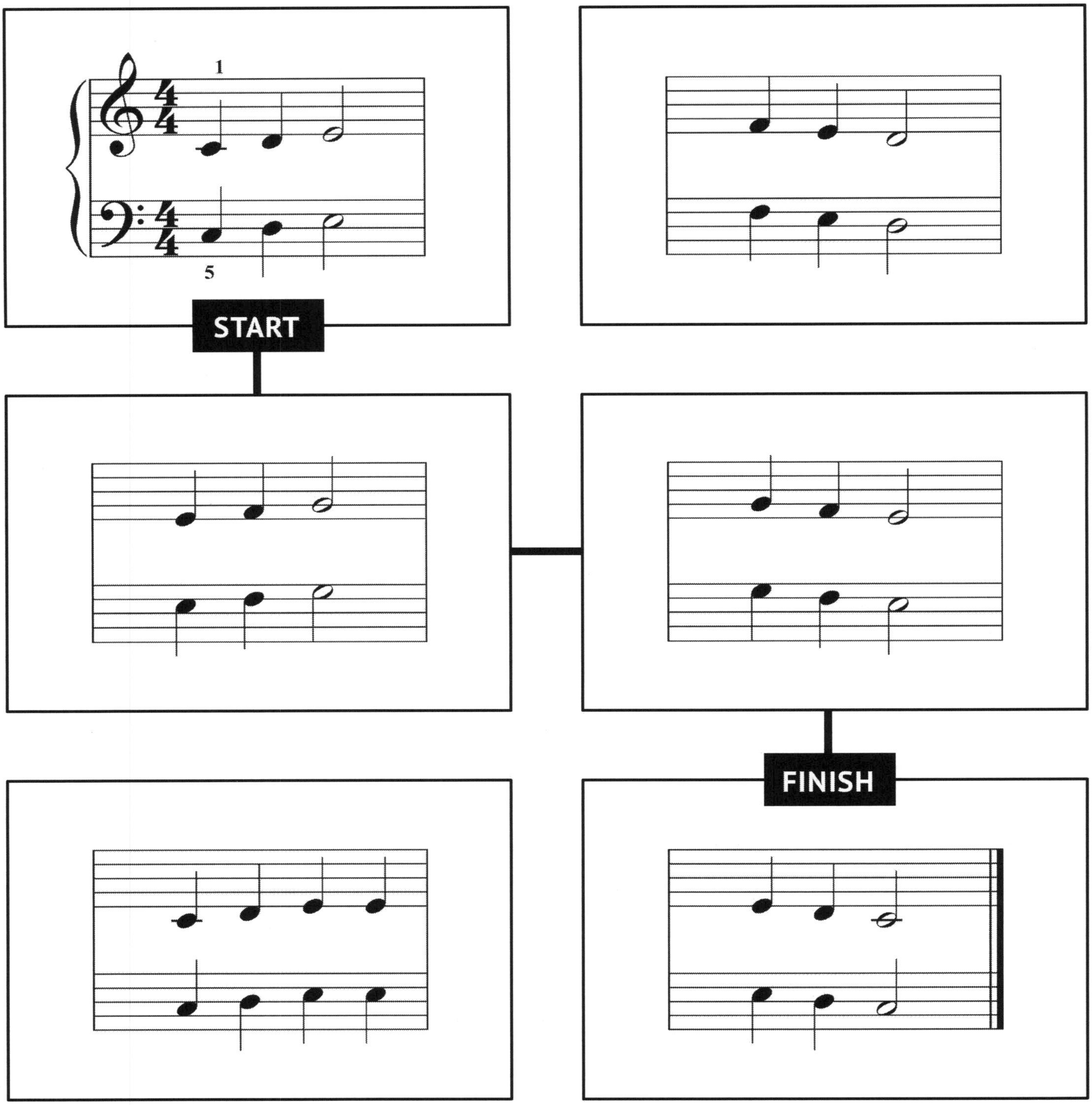

SET 4 | PART 2

Look at Sight Reading Two. Beginning at the START and ending at the FINISH, play the four measures that rest on the path. Use a colored crayon to draw a new four-measure path. Play again.

SIGHT READING TWO

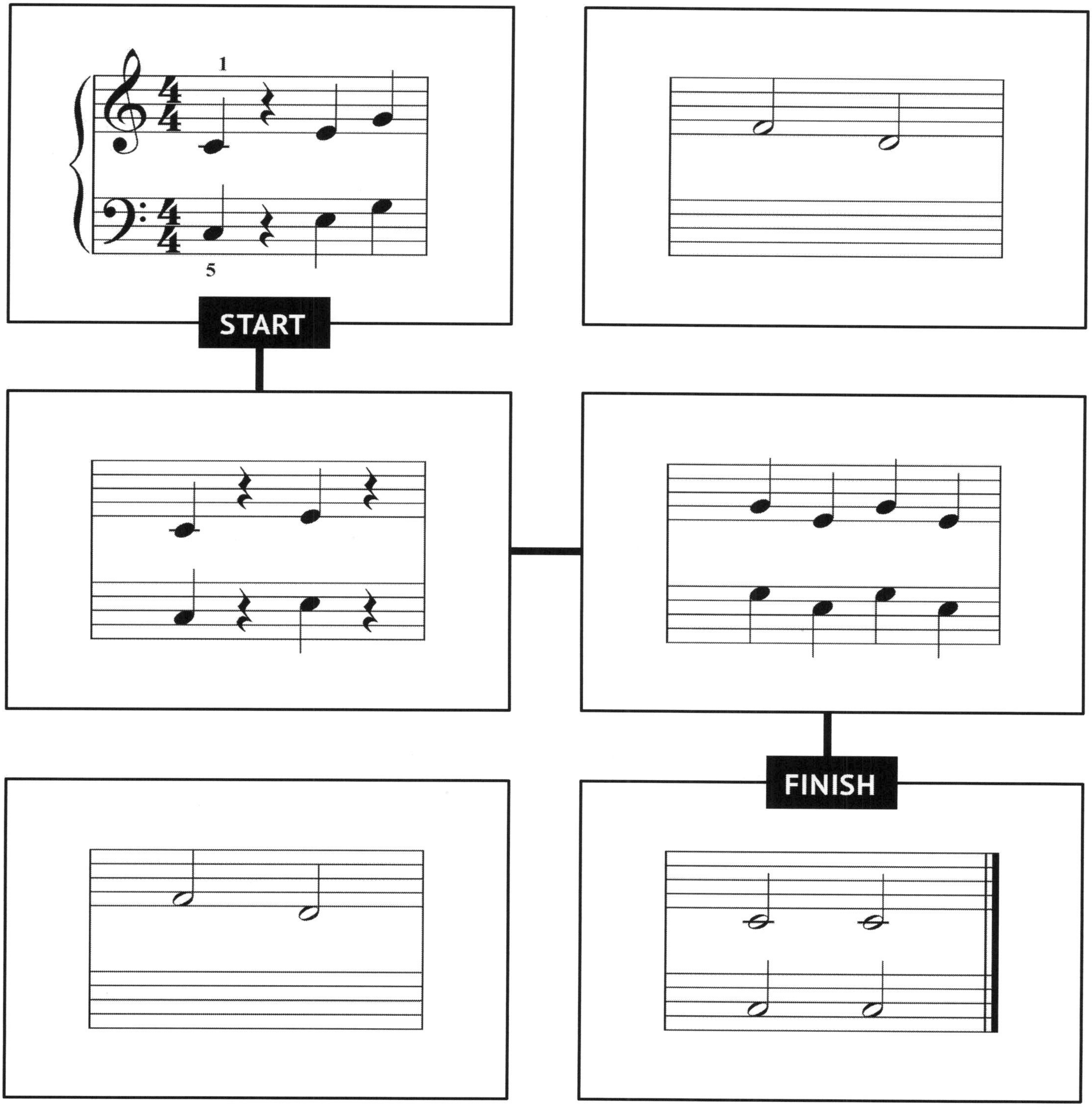

SET 05

UNIT 6

QUARTER RESTS

Color in one lettered box each time you practice a line of music.
After all of the boxes are colored, you will be one AWESOME piano player.

SPROCKET ROCKET

A	W	E	S	O	M	E

SADDLE UP

A	M	A	Z	I	N	G

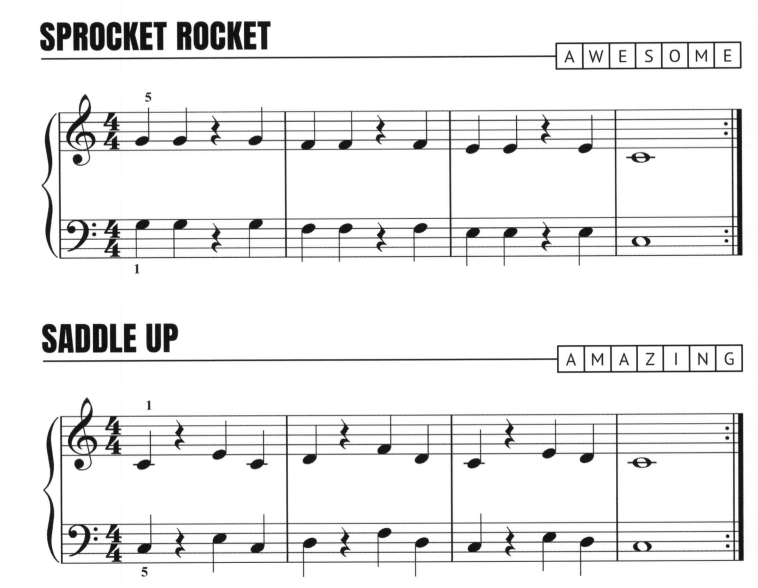

HIGH GEAR

W	I	N	N	I	N	G

HOP AND HOVER

P	E	R	F	E	C	T

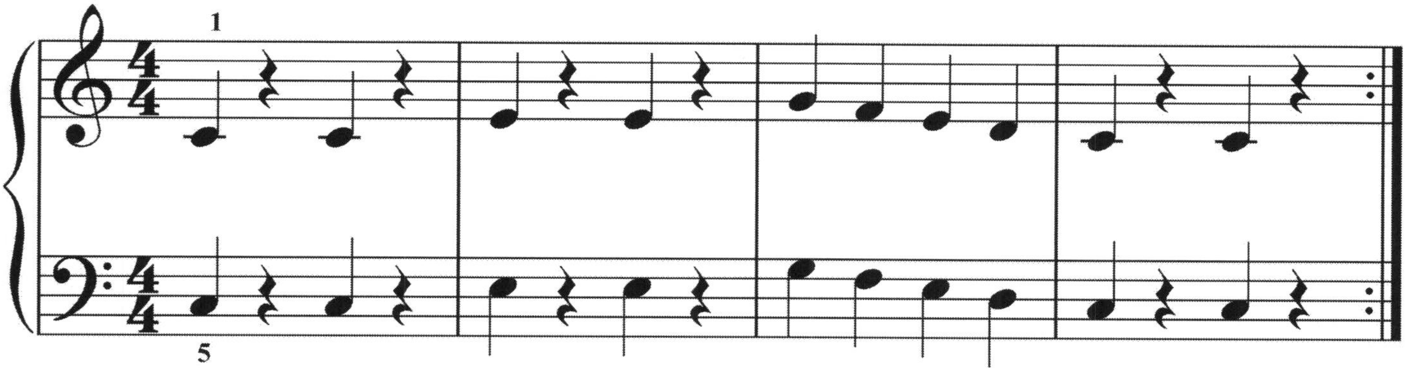

PEDAL POWER

S	T	E	L	L	A	R

SET 06

UNIT 6

NEW!
HELD FIFTHS

Color in one lettered box each time you practice a line of music.
After all of the boxes are colored, you will be one AMAZING piano player.

SWITCH UP

A M A Z I N G

STAY AND AWAY

A W E S O M E

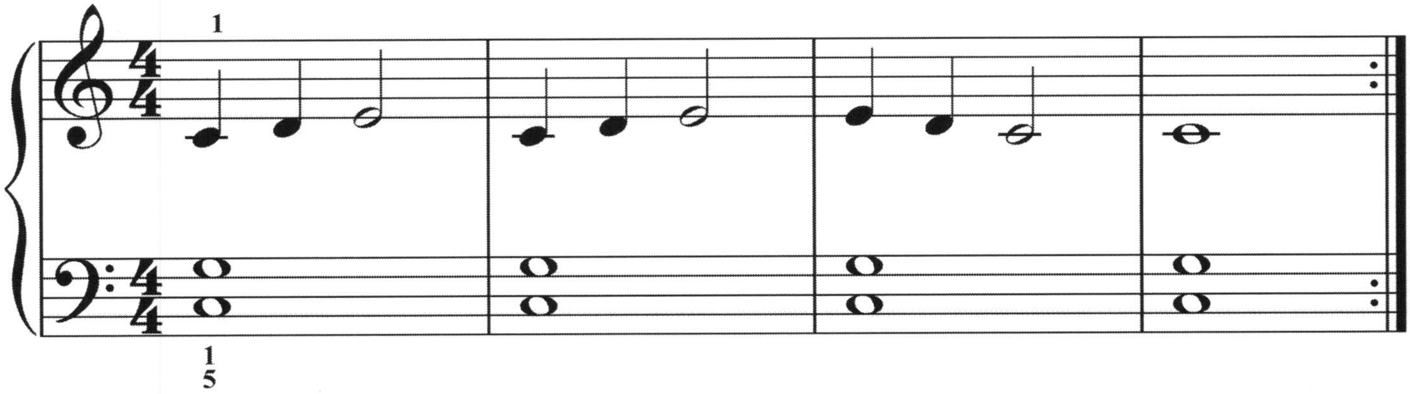

OUT AND BACK

W I N N I N G

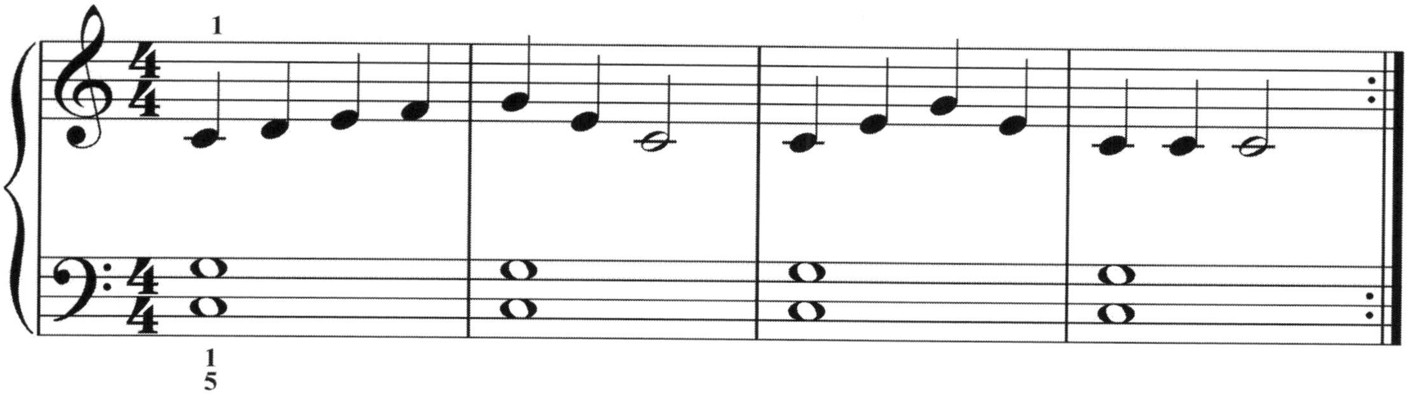

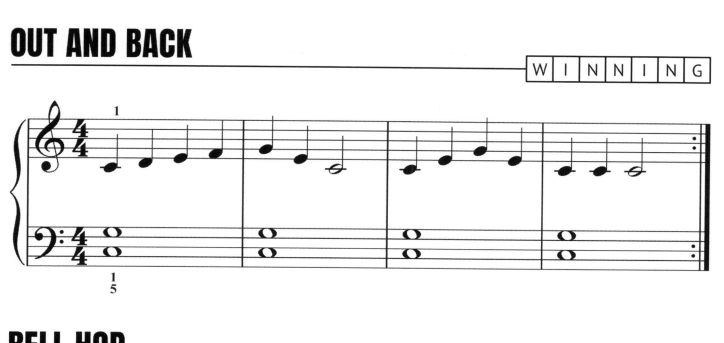

BELL HOP

P E R F E C T

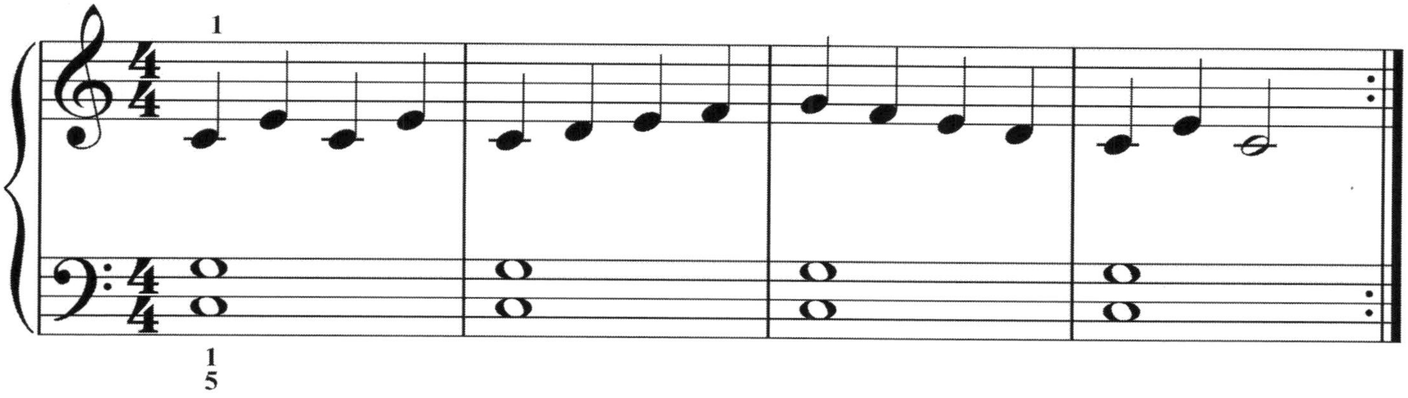

ROLLOVER

S T E L L A R

UNIT 6

NEW!

HELD WHOLE NOTES

Color in one lettered box each time you practice a line of music.
After all of the boxes are colored, you will be one PERFECT piano player.

TOP HOP

P	E	R	F	E	C	T

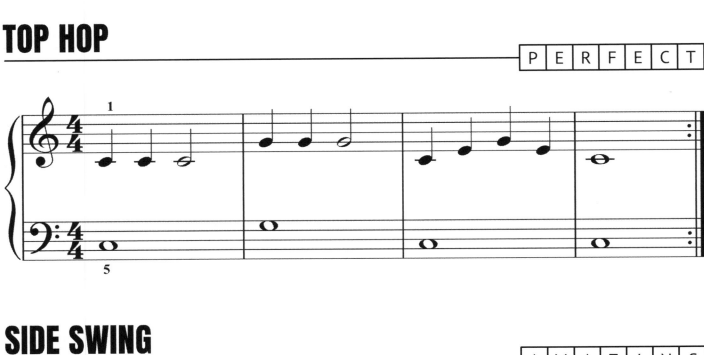

SIDE SWING

A	M	A	Z	I	N	G

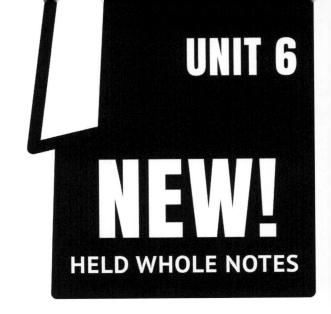

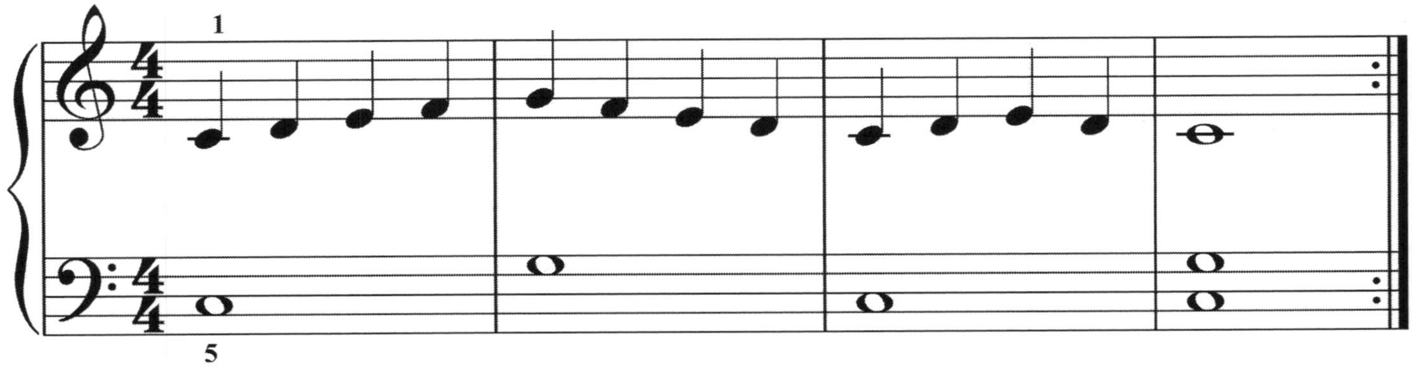

STRADDLE CROSS

W	I	N	N	I	N	G

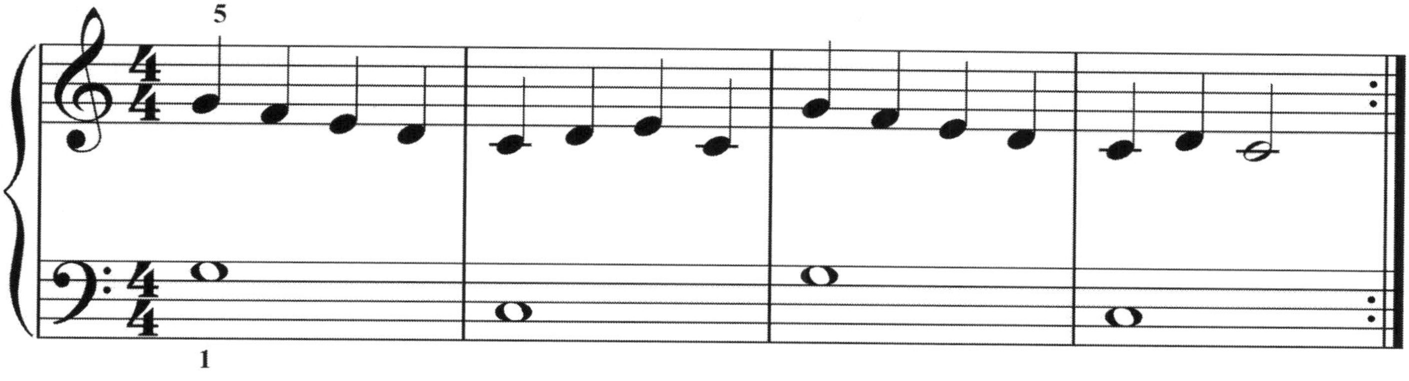

REBOUND

A	W	E	S	O	M	E

BOUNCE PASS

S	T	E	L	L	A	R

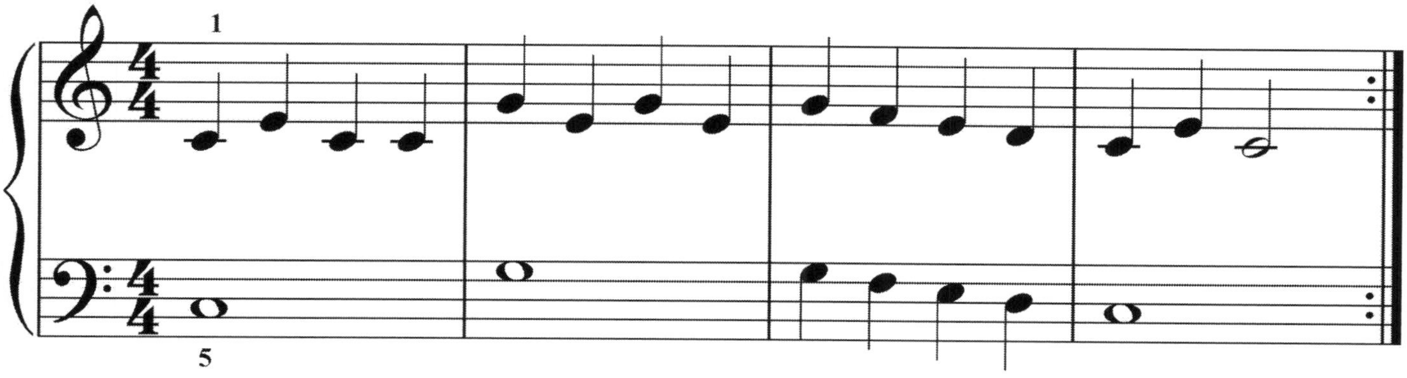

SET 08

UNIT 6

OUT OF POSITION

In each exercise, use the finger number clue above the treble staff and the finger number clue below the bass staff to find your starting position.

MOVE AND GROOVE

S	T	E	L	L	A	R

SPACE TRAVEL

A	M	A	Z	I	N	G

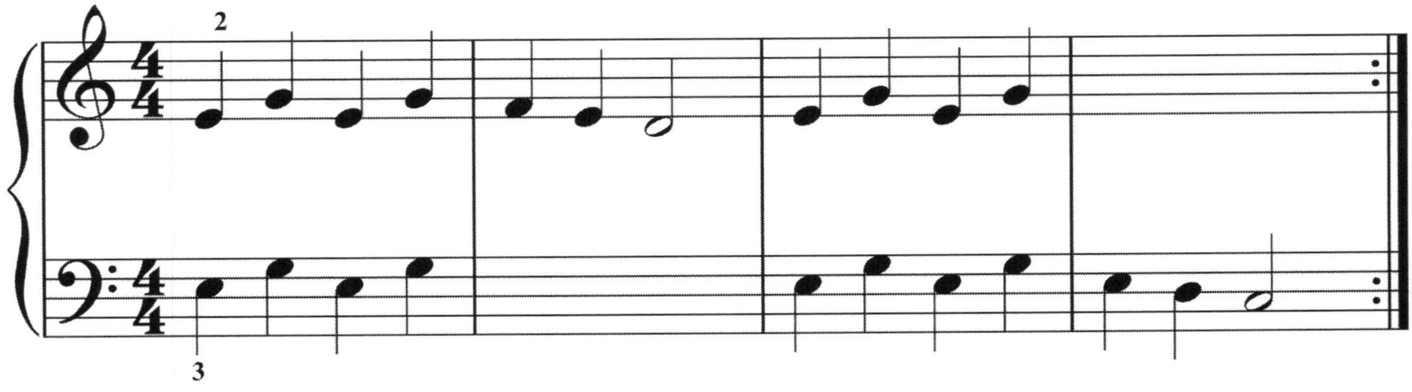

SHIFT WORK

W I N N I N G

CHALLENGE PIECE 1

P E R F E C T

CHALLENGE PIECE 2

A W E S O M E

SET 09

UNIT 6

RHYTHM

Look at the first line of rhythm below. Stem-down notes are performed by tapping both hands on your lap. Stem-up notes are performed by clapping your hands together. After performing the first rhythm, complete the remaining exercises.

RHYTHM CHALLENGE 1

A	W	E	S	O	M	E

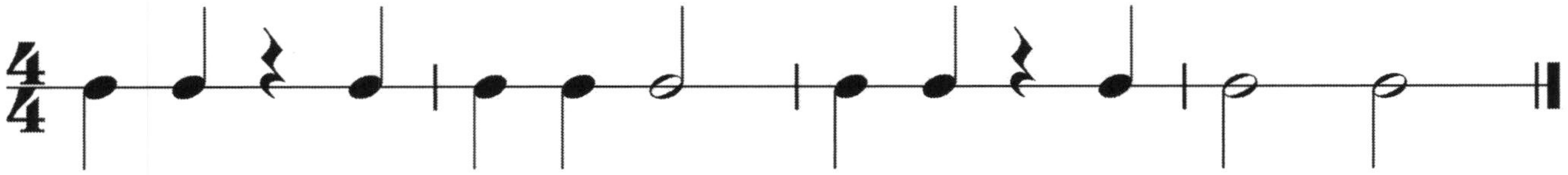

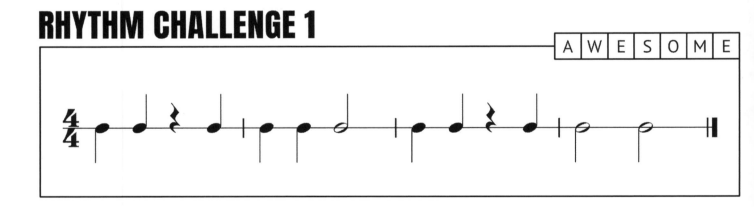

RHYTHM CHALLENGE 2

S	T	E	L	L	A	R

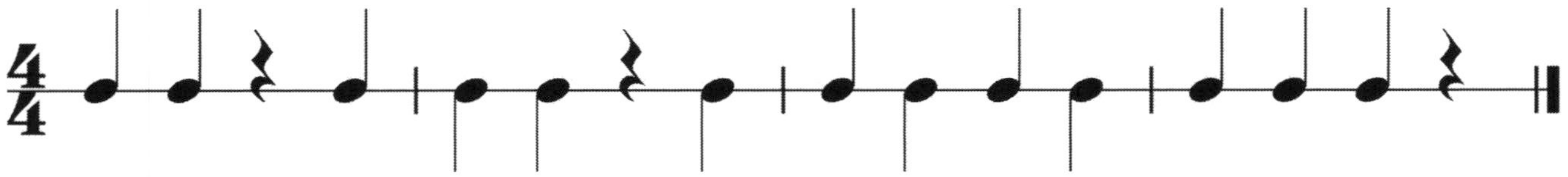

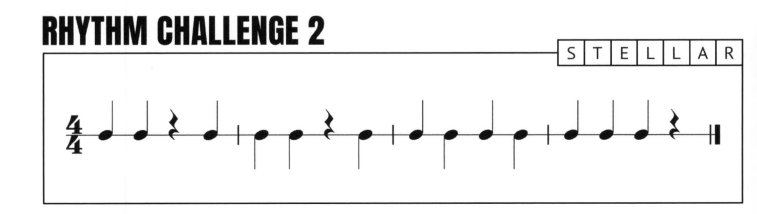

RHYTHM CHALLENGE 3

S U B L I M E

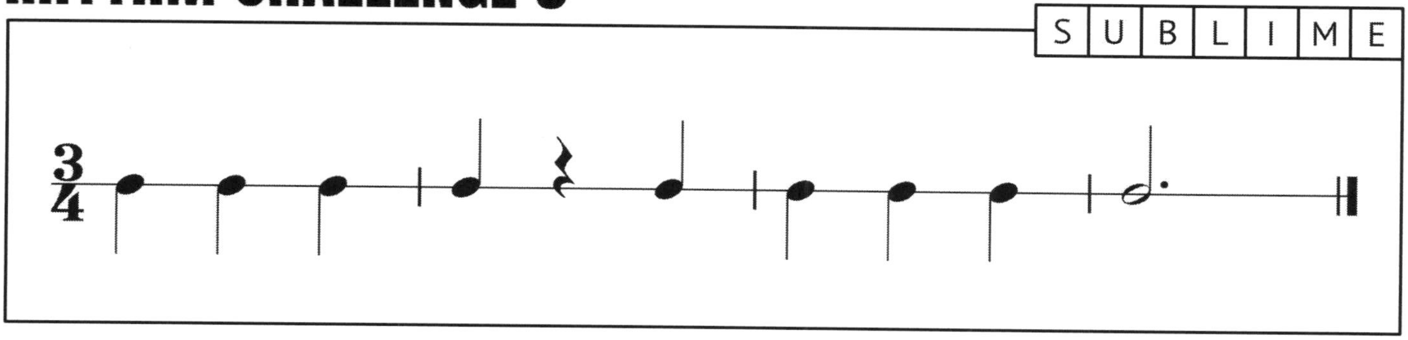

RHYTHM CHALLENGE 4

P E R F E C T

RHYTHM CHALLENGE 5

W I N N I N G

RHYTHM CHALLENGE 6

A M A Z I N G

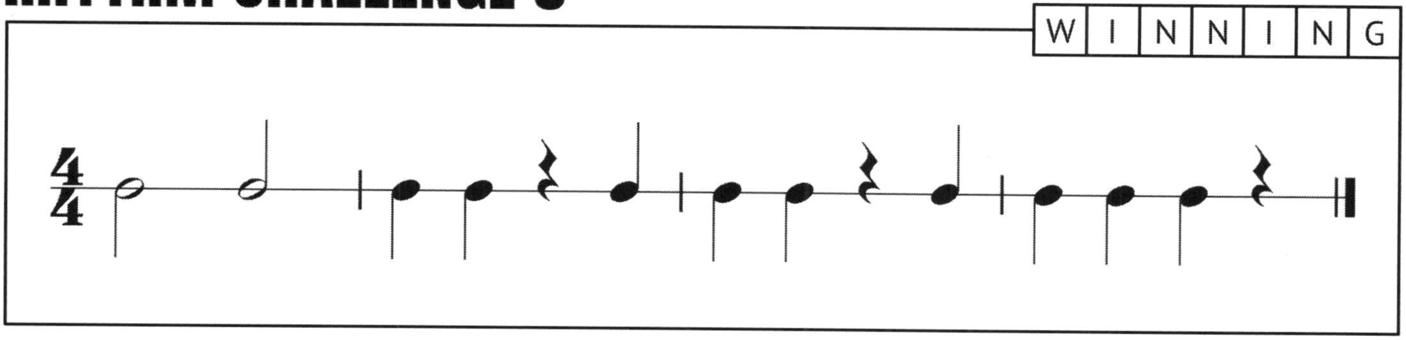

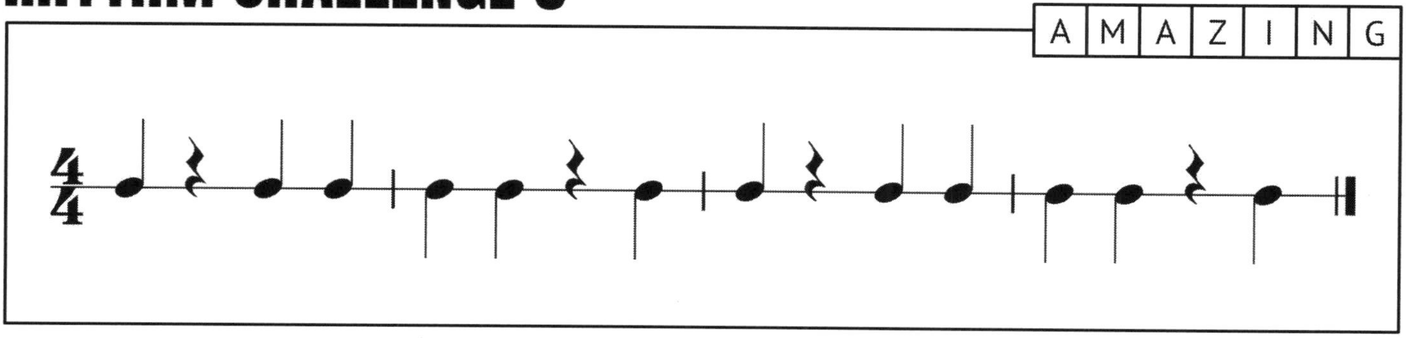

SET 10

UNIT 6

CHALLENGE SET

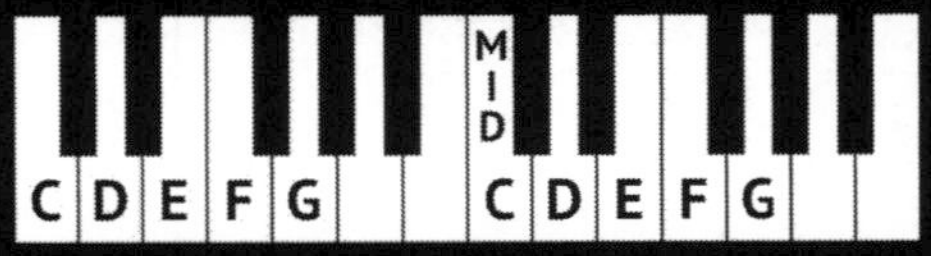

The following contrary motion exercises are intended for older beginners and students who want to test their skills.

SIDE BY SIDE

A W E S O M E

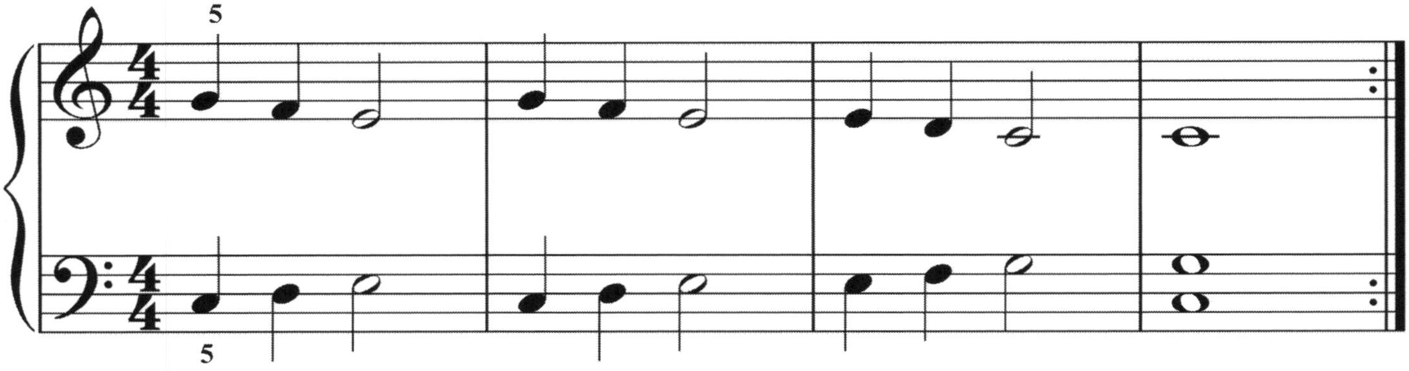

POWER DOWN

S T E L L A R

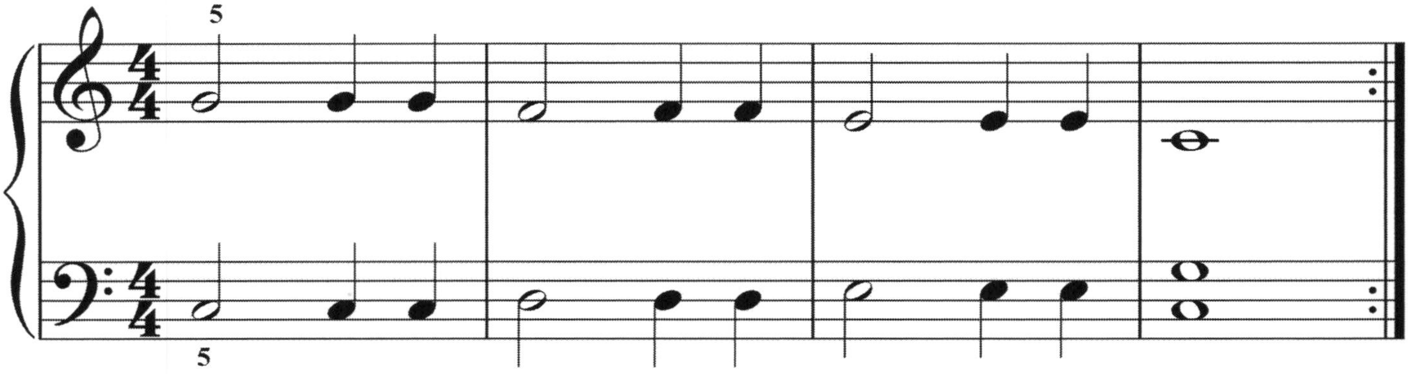

HURDLE HOPS

W I N N I N G

WOODCHOP

P E R F E C T

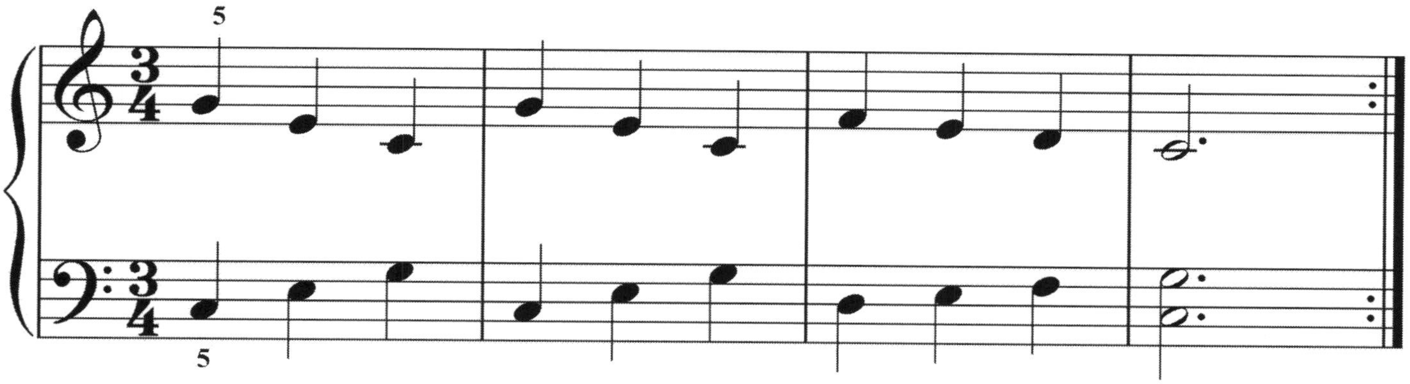

DOUBLE NO TROUBLE

A M A Z I N G

Printed in Great Britain
by Amazon

61288554R00059